KEEPING PACE: INSPIRATIONS IN THE AIR

BY ERNEST A. FITZGERALD

Pace Communications, Inc.
Greensboro, North Carolina

Keeping Pace: Inspirations in the Air was printed by Arcata
Graphics Company and published by Pace Communi-
cations, Inc.
Book design: David McClure
Project coordinator: Carol A. Mann
Production director: Joy Freeman Nead
Editorial staff: Sarah Lindsay (coordinator), Roland Banks,
Mary Best and Melinda L. Stovall.

In appreciation for Dr. Fitzgerald's contribution to all of us,
the net proceeds from this book are going to the Endowment
Fund of the Triad United Methodist Home in Winston-Salem,
North Carolina. This fund is used to help worthy persons re-
side at the home if their financial resources would not normally make it possible otherwise. Dr. Fitzgerald was
instrumental in getting this project under way.

Pace Communications, Inc.
1301 Carolina Street
Greensboro, NC 27401

Table of Contents

Foreword

Mrs. Walter Eugene Johnston, known to friends as "Bessie," suggested 14 years ago that PACE magazine needed a column that was both inspirational and uplifting. She recommended Dr. Ernest A. Fitzgerald as a possible author for that column. Since that date, Dr. Fitzgerald, now a bishop, has become one of the most beloved and popular columnists in PACE magazine. He has reached out to touch the lives of countless people from a somewhat unlikely place, an in-flight magazine.

Bishop Fitzgerald has a hundred stories to tell, and a hundred ways of making us look at things and see them differently. He can find insight in the stars, or his daughter's box of toys, or the little mountain stream he camped by as a boy. But he's not writing for the saints and sages—he's writing for all of us.

These little essays—both nonsecular and nonsectarian—can inspire and uplift every reader. Bishop Fitzgerald speaks not only of sunshine, nor does he see his mission as merely to make us all feel good. "Books on how to succeed are important," he has written, "but I often wish someone would offer a bit of direction on what to do when you have tried and failed." He doesn't mince words about the timeless troubles of the human condition. But he never fails to offer hope. Above all, he addresses our values—that priceless part of ourselves we all need to develop and share.

Many of Bishop Fitzgerald's airborne readers have asked for a collection of the essays that have appeared month after month for 14 years in Piedmont Airlines' seatback pockets. These "inspirations in the air" have been all over the country; now here they all are in one place for the first time. The sources of inspiration never grow old—and neither does our need to be inspired.

A special thank you from all the employees of Pace as well as the employees and passengers of Piedmont Airlines for continuing to touch our lives.

Bonnie McElveen-Hunter
President and Publisher
PACE Magazine

1

Preface

It has been my privilege to write a column in PACE magazine for many years. I have been constantly surprised at the number of people who read the magazine and take time to respond. Hundreds of letters have been received from all over the world. I am deeply grateful to every person who has taken time to write, or to read the articles.

I am greatly honored that the editors of PACE are now publishing all of the articles in a single volume. It is my hope that this publication will not only reach those who have read the articles originally, but others who may not have seen the magazine.

I am indebted to Fisher-Harrison Publications for affording me the opportunity to reach thousands of readers; and to Piedmont Airlines, which has provided me a forum, enabling me to speak to thousands of travelers who regularly board one of America's leading airlines. I am especially grateful to Mrs. Betty Coleman, my secretary, who has edited the articles from month to month. Most of all, I am grateful to my wife, who constantly inspires me to higher and better things. The articles in this volume now go forth with the sincere wish that because of them life may be a little brighter for someone looking for a ray of sunshine.

Ernest A. Fitzgerald
Atlanta, Georgia
August 1988

When Do You Begin to Live?

"He retired at 65 and died at 66!" That's an ironic circumstance which happens all too often in this unpredictable world. But it does happen, and I'm in the position to know. A part of my work is holding funerals. I am a minister.

Recently in a medical journal there was an article about some studies being made on the sensitivity of the human brain. As a result of these studies, extensive experiments are being made in what the scientists call "sensory overload." They have discovered that man is capable of receiving only a limited amount of sensory data. Beyond a certain point, the brain goes blank and refuses to function normally. Dentists have been toying with some of these discoveries. Earphones are placed on the patient, and the sound level is turned up until the sensation of pain no longer is felt.

While this can be an obvious blessing, the principle of "sensory overload" can have ominous implications. The complexities of life in this "pressure-cooker" world can so overload our minds that beauty, happiness and gratitude can also be blocked out. We are caught up in such a whirlwind of activities that there is no time for appreciation of life in the present.

One of the common results of the mad pace of contemporary man is the imaginary notion that the best of life is over the next hill, a few years ahead or just down the road. The only trouble is when we condition ourselves to believe that happiness is always in the future, the future never comes. There is an old saying which reads, "If you aren't happy now, you never will be." The point of that is clear. We need to find the good things in life as we go along. All too often we spend our time getting ready to live and then discover there is no time left to live.

Howard Murry has a story about an old mountaineer who offered a friend a bit of sage advice. The traveler had come by to ask directions and appeared to be in a great rush. "What's your hurry?" asked the mountaineer. "You're gonna run by more'n you'll ever catch." This is a quaint way of suggesting that it is possible to miss the best things as we go along and never live to find the good days we so relentlessly pursue.

One of the oldest stories in the world is about a boy who lived a long time ago in a remote corner of the world. His home was a rocky hillside farm. Somewhere in the distance was a city; its towers glittered in the sparkling sunlight. He thought life would be better over there; so off he went with all he had, only to discover that life was as hectic in the city as it had been at home. He slowed his pace a bit and looked back. In retrospect he saw the old home place in a new light. Sober reflection convinced him that he had run away from the very things he had wanted to find.

Life ought to be lived in the *now*. Mac Davis sings a popular song, "Stop and Smell the Roses." There is a haunting reminder in that line. The pressures of day-to-day life can reach such magnitude that the things we ought to find are blacked out. It's a shame to spend 65 years getting ready to live and then in 12 months find yourself attending your own funeral.

However, the question is, "How can I really live as I go along?" Recently I asked a friend who is a psychiatrist about this very thing. His answer was simple and pointed. "It's a matter of establishing priorities." The problem is not a matter of having more time. There are 60 minutes in each hour and 24 hours in every day for all of us. The solution is in the use of the time we have. Marconi, the Wizard of the Airwaves, was a young man when he invented the first radio. From that day his life was complicated by fame and fortune. But children were always a welcomed distraction for him. Once, while in Ireland, he was late for a news conference. The reporters milled about, miffed over the inconvenience. Later, they discovered that Marconi was busy mending a doll brought to him by a six-year-old girl. He would not leave the job unfinished. Marconi took time to "smell the roses."

A dozen years ago a widely known news reporter made an apt observation. "While you are getting all the things money will buy, it's a good thing to stop and ask if you are losing the things money won't buy. If that is true, then you ought to sacrifice a few of the first for a few of the latter." What rare wisdom and good common sense.

It really doesn't take a radical reordering of our lives to "smell the roses." It takes only a moment to feel the freshness of the crisp morning air, or to glance at a tree laden with the crystals of new fallen snow. A moment spent gazing out the window of a plane at the sunset can put you in touch with what life is really about. An evening by the fireside with family or friends, who so often want something more than money can buy, can be an unforgettable experience. It isn't how much time you take to "smell the roses." It's how you use the time you have.

The holiday season, despite its whirl of festivities, is a good time for a little reflection. If you have been missing life as you go along, you may well miss it altogether. Many of us are passing by what we are really trying to find. The uncertainties of life press the question upon us. If you have your health, enjoy it while you have it. If you have a family, take some time with them while they are still around. If there is a bit of beauty nearby, pause a moment to enjoy it. That is a good way to celebrate Christmas and a splendid resolution for the New Year. Start living now! It may be all the living you will have time to do.

Chased by Your Own Heartbeat

There was recently a story in an Atlanta paper about a woman in Peterborough, England, who had worked herself into a state of near collapse. She imagined that wherever she went there were people following her. When she looked back, no one was there. Yet she always heard footsteps. Finally, in desperation, she sought out a psychiatrist who solved the mystery. The doctor discovered that the woman had been wearing her hearing aid backward, and the footsteps she was hearing turned out to be her own heartbeat.

This story is most likely fictitious. If it isn't, the lady had problems other than just a backward hearing aid. But here is a lesson about life and the way many of us live it. We describe our age as the "age of tension," and that's probably accurate. Someone has said that one out of every four hospital beds could be emptied if we could learn how to live under pressure. The important point is that the world need not be all that complicated. Many of our tensions are self-induced. The pressures chasing us are often manufactured in our own minds. We make life more complex than it really is. All of us could profit by taking a bit of time to analyze the way things really are. The tensions of life fall into three general categories. It helps to know which ones are following us.

First, there are tensions none of us can avoid. There is a maxim in science which is universal in its application: "All growth takes place in a resisting medium." Muscles are strengthened by exercise, movement involves the conflict of friction, and education takes place as the result of study. Any sense of accomplishment is achieved as the result of effort. We live in a world where drifting brings nothing except troubles.

The editor of one of our nation's greatest newspapers was asked once how he managed to be so successful in so short a time. He said, "I owe my success to uncommon ability, hard work, and to the fact that my father owned the newspaper." Most of us imagine that the last situation is the most significant. It really isn't. Luck plays a minor role in determining what we are. If you read the biographies of truly great people, it is clear that fate may put them in a fortunate environment, but to stay there requires a lot of backbone. If you have a happy home, you have to work at it. If your vocation is rewarding, no matter how you got it, you have to put forth the effort to keep it meaningful. A reputation has to be earned. No one can give you that.

There is a second kind of tension. *There are some pressures we don't have to face.* There is an old story about a farmhand who applied for a position with a well-to-do farmer. The farmer asked if he could do

7

the work. The laborer replied, "I can sleep on a stormy night." "But can you take care of my cattle?" Again came the reply, "I can sleep on a stormy night." The farmer decided that the laborer was a bit daffy, but he hired him anyway. A few nights later the farmer was awakened by a violent storm. He tried to arouse his new assistant, but the man was sound asleep. So the farmer rushed out to the barn to get things in order. To his surprise he found the barn doors closed, the cattle safely inside, and the hay stacks neatly covered. The employer then understood what the man had meant when he said, "I can sleep on a stormy night."

A lot of our troubles we make for ourselves. Many of the tensions in our lives could be eliminated if we would take a few moments to hold a conversation with our conscience. Knowing what we ought to do is not always easy. Decisions are often difficult. But sometimes it helps to ask ourselves the simple question, "Can I sleep on a stormy night?" You can be sure that the stormy night will come. It comes for everyone. If you've played by the rules, inner peace will be yours. And that's better than a fortune. Without this peace, a fortune is useless. With it, you are always rich.

Finally, there are some tensions we should not avoid. What brings life's greatest satisfaction? The past president of one of our international civic clubs said that one night he came out of a hotel and found a ragged little boy crying. When the executive inquired as to the reason, the boy said, "My father sent me to the corner grocery store, but I have lost the money he gave me. My dad is drunk. If I don't find that money, he will beat me half to death." The man reached into his pocket, pulled out some money and gave it to the bedraggled child. The little fellow looked up with shining eyes and said to him, "Gee, mister, I wish *you* was my dad." The man said he walked four blocks in the rain that night hoping to find another little boy he could help.

We have become paranoid in our times trying to get rid of tensions. But there are some troubles we should never avoid—among these are the burdens others carry. By helping a bit with problems that are not our own, we find what real living is. A friendly smile to the people around us or a simple word of thanks can make the day for someone. And if you make it a good day for others, it will be a good day for you. The strangest paradox in life is this: As you bear the tensions you don't have to carry, the tensions you must carry become easier. There is no way to explain why this happens. You have to try it to know that it's true.

There is a prayer often attributed to Reinhold Niebuhr, but it goes back a lot further than that. The prayer has survived the years and has become widely known. "God, grant me the serenity to accept the things I cannot change, the courage to change the things I can, and the wisdom to know the difference." There is no way to avoid tensions in this world. You face the ones you must carry, choose the ones you should carry, and never let yourself be chased by the ones you make for yourself.

How to Be a Failure

For the past 50 years or so, book publishers have been making fortunes selling books on the subject of success. The American mind has been saturated with an endless parade of do-it-yourself plans to get to the top. No generation has ever been subjected to greater pressure. The businessman is supposed to out-produce everyone else, and if he can't "cut it" he isn't needed. Every young person is expected to make *Who's Who*, be involved in multitudes of social activities, and still graduate at the head of the class. The housewife is under duress to be a good mother, an ideal wife, and a community leader, and to keep the entire family in the proper social register. Ours is a success-oriented society, with applause only for the winner.

As a minister, I talk with a lot of people. One thing I observe is that we are so steeped in the idea of success we don't know how to handle failure. A great part of my time is spent in counseling with people who have unfinished dreams, incomplete plans and unrealized hopes. It is perfectly clear to me that everyone won't and can't make it to the top. Books on how to succeed are important, but I often wish someone would offer a bit of direction on what to do when you have tried and failed. A lot of us know more about losing than we know about winning. What would you say to someone who has really tried and hasn't made it? How would you help that person make sense out of agonizing defeat? There are three things which need to be remembered.

First, failure is always relative to perspective. There is an old Norwegian tale about a fisherman who, with his two sons, went out on a daily fishing run. The catch was good; but by mid-afternoon a sudden storm blotted out the shoreline, leaving the men groping for the direction of home. Meanwhile, a fire broke out in the kitchen of their rustic cottage. Before it could be extinguished, the fire had destroyed the family's earthly possessions. Finally, the father and sons were able to row their boat ashore. The man's wife was waiting to tell him the tragic news of the fire. "Karl, fire has destroyed everything," she said tearfully. "We have nothing left." But Karl was unmoved by the news. "Didn't you hear me?" she asked. "The house is gone!" "Yes, I hear you," replied Karl. "But a few hours ago we were lost at sea. For hours I thought we would perish. Then something happened: I saw a dim yellow glow in the distance. It grew larger and larger. We turned our boat toward the light. The same blaze which destroyed our home was the light which saved our lives."

Little commentary is needed on the lesson of that story. Failure is often success when seen from a different point of view. History is full of this kind of thing. Columbus, looking for a new route to India, failed in his intended mission but unintentionally opened a new world. In

1872 a severe hot spell in California shriveled a farmer's entire grape crop. He sent his "dried-up " grapes to a grocer who advertised them as "Peruvian delicacies." They sold at a good price, and we've been eating "raisins" ever since. Failure is largely determined by your point of view. It is almost impossible to think of anything, no matter how bad, which doesn't have some good in it—if you look for it.

Second, failure is relative to our use of it. No one can evaluate the place of any eventuality in life. Whether it is good or bad depends on how a circumstance is used. In John Wooden's biography there are a couple of meaningful lines: "Things turn out best for those who make the best of the way things turn out." About a hundred years ago, in Tuscumbia, Alabama, a 19-month-old child was deprived of sight and hearing. The child soon became mute. Yet, 24 years later, this child graduated cum laude from Radcliffe College. Helen Keller's closed eyes have opened the eyes of millions. There are times when the blind *can* lead the blind. Helen Keller did! Beethoven's deaf ears have helped multitudes hear immortal music. Catherine Marshall's broken heart made Peter Marshall immortal. Nothing is good or bad within itself. Value has some relationship to use. The worst can be made to serve the best purposes if we know how to utilize it.

Third, failure is relative to time. Did you ever consider the fact that no one really knows when he has had a good day? Wallace Hamilton tells an old story about a Chinese landowner who had a large estate. One day some wild horses wandered onto his property. The horses were worth a fortune. The neighbors gathered to congratulate him on his good luck. The man stoically remarked, "How do you know I am lucky?" Later the man's son was trying to break one of the horses. The boy was thrown and his leg broken. The neighbors tried to console the man on his misfortune. He asked again, "How do you know I have been unfortunate?" A while later the king declared war, and the landowner's son was exempted from military duty because of his broken leg. The neighbors came in to say how fortunate the man was. He asked the same question: "How do you know I am fortunate?"

How do we really know when we have had a good day? All of us have looked back on some happy experiences which seemed good at the time. But those experiences have turned out to be not quite so happy. We have had some bad days, but far down the road we have been compelled to say, "It seemed terrible at the time; but as I look back, it was the best thing that ever happened to me." Time turns a lot of failures into successes. The fact is, you never really know when you have failed.

We need some new standards by which to measure success. Genuine success is not climbing to the top of the heap and staying there. I know a lot of people who have "arrived," but they aren't very happy. Success is doing what you can, with what you have, where you are. People who succeed can look back at life and not be ashamed of what they see. No one who can do that is a failure!

The Elusive American Dream

There is a story told by Roy Putman about a soldier who was serving his term of duty on the battlefield. He kept getting long, nagging letters from his wife back home. One day, his patience completely exhausted, the soldier fired a letter back to her. "Quit nagging me," he wrote, "and let me enjoy this war in peace." That soldier's letter sounds like an absurd contradiction, but it really isn't. There is a hint of something here about life that many of us just don't understand.

It is difficult to know where the notion got started, but the American Dream seems to be that of being happy. When our forefathers penned the Declaration of Independence, they affirmed the right of every citizen in this land to "pursue" happiness. That's an admirable goal; but I sometimes think we don't understand what they meant, or we have some strange ideas of what constitutes happiness. A recent anthology of quotations contained some 30 references under the word *happy*. Twenty-four of these quotations were cynical. Apparently the majority of the authors referred to in this anthology felt happiness to be an impossible dream.

Could it be that many of us don't understand the meaning of the word and thus spend our time looking for the wrong thing? Pick up a dictionary sometime and look at the definition of happiness. Webster suggests that the word comes from an older word meaning "to be fortunate, lucky or favored by circumstance." Happiness in its strictest definition, therefore, appears to mean a sense of well-being based on one's outer situation. If that's what we are seeking, no wonder we can't seem to find it. If happiness means an ideal environment where all struggles, tensions and strivings are suspended, we will probably never find it this side of the cemetery. As a minister I've talked to enough people to know that the world is a battlefield for almost everyone. There is no place on this earth where everything is tranquil. If you find any peace at all, you will have to find it under pressure. It's peace in the middle of war, or no peace at all.

Of course, the real question is, "How do you manage to find peace in a world of muddled confusion?" No one has all the answers, but there is one thing absolutely essential. Many years ago, Benjamin Disraeli, known for his calm courage even under fire, made a speech before Parliament. He said something which touched a tender nerve. Suddenly the hall came alive with shouts of anger. The House of Commons would not be silenced. He tried to speak but was shouted down. Disraeli closed his manuscript and waited for the noise to subside. Then, with complete composure and in the dead silence, he made a final comment: "Though I sit down now, the time will come when you will hear me." It's easy to understand Disraeli's confidence. He knew

11

he was right—dead right—and no matter what anyone said or did his cause would prevail. He was at peace.

Think about that story for a moment, and you discover it contains a significant clue to the pursuit of happiness. There is no way to achieve peace until you make peace with yourself. A while back someone made a study of Americans who travel all over the world looking for places to relax. An enterprising news reporter followed some of these people around and observed them on remote islands and in hideaways half-way around the globe. His report was this: "Wherever these people go, they are soon leading hectic lives. They carry their confusion with them." That's the way it always works. People who are wrong on the inside never find a world that is right on the outside. And if they did, it wouldn't be right for long.

Deep inside all of us, the Creator has placed an inner voice. It's a quiet voice, so quiet that many of us have allowed it to be crowded out and distorted by the clatter of a noisy world. There are times, however, when every distraction needs to be shut out and that inner voice heard. If you listen carefully, that voice will be pointing the direction, saying this is what you ought to do and what you ought to be. Sometimes it takes a while to understand what that voice is saying, but after a while the signal will finally come in loud and clear. If you are obedient to that signal, nothing can really get to you. There comes an inner confidence which not even the shouting of a jeering world can shake, and you can weather any war in peace. And even more important, you don't have to spend your life pursuing happiness. If you know you are doing what you ought to do and being what you ought to be, you will find happiness where you are, and the elusive American dream will be yours.

How to Know When You Have Done Your Best

"When you have done your best, forget it!" That's standard advice to people who are harassed with all kinds of complicated problems these days. The reason for such counsel is that we are concerned about our friends who appear to be worrying themselves toward the ragged edges of a breakdown. This is why we keep saying to them, "When you have done what you can, all the anxiety in the world won't help." That's sound advice, of course; and most of us could follow it except for one thing. Who really knows when he has done his best? People worry a lot about that. If you don't believe it, come spend a while with me. Every day I, as a minister, see people who are troubled with some difficult problem. They ask the same questions: "Have I done all I can do? Is there a stone anywhere that I have left unturned?"

It goes without saying that no one has turned every stone. Who really has done all that could be done? All of us have our limitations. How, then, do we ever find any peace, always wondering if we have given our all? There ought to be some rule of thumb by which to judge our performance, some way to know when we have done our best. My years as a counselor have taught me a few things worth remembering.

First, try to keep in mind that our best is always limited by our circumstances. A few years ago the wire services carried the story of a man who knocked down the locked door of a burning apartment house to rescue his small child. Flying glass cost him one eye completely and severely damaged the other. Because of his injury, the man could no longer continue in his occupation and was forced to resign. He had great difficulty in finding other work, and his family suffered significantly as a consequence. In the story was a touch of irony. Firemen discovered that the rear entrance to the building was unlocked. They reported that the man, had he known, could have entered the building without effort and in safety performed his mission. Nevertheless, this father had acted on the best knowledge he had at the moment.

There is a lesson here. It's easy to say, "If I had only known." But the fact is, no one can know everything. We have to make decisions and plot our courses based on the evidence at hand. To look back is senseless. It's enough to say that I did what I could with what I had, realizing that no one can do better than that.

There is another thing to consider. Going the second mile today makes tomorrow a happier day. When Marshal Ney was sent by Napoleon to guard the Russian front, Ney held until he had lost every soldier in his command and barely escaped with his own life. One cold night he went to the emperor and reported that he had tried and failed. Napoleon, known for his insistence on complete sacrifice, inquired, "Marshal, how do I know you have given your best for France and your emperor?" The marshal stood erect in his tattered uniform and with complete confidence replied, "Sir, I would ask of you no more than I have done."

It's mighty helpful now and then to ask the question, "Would I expect more of another than I have asked of myself?" It's amazing how that helps one's peace of mind. If you demand no more of others than you demand of yourself, if you have worked as hard as you would expect another to work, you will find it easy to sleep at night. The people who are at peace with life are those who have gone the "second mile," who have done a bit more than was expected. The freeloader may have an easier life, but if he ever stops to reflect, he will have a troubled heart.

Finally, you must be prepared to wait for your efforts to produce their harvest. Minton Johnson somewhere tells about some African violets his wife brought home one night. She set them in the window and remarked how beautiful the white blossoms would be. Looking at the plants, Johnson discovered that they looked just like those plants which produced crimson blooms. "How do you know these flowers will be white?" he asked. "That's easy," declared his wife. "White is the kind the florist planted." The logic here is simple. Nature is dependable. The right plants produce the proper flowers.

Most of us are too impatient. There is a highway in the Great Smoky Mountains which runs from Cherokee to Newfound Gap. It's a crooked road and winds up the valley, often across high cliffs of mountain rock. Whenever you travel that highway, you discover that at times your direction seems exactly opposite from the way you want to go. But standing at the top and looking back, you can understand the reason. The mountain is so steep that engineers often had to turn the road back in order to gain the higher elevations. Life is sometimes like that. You do what you can with what you have, going as far as you would expect others to go, but things still don't go as you had planned. But you must remember that seeds grow a long time underground before you can see them. Learn to wait for the flowers to bloom. It is true that if you take the right road and hold it, you will get to the right place—sometime, somewhere! That principle holds in the world of nature. It is no less true in life.

How to Make People Treat You Right

We met on the street the other day, and he was really "steamed up." He had had a tough morning at the office; things had started wrong and gotten worse. "It's a hard world," he said. "How can we make it treat us right?" I stepped back to give him a lecture, but he was in no mood; so I let the moment pass, and we went our separate ways. His question lingered with me, however, because it's one all of us ask now and then when we have been dealt a bad hand.

How *do* you make people treat you right? Is there really an answer to that question? There may not be if you are talking about a particular person who seems bent on doing you in. But there is a principle which prevails more often than not, and it's been working successfully a long, long time. Who stated this principle first, we don't know. The ancient Greeks, the Chinese and the Egyptians all had it in one form or another. We remember it best, however, as stated by a Nazarene carpenter. He said, "Do unto others as you would have them do unto you." For most of us, this is a simple and lovely little instruction on living which is good to know but not of much value in the practical affairs of life. The truth is, this maxim is the most penetrating insight into the nature of things ever written in the wisdom literature of the world. The Golden Rule is not a statement of the way we should live but an accurate description of the way life works.

Someone has said that much of the trouble in our world results from the confusion over the difference in definitions of the two words *rule* and *principle*. The word *rule* implies an arbitrary regulation imposed upon us by legislation. A few years ago the government of Sweden decided to change the side of the road on which its motorists drove. After years of using the left side of the highway, a decision was made to reverse the procedure. Reports indicate there was some confusion at first, but after motorists made the adjustment traffic moved along quite well. Of course, we would expect that. One side of the road is as good as the other so long as all agree. It is a matter of legislation. Much of life is governed by rules. People get together and by common consent establish a procedure, but such procedures can be changed at will so long as there is agreement.

The word *principle*, however, implies a regulation which springs from a deeper level. Some things are written into the scheme of the universe, and are not up for popular vote. The principle of gravity is inherent in creation. No legislative vote can change that. Principles are never disobeyed, and any effort to do so only proves them.

Across the centuries those who have observed life suggest that the Golden Rule is not really a rule but a principle. The most accurate statement of the axiom, therefore, is this: Whatever you do unto others, they will do unto you. There is a lot of evidence to support that. Anders Nygren once said that everything in creation obeys the law of reciprocity. Everything obeys the law of give and take. A bee pollinates the flower from which it takes its honey. There is a continual interaction between plant and animal life, and because of it life continues on this planet.

It is precisely because we fail to keep in mind this law of give and take that life is so rough for so many of us. Not long ago I visited a hospital patient who said that no one ever visited him. We chatted for a while, and the reason became apparent. He had never visited anyone else. Someone told of a man who went to church and sat through the entire service with his hat on. An usher finally asked him why. "People never speak to me, so I decided to make them do it." The usher responded honestly, "There is a better way to make that happen. You could have spoken to someone yourself."

Now you can press this truth too far. Life is not a matter of exact dividends on investments. It is a fact, however, that the world never permanently hates one who consistently loves, nor does it consistently love anyone who permanently hates. Time has a way of sifting things down to the right place. Two thousand years ago, there were two people in the city of Rome. One of those people was the emperor of the empire. He was selfish and mean. The Romans revered him, but it was a reverence born of fear. He punished any insubordination with death. In Nero's empire there was another man, named Paul. Paul was gentle and filled with boundless good will for everyone. Even after Nero imprisoned Paul, Paul still refused to hate. When, according to the legends, Nero ordered Paul's execution it appeared that Nero had won and Paul had lost. But 2,000 years have passed, and the scales have been balanced. Nero has the admiration of no one; we even name our dogs for him. Paul is now remembered as a saint, and one of history's most important forces. If you give time a chance, it will at last bring back what you put out.

It will work in the general flow of life—this "Principle of Gold." What you give, you will receive. Perhaps not with day-to-day precision but in the long pull. If you are having a bad day and getting the brunt of the hostilities of others, it could be that the place to work is not on other people but on yourself. It's amazing how the principle works. Will Rogers once said that he had never met a man he didn't like. It's not surprising that the world loved him. Doing unto others as you would have them do unto you is not something you *should* do. It's something you *must* do if others are to treat you right.

The Set of the Sails

Recently a national magazine published a series of articles about the widespread fascination of Americans with the occult. Interest in astrology, crystal gazing, fortunetelling, palmistry and phrenology has resulted in the publication of numerous books in the field. An astonishing number of newspapers and periodicals publish horoscopes daily. Popular magazines abound with advertisements for amulets, Ouija boards and crystal balls.

We are not the first people to be attracted to such studies. The ancient Babylonians, the Egyptians and the Greeks were said to be skilled in the magical arts. In later times Chaucer, Shakespeare and Milton are thought to have been semibelievers. Adolf Hitler and his henchmen reportedly consulted the astrologers regularly. To state categorically that they were wrong would require more knowledge than any of us possess. Our lives could be affected by outer and mysterious influences. But the weight of evidence suggests that the determinative factors in our lives are more internal than external, and we have more to do with what happens to us than does the movement of the stars.

The other day I saw a sentence worthy of serious thought: *If you find life worthwhile, it's not because you found it that way but because you made it that way.* A recent cartoon pictured a small lad looking at his report card. He is saying, "My environment is all right. It must be heredity." A lot of us think this way. Whatever is wrong with our lives, we imagine it to be the result of what we have inherited or the circumstances under which we live. The truth is that none of us live in a perfect environment, nor do we have an unblemished heritage. Making life worthwhile must be accomplished in spite of these things. Three ideas need to be considered.

First, *the meaning of life is determined by the set of our minds.* Ella Wheeler Wilcox once wrote some lines in which she compared life to a sailing vessel. "'Tis the set of the sails and not the gales which decides the way to go." Sailors with skill can move a ship in any direction driven by the same wind. The same winds of adversity which destroy some of us can push others of us to the top, and the difference is in the way we think.

Several years ago an eastern newspaper covered two separate stories which were identical in many ways. Two soliders had been jilted by their fiance'es. One of the soldiers jumped from the Golden Gate Bridge; the other, in his depression, wrote a mournful little song entitled "Goodnight, Irene." His song made the hit list from coast to coast and netted him a fortune. "'Tis the set of the sails and not the gales which decides the way to go."

Most of us think our way into trouble and despair. It never occurs to us that every adversity has its opportunity! And there are no exceptions to that. A large part of the most important book in the world was written by a man in jail. Paul used the adverse winds to write. We can be glad about this. If Paul had been a free man, we might never have remembered him. But as it was he became the author of much of the New Testament. If life is worthwhile, it isn't because you found it that way. You made it so.

There is a second clue to the meaningful life. *It is the intensity of our struggle.* It is often reported that Walt Disney was not only a remarkable man but also a remarkably happy man. Somewhere recently there was a story about his early years. When he started out in Kansas City, he couldn't sell his cartoons. Some hinted that he had no talent. But Disney had a dream, so he set out to conquer his foes. He found a minister who paid him a small amount to draw advertising pictures for his church. Disney had no place to stay, so the church let him sleep in a mouse-infested garage. One of those mice, which Disney nicknamed Mickey, became famous—as the world knows. How satisfying life must have been for Disney when he remembered the hard struggle from lean years spent in a church garage.

None of us ought to make mountains for the sheer purpose of enduring hard times. But let it be said that those who struggle most find achievement proportionately satisfying. This ought to be clear to Americans. Ours is a land where the struggle for life is less and where unmet needs are fewer than in any nation on earth. It is also a land with the greatest incidence of emotional and mental disorder. Surely this should set things in perspective for us. Never retreat from the struggle if the mountain needs to be climbed. The hard climb will make reaching the peak more satisfying. We don't *find* life worthwhile. We have to *make* it that way.

There is a final thing necessary for meaningful life. *It is an abiding faith.* I knew a man many years ago who lived in one of the isolated corners of the Blue Ridge Mountains. Life was hard, and every day his little hillside farm was at the mercy of drought, wind and cold. Yet he was about the most serene and deeply contented man I've ever known. I asked him one day if he ever had any troubles and if he had ever spent sleepless nights. "Sure, I've had my troubles," he said, "but no sleepless nights. When I go to bed I say, 'Lord, you have to sit up all night anyway. There's no point in us both losing sleep. You look after things and when tomorrow comes, I'll do the best I can.'" Nothing sophisticated about his vocabulary, but his idea is as sound as creation itself. You can only deal with the outer world when you are sustained by an inner faith.

President Dwight D. Eisenhower once said, "Faith gives you the courage to make the decisions you must make in a crisis and then the confidence to leave the results to a higher power. Only by trust in oneself and trust in God can a man carrying responsibility find

repose." The only way to peace in this uncertain world is to give y
best and then trust a higher hand to bring you out at the right plac
If that doesn't work, nothing else will.

Time to Cross a River

Not many miles out of the beautiful town of Sylva, North Carolina, there is a spot known as the Crest of the Blue Ridge Mountains. Here the eastern half of the North American continent is divided by the misty and majestic peaks of a mountain chain said by many to be among the most beautiful mountains of the world. As one approaches this dividing line, a little spring by the side of the road can be observed. The water trickles forth and forms a sparkling little stream which makes its restless way down the lush green hills. For ten miles down that stream, one can cross it in a single step. Somewhere down the valley, the little stream is joined by another brook and becomes the Tuckasegee River. Now the Tuckasegee travels a turbulent channel and merges with such rivers as the Oconaluftee and the Nantahala. The names of the rivers change as they are joined by other streams. After a while the waters of that little brook meet the mighty Mississippi. As the Mississippi reaches the sea at New Orleans, the great ocean-going vessels of the world float on its vast waters.

As a boy I used to camp by that little mountain stream. In the late evenings when the world was hushed, I'd sit and think of the long journey the water made to the sea and the ever-widening channel through which it flowed. In later years those reflections have fixed a thought in my mind which life continually impresses upon me: "The time to cross a river is before it gets too wide."

One of the interesting things about life is that there are moments when directions are easily changed. It was James Russell Lowell who said, "Once to ev'ry man and nation/ Comes the moment to decide,/ In the strife of truth with falsehood/ For the good or evil side." the choice goes by forever/ Twixt the good and evil side." Now Lowell's lines are not without point, and yet life is hardly as rigid as he might have us think. Someone has said that life is a series of alternatives, and the business of living is to choose a proper direction. All of us make such choices. We do it in our vocations, our patterns of living and the habits we form. We even do it in our attitudes toward life. For some, life is a game to be lived for all it's worth; and they take from it everything they can get. For others, life is a trust to be used; and they try to put back a little more than they take. Life is a series of alternatives, and for a while, at least, there are countless opportunities to reverse one's field and take another direction. In the earlier stages of such decisions, the options remain open. It is easy to cross the river when it is not too wide.

But have you ever observed that directions tend to become fixed as the years go by? In New England there is this sign posted at the beginning of a muddy road: "Choose your rut carefully; you'll be in it for the next 20 miles." That's true not only of roads but also of life. Habitual patterns establish their own grooves. There is a law in physics known as the "principle of inertia." This means that an object tends to move in a fixed direction unless it is subjected to an opposing force of sufficient magnitude to deflect it. It's the same principle involved in that story of the mountain stream: "The farther you travel on one side of the river, the more likely you are to continue on that side."

Consider how little things become fixed directions. There is in the game of baseball something called the "seventh-inning stretch." It is said that the practice began when President William Howard Taft was attending a baseball game in Washington. Just after the seventh inning, he stood up to rest his knees. The fans—thinking he was leaving—stood, too, out of respect. But the president sat down to watch the rest of the game. Today, the "seventh-inning stretch" is as much a part of baseball as helping the umpire and scrambling for foul balls.

Habitual patterns tend to become fixed, and we easily fall into our ruts. We get hooked on status symbols, thought patterns and putting off until tomorrow the things we should do today. Even in our businesses, we hang to one side of the river long after changes should have been made. We try to work today with yesterday's tools and hope to be in business tomorrow. Our personal lives are no less susceptible to ruts. We have good intentions to spend more time with our families, to take a bit more time to "smell the roses," to visit old friends. But patterns of living have a way of getting fixed. Before long, we have developed a mind-set. Work becomes a mania, occasional practices become habits and experimental methods become traditions. It happens because we go down one side of the river too far. The principle of inertia takes over and directs our lives.

The troublesome thing about all of this is that the price of crossing the river gets higher as the river gets wider. There is nothing complicated about that thought. A tiny stream can be crossed in a single step, but crossing a river calls for a huge structure of steel and concrete. That's a matter worthy of serious reflection. It ought to force a consideration of the things in our lives that should be changed. Maybe we need to rethink our vocations. Are we doing in life what we should be doing? Not all of us can find the work we most enjoy. But many of us can, and the rest of us can find ways of doing our work in more effective and satisfying ways. Perhaps there are life patterns that ought to be reversed. Countless Americans are caught up with status symbols and never realize that the price of keeping pace becomes more demanding as the years go by. For some of us, there is a need to rethink our priorities. We don't take enough time to see the flowers along the way. Our friendships fade; the fun we should be having with our families gets pushed aside by less important things. How easy it is to spend one's life on roads that go nowhere. An ancient writer once asked, "Why spend your money for that which is not bread?" What he meant, of course, was that many pursuits in life bring no lasting satisfaction. The farther you go, the more difficult it is to cross the river. The time to cross is before the river gets too wide.

There is, however, one magnificent truth about life: No circumstance is hopeless. The river never gets so wide but that some changes can be made. We can't always start over, but we can start from where we are. Perhaps we can't take a new direction overnight, but at least tomorrow can be slightly different from today. Just as old ruts get fixed by repetitious use, new roads can be built if we are willing to pay the price. There is a story of a man who lived long ago. He spent the early years of his life in the wretched business of executing undesirable people and was both hated and feared by most of his contemporaries. One day on a desert journey, he decided to cross the river. And he did! It took a long time, but he finally made it to the other side. Few men have had a greater influence on history than St. Paul. We owe to him a major part of the world's most powerful and influential book—the New Testament.

Paul crossed the river when it was a mighty stream. Had he done it earlier, it would have been easier. The time for most of us to cross a river is before it gets so wide.

Selling Out Too Soon

It was established nearly a hundred years ago—the famed Temple University in Philadelphia. The founder was a 41-year-old native of Massachusetts who started a small night school. Not only will Russell H. Conwell be remembered as the founder of a university, but he also will be remembered for a famous lecture entitled, "Acres of Diamonds." That speech was given more than six thousand times across this land, and from it the author earned nearly eight million dollars. A lot of that money was used in the building of his school.

"Acres of Diamonds" is an impressive lecture which caught the imagination of America. In it Conwell insisted that, if only we would use it, most of us have in our hands more than enough to make life meaningful. He told the story about a man who discovered gold in western Nevada. The man worked his claim for a while, thought it was running out, and sold it for eleven thousand dollars. But the history of that gold mine was not to end there. An unexpected discovery opened the "Comstock lode," which proved to be one of the richest gold and silver deposits ever discovered on this planet. Thirty years later the purchasers had earned three hundred million dollars on their investments. One night Conwell labeled that story, "the man who sold out too soon."

Have you ever thought how often this circumstance is reenacted in life? One of the deadliest enemies to human accomplishment is the chronic temptation to become too easily discouraged. It happens to all of us now and then. We struggle for a good cause, work at something that should succeed and find ourselves grappling with problems which need to be solved. But the road gets rugged, the load heavy and the problems complicated. We throw in the towel and sell out, but a lot of times we sell out too soon. Just a little more effort, another bit of push, and the "gold mine" could be ours. Have you ever wondered how you could get the strength to push on? Well, a part of that strength can come from the way you think. The next time you are tempted to turn back when you know you ought to push on, try remembering two or three things.

Remember, for instance, that *the perception of life at any given moment does not always reveal its true meaning.* The trouble with most of us is that we judge life by too short a segment of time and too few events. William Sangster tells about a friend who complained that it always rained on his day off. Finally, tired of his friend's murmuring, Sangster challenged him to check the records at the weather bureau. Investigation revealed that it rained no more on this day than on other days. The man's problem was that he remembered more vividly the days when bad weather interfered with his plans. A lot of us live that way: judging everything by too few things, reading the whole of life in terms of isolated events.

Even when the bad days come too frequently, they don't always tell the whole story. Years ago in England there was a frail, freckle-faced lad. He disliked study and appeared dull. It took the lad three years to complete the first grade. His father soon decided the boy could never master law and suggested a military college. Before being admitted, he failed the entrance examination three times. He had a terrible speech defect which plagued him everywhere he went. But to have judged this lad's life a failure on the basis of those facts would have been a mistake. There came a day when Winston Churchill cast a timeless shadow across the pages of history. You cannot always tell what's going on by looking at any given day. Sometimes it takes a while before the real gold mine can be uncovered.

Another thing we need to remember is that *unexpected events can change the significance of even our darkest hours.* If there is one predictable thing about the future, it is that the future is unpredictable. An ancient writer once said, "We know not what a day may bring forth." This isn't to say that planning is unimportant. In more ways than we imagine, we make our future. But we should never forget that the unexpected often foils the best-laid plans. This isn't all bad. As the unexpected sometimes causes good plans to go awry, so it can change the dark days into our finest hours. Do you remember that story of a boy in Decatur, Illinois? He answered an ad in a magazine, requesting a book on photography. The publishers made a mistake and sent him a book on ventriloquism. That blunder made Edgar Bergen and Charlie McCarthy household words across the land.

There is a monument in Coffee County, Alabama, which must be one of the strangest in the world. It was erected to the boll weevil. Alabama had been cotton country for years, and one day the boll weevil came along, stripping the cotton of its leaves. Just when all seemed hopeless, the people in that troubled county found a new crop, and with the peanut came new prosperity. Inscribed on the memorial are these words: "In profound appreciation of the boll weevil and of what it has done as the herald of prosperity, this monument is erected by the citizens of Enterprise, Coffee County, Alabama." Think about that the next time you are tempted to turn back but know you should go on. Sometimes just over the next hill and another day away, the unexpected will open the gold mine.

One other thing to remember is that *no matter what happens, it can be used for something good.* There is a story told of a former governor of a southern state. During college days, he took a summer job selling magazines. Somewhere in his travels, he met a lovely girl. He decided to ask her to be his wife. One moonlit evening, he found the proper time to propose. "Will you marry me?" he asked. "No!" she replied. "Well," he said quickly, "will you subscribe to my magazine?" There is a profound lesson in that story. The real business of life is to concentrate not on our troubles but on how we might deal with them. The people who find life exciting are not those who have everything going their way. Real living is the business of taking what life hands us and working with it until we find the gold mine. It's a bad thing to sell out too soon. The people who win are those who hold on until the gold mine is theirs.

The Man Who Missed the Boat

He was about the happiest fellow I've ever known. I met him years ago in a little mountain town, and he didn't seem to have a lot to be happy about. His home was modest; he worked at a sawmill, and that's never been a very glamorous profession. He did, however, have the soul of a poet. He saw beauty when the rest of us missed it, and he heard songs when the only musicians were crickets and cicadas. He was an old man when I first knew him, but his spirit was as youthful and fresh as a spring morning. He had come here from Scotland in the year 1912, and often said life began for him that year.

Remember what happened back then? A ship was built by the White Star Line. In mid-April of that year, this ship began its maiden voyage as the luxury liner of the world. On the night of the 15th, the ship was on the high seas 1,600 miles from New York Harbor. The *Titanic* had aboard some 3,000 passengers. The iceberg came up like a ghost in the night. When the morning came, the "unsinkable ship" was gone, taking with it some 1,500 people. As the news of the ill-fated voyage swept around the world, people everywhere paused in sadness. There was one man, however, whose sorrow was tempered with gratitude. A young man from Scotland had booked passage on the *Titanic*. He was eager to begin a new life in a new world, but illness forced him to cancel his reservations. He often said to me, "You never know when you have had a good day."

Did you ever notice that along about this holiday season a strange sense of excitement seems to get hold of us? People who have been grumpy and bored the whole year through are seen scurrying along to parties and family gatherings. They are busy with shopping and the other chores related to the season. Everyone complains about having too much to do, but you get the feeling that such complaints are not really serious. There is an excitement in the air, and a lot of usually sad people suddenly seem to be having a great time. What is it that happens to us? Is it the anticipation of gifts, the hope that someone will give us that long-wanted something we would not or could not buy for ourselves? That may be a part of it, but it's not the whole story. Something happens to us, and it has to do with the way we think.

We remember, for instance, that we are far richer than we imagine. We spend most of our lives thinking about the things we don't have and wishing they could be ours. Long ago a wise man said, "There are not enough things in the whole world to keep any of us happy for 20 minutes." What he meant was that more often than not the possessions we seek somehow lose their glamour and appeal once they are ours. We push along for the next promotion, thinking that will be enough, only to discover that the ladder to the top has no top, and every rung attained reveals another to be climbed. There is that dream house in the city which promises to be the ultimate goal. Once there we immediately begin to devise ways to get away from it all for a weekend in the country. All in all we are pretty miserable people because our minds are always reflecting on the things beyond our reach.

But about this time of year we are reminded to look in a different direction. The very nature of the holiday season helps us to do it. We take time to be with friends and family and find ourselves reflecting on these priceless things. Almost always at Thanksgiving and Christmas, you will find someone who is having it tougher than you are. In spite of yourself you will likely run into something which makes you appreciate what you have. If only for a day, you will find yourself thinking, "I'm a pretty lucky guy."

Something else happens to us during these holiday celebrations. When you count your blessings, you realize that many times you didn't know what your real blessings were.

On November 28, 1942, according to Fulton Oursler, there was excitement in the city of Boston. It was a blustery afternoon, but thousands of sports fans were filing into the stadium for a crucial game between Holy Cross and Boston College. For the first time Boston College had won every game that season. Holy Cross had won four and lost six. They would be a pushover. The Boston team had planned a gala celebration and had rented a famed nightclub for the evening. But everything went wrong from the beginning whistle. Boston College took one of its worst beatings. The team left the stadium dejected and disappointed. There would be no bowl bid, and no one felt like celebrating. The next morning the team saw the headlines. The Coconut Grove Nightclub—the place of the intended victory rally—had burned. It was one of the most terrifying fire disasters on this continent. Four hundred and ninety-one people died. Now don't press the story too far, or you will soon be pondering questions beyond the scope of human understanding. But one thought is readily evident: We don't always know what our real blessings are. A man misses his ship and discovers his misfortune to be his most fortunate day. A lot of victories turn out to be losses, and a lot of losers become winners. The holiday season has a way of making us count our blessings. When you really get down to this, things are never as bad as they seem.

But even more important is that during this season we are reminded of those things which will ultimately prevail in our world. Somewhere in all of the festivity of the closing year, we will be reminded of a man who lived a long time ago. He came from an obscure little town in a faraway part of the world. His heritage gave him no claim to fame. Born of peasant parents, he received his schooling in a carpenter's shop. His friends were fishermen, storekeepers and the like. His travels never took him more than 150 miles from home. At his death he left only a robe, which was given away by the rolling of dice. Somewhere near the end of his life, which lasted only some 33 years,

27

he became a threat to those who had achieved power by unscrupulous means. They decided to do him in. They had the authority and knew they could stop him; so they fixed him to a cross and watched him die. When he was gone, they congratulated themselves on a job well done. They would no longer be threatened by a man who talked about love in a world where only force seemed to count. It's been 2,000 years since those days, and we now know who won. Every time you write the date, you acknowledge his place in history. We count time from the year of his birth. The manger, the place where he was born, is a shrine erected wherever Christmas is celebrated. In fact, the very word *Christmas* contains his title.

In a world often baffled and confused to the point of despair, we need to remember that man. He stands as an eternal reminder that James Russell Lowell was right when he wrote the following lines:

> *Though the cause of evil prosper,*
> *Yet 'tis truth alone is strong;*
> *Though her portion be the scaffold,*
> *And upon the throne be wrong,*
> *Yet that scaffold sways the future,*
> *And, behind the dim unknown,*
> *Standeth God within the shadow*
> *Keeping watch above his own.*

Most people will be a bit happier during these holidays. We will pause to think about our real riches, to appreciate the blessings which come from even bad things, and to remember that at last the good and beautiful prevail. If we could think about these things more often, every day could be as happy as the holidays.

Sweating the Small Stuff

"Don't make mountains out of molehills!" How many times have you heard that, especially when you have been up-tight about a world of little things which keep pressing you for action and decisions? It's sound advice, of course, at least most of the time. Far too many of us spend our lives "sweating the small stuff," never having time to look at the larger matters which should claim our attention. But the trouble with most old sayings is that they lose their meaning when pressed too far. This is especially true of that "mountain/molehill" proverb. Sometimes the "small stuff" is the fabric out of which history is made.

If you wander back through the pages of the past, you will discover many places where the course of nations and even the world hinged on a insignificant detail. On April 14, 1865, at Ford's Theater in Washington, DC, Abraham Lincoln was shot by a young actor named John Wilkes Booth. There is a strange story about that fatal night. The Lincoln family had planned to spend the evening at the National Theater watching a play about the antics of a famed show horse. Early that afternoon, however, Mrs. Lincoln decided that she and her husband would attend another play being staged at Ford's Theater. She sent a messenger to obtain tickets. As the messenger made his purchase, Booth overheard the transaction. In that moment Booth decided to conclude one of the most wretched plots in American history. A few moments after ten that night, he fired the fatal shot. The next morning Lincoln was dead. It's far too simple to suggest that the course of our country was altered because of a last-minute change in theater plans. One wonders, however, what might have happened if President and Mrs. Lincoln had seen the other play.

You run into something like this in lots of places. Not too many years ago a man was walking down a street in New York City. Lost in his thoughts, he came to a busy intersection. Unaware that the lights had changed, he stepped into the path of passing traffic. Nearby stood a cabdriver who saw the man in danger. At the last moment the driver pulled the man to safety. The world may not remember the name of that cabdriver, but it will never forget the man who was pulled to safety that night in New York. In the darkest hours of this century, he pled with his world to die rather than surrender. History still recalls this man's gravelly voice as he stood in the British Parliament and promised England its "finest hour." But on that night in New York, the life of Winston Churchill was in the hands of a cabdriver.

We never really know the significance of an event, whether it seems great or small. Sometimes what appears to be a detail becomes a matter of crucial importance in our lives. Back in another generation one of America's most successful men used to lecture his employees, "Manage the pennies, and the dollars will take care of themselves." Isn't it equally true to say that if we manage the details, the larger matters will run to the right conclusion? Most of us make or break ourselves by the way in which we handle the "small stuff."

Do you remember the story of the lad who saved Holland? One day as he was playing near the dikes, he discovered water trickling through a crevice. Aware that the water would continue to flow until it became a torrent, and that his country lay below the level of the sea, he knew his country could be destroyed. As I recall the story, the boy sat down by the crevice and with his hand held back the sea until help could arrive. There are a lot of lessons in that story, but among the most important is this: A detail overlooked or ignored can become a disaster.

In my work as a minister, I see a lot of people with tangled and jumbled lives; and a lot of them have made it that way themselves. I have discovered, however, that in most instances their problems didn't happen overnight. They usually developed one step at a time—a surrendered principle, a short venture across the line of conscience. A friend tells about a puppy he once owned. One day the dog discovered the thrill of chasing cars. At first he stood on the curb and barked furiously as the autos went by. Then he began to venture into the street. He became bolder and bolder, and finally he was running the block with every car that passed. One day he was chasing a fast one. Hypnotized by the turning wheels, he failed to see the car coming in the other direction. It happens that way to people too. We ignore the "small stuff," and the molehill becomes a mountain.

But one of the amazing things about life is the way in which the small things make living beautiful. Charles Kettering once said, "You don't buy a fiddle today and play in Carnegie Hall tomorrow." He was right about that. But little by little the daily toil of practice will produce its harvest. In the early days of piano lessons, a child will struggle with scales and notes, painfully putting together each chord. Each lesson is rehearsed over and over. Then one day with perfect ease those hands sweep the keyboard, and the piano responds with the strains of immortal music. It was the "sweating of the small stuff" that made the greater harvest possible. The molehills became mountains and lovely ones at that.

Isn't this principle valid in business? Most great businesses are built not by big deals but by hundreds and thousands of little deals. Every customer—no matter how small—is treated with honesty and integrity. His complaints are heard and handled with concern and respect. Such a reputation builds confidence, and confidence breeds success. But let a business neglect its attention to details and the people it serves, and it may run for a while on past momentum, but one day the molehills become mountains over which it cannot climb.

This same principle is equally effective in the relationships between people. It's the thoughtful person who smooths the troubled waters of conflict. Too many of us want to spend our energies pondering complicated theories of interpersonal dynamics. We don't have time for things like a friendly greeting, a brief inquiry about another's concerns or a bit of attention to his problems. But think about it. The people who mean the most to us are those who remember a birthday, who take time for a friendly phone call or who remember the names of our children. It's amazing, isn't it, that the greatest people are those who find time to "sweat the small stuff."

Perhaps the most important thing about the principle, however, is the way in which it changes the world. A long time ago a carpenter from Nazareth told his friends that the way to change the world was by way of the "small stuff." They were looking for big things to do. He said, "The way to do it is by a crust of bread to the hungry, a glass of water to the thirsty, a helping hand to someone in need." Just help the people you meet along the way, and if enough of us do that the world will be a better place. Long ago G.A. Studdert put it this way:

> *Sometimes I wish that I might do*
> *Just one grand deed and die.*
> *And by that deed reach up*
> *To meet God in the sky.*
> *But such is not thy way, O God,*
> *Not such is thy decree.*
> *But deed by deed and tear by tear*
> *Our souls must climb to thee.*

It works just that way. Our lives and our world are sometimes changed by massive events of grand importance. But most often the change is gradual. People who take time to "sweat the small stuff" are usually the winners, and the world is a better place because they lived.

Those Inevitable Footprints

Several years ago a prominent citizen in Atlanta picked up an afternoon newspaper. Glancing down the front page, he was startled to discover his own picture and underneath a headline reporting that he was dead. How the article came to appear in the paper, no one really knew. The man had been scheduled to speak at a meeting in the city but, because of a mixup in dates, he had failed to appear. Somehow word got around that he had been stricken with a fatal heart attack. A reporter picked up the story and under the pressure of a deadline failed to check the facts. So there it was—the story of the death of a man who was alive and doing well.

The "dead" man read the story and on impulse decided to walk around a bit to see how Atlanta was taking the news. To his dismay, he discovered that things were going quite well. The traffic was proceeding as usual, and people were going about their daily affairs. "It is disconcerting," said the man, "to discover that you are dead, and it makes no difference."

Now the point of that incident has been made often enough. It is altogether possible that we overestimate our role in holding the world together. I read somewhere about a man who had become involved in a multiplicity of things, all of which seemed important. Pushed and shoved by too many demands, he feared himself on the verge of a breakdown. He wondered what would happen to the world when he was gone. One night he had a dream in which he imagined he heard God saying, "That fellow is about to be sick. How will I ever manage things without him?" Once in a while we need to take ourselves less seriously. It is conceivable that the world might go on without us.

The trouble with that kind of thinking, however, is that we may well press it too far. To say that there are no indispensable people is not the same as saying that people are unimportant. One by one we do count for something, and whether we live or die makes a difference. There is a line in an old book which reads, "No man lives alone, and no man dies alone." This author may have had in mind many different things, but he does suggest that we are inseparably linked together. It's a grave mistake to believe that the individual makes no difference.

We ought to sense this by simply observing the world around us. There is a kind of interrelatedness inherent in all of creation. Every bit of matter, for instance, is infused with some gravitational attraction. The stars are held on their courses by other stars so that the movement of one is determined by the others. Even a golf ball has its own gravitational field. It's infinitesimal, of course, but it is sufficiently present so that if it is dropped to the earth, the earth rises ever so slightly to meet it. The moon not only pulls at the earth but also the earth pulls at the moon. Nothing in creation exists without having some effect on the rest of it.

We used to believe that Mother Nature was extravagant and wasteful in her processes. We are not so sure of that now. She is far more exact than we imagined. Little things such as the use of improper insecticides and the exhaust fumes from poorly designed machines are about to wreck the whole life support system of our planet. Sir Isaac Newton had a point when he said that for every action there is an alternate reaction. A change here means a change somewhere else—be it ever so small. Why is it so difficult for us to believe this about people? To say, "I do not account for anything" is logically impossible. We do count—one by one—and the world is not quite the same without us.

In recent years there has been a rash of books written on how to influence people. That very notion is misleading. We don't have to learn how to influence people. We do that with every day that passes. We have an inevitable effect on our environment. The choice is not *whether* we influence others but *how* we influence them. We may discover methods of making our influence more forceful, but we cannot eliminate the shadows we cast on the lives of others.

Wallace Hamilton told that old story of a family traveling by Pullman out of Louisville one night following the Kentucky Derby. The car was full of people who were celebrating with unrestrained levity. One berth section had been made up for a four-year-old boy. He stood in the aisle, wide-eyed, clad in his wee pajamas. Just before he climbed into bed, he knelt and began, "Now I lay me down to sleep . . ." For a moment the noise continued, and then the place became strangely still. Men and women, long past their childhood, began to wander back to faraway days and reflect on precious things lost in the scramble for position and success. In the stillness someone muttered "I'd give a lot to have those things again." A four-year-old and his shadow— consciously or unconsciously, we touch the lives of other people. There is no way to stop it. We can only decide how we will touch them.

We need to remember this as we devise our schemes to manipulate people. Influence is not something we turn on or off at will. It goes on all the time. Even our attitudes affect our associates in our businesses, our families in our homes and our neighbors in the community. They hear what we say, watch what we do; they even read the expressions on our faces. Everyone counts for something: good or bad, great or small. Be assured that the world will be different when we are gone. Even more importantly, we keep on counting for something after we are gone.

Shakespeare once said that the ill men do lives after them, and the good is oft interred with their bones. That's only partially true. One of the teachers in our church school spoke to our staff recently. She mentioned some of the trials of her profession: "It's a tough job to be a teacher." She said, "But we have our compensations." Her clos-

33

ing thought was from a book by Alice Lee Humphreys: "My priceless legacy is the ability to live on in the lives of my children. Who knows? Perhaps I shall be a doctor, homemaker, minister, nurse, artist or even a moon explorer. Long after I'm dust, I shall enjoy a timeless existence through my school children."

We do live beyond our years. Remember that story of the wealthy British family whose child was rescued from a swimming pool by the gardener's son? In gratitude the family sent the lad to school where he chose to study medicine. Years later when Winston Churchill was ill with pneumonia, the King of England instructed that the best doctor be found for the prime minister. Said Churchill later, "It is rare that one man owes his life twice to the same rescuer." How many of the rest of us share in that legacy, especially since the gardener's son was the one who discovered penicillin?

Is there really any way to stop one's influence in the world? It travels a timeless course, sometimes in bold and discernible dimensions; at other times it is enmeshed in the flowing tide of history adding only a tint of color here and there. But for good or ill, it is never lost. Henry Wadsworth Longfellow, you recall, caught the significance of that in his immortal poem, "A Psalm of Life."

> *Lives of great men all remind us*
> *We can make our lives sublime,*
> *And, departing, leave behind us*
> *Footprints on the sands of time.*
> *Footprints, that perhaps another,*
> *Sailing o'er life's solemn main,*
> *A forlorn and shipwrecked brother,*
> *Seeing, shall take heart again.*

We do leave our footprints—all of us. For some of us the city stops, and the flags fly at half-mast. For others of us, only a handful of people sense the significance of our lives. But all of us leave some kind of print somewhere. We are making it now! The question is, "What kind of footprint will it be?"

Riding the Top

A few months ago we passed the 13th anniversary of the assassination of John Fitzgerald Kennedy. If you recall those traumatic days, you will remember that on the Sunday following the president's death, churches all across the land were packed with people. The presence of so many folk in their churches on that day confirmed a long suspected hypothesis: "In troubled and uncertain times, most people are inclined to pray." One of America's better-known columnists observed, "We were made acutely aware of our inability to manipulate the events that control our destiny. Americans know how to handle success, but they are completely bewildered by adversity."

Now anyone recognizes the point of that columnist's comments. It is true that most people—including Americans—have trouble coping with hard times. It is not quite accurate, however, to suggest that we are completely adjusted to success. I hear it often in my work from people who have made it to the top: "I'm overcommitted, harassed by too many obligations, and not happy over the kind of life I'm forced to lead. The top isn't all that exciting. It's more fun getting there than being there." A lot of people who have arrived feel that way. They struggle all their lives to be number one, only to find that the high rung on the ladder is a tough place to stand. Some of these people come apart, and the rumor mills make their judgment: "He just couldn't stand prosperity! He didn't know how to handle success!" All of us have heard this assessment of someone who has folded under the load. Sadly enough, it is sometimes true.

Do you ever wonder why so little is said about this? Businesses and corporations devote millions to the study of "people motivation." Seminars, institutes and sales meetings are held everywhere with the single objective of inspiring people to reach for the top. We have devised all kinds of methods to get better production from employees and encourage them to outrun the competition. But there is one glaring and obvious omission. We haven't said much about helping people handle the top when they reach it. Breakdowns, dropouts and suicides happen all too frequently among those who seem to have everything. It is true, is it not, that a lot of people don't know how to "ride the top."

A part of the problem is a confused and improper motive for success. So many people don't know why they are shooting for the number-one spot. In a lot of instances, the game is success for the sake of success. That never works, and the reason is that the top slot is an ever-moving and retreating target. It is an endless ladder where the high rung can never be identified. Remember that old description of the hungry tycoon: "He only wants what's his and what lies next to it." The trouble is that these people never get enough. It wouldn't be so bad if their dissatisfaction diminished in proportion to the degree of success achieved. But more often than not the more they get, the more greedy they become. Soon these people are overextended and their lives fragmented as they try to hold on to more than any one person can hold. Their empires are built on sand, and they go down with a resounding crash. It's a time-proven axiom in history. Power for the sake of power never lasts. It perishes in the ever-moving ravages of time.

In one of the oldest books in the world, there is a curious sentence: "He that would be greatest among you, let him be the servant of all." That's not dreamy idealism but a hard and realistic description of the way it works. Fame and fortune are never valid goals in themselves. The great people who have ridden the top successfully are not those who sought success, but those who sought a great cause. Abraham Lincoln stands at the pinnacle of American history not because he sought success but because he championed a noble cause. That's the way it always works. Genuine success is achieving something lasting and useful. If fame and fortune come in that process, they are incidental to the central objective. Only those who accomplish worthy and important goals ride the top with an inner sense of fulfillment.

Another thing essential to satisfying success is the necessity of remembering our dependence on those who helped make it possible. Our forefathers often used a quaint but descriptive phrase: "A fellow can get above his raisin'." What they meant, of course, was that on the high tide of success, it's easy to forget our indebtedness to those who helped us get there. This, in part, explains why so many people at the top lose their sense of inner peace. In its place there is guilt— guilt which comes from using other people as pawns.

It is reported that the great Albert Einstein once declared, "With each passing year, I recognize how dependent I am upon countless people who went before me." Einstein simply reported what has always been evident. No one hits the top alone. The self-made person is a myth long since exploded by those who understand the interrelatedness of people. To pass your benefactors in thoughtless ingratitude not only builds resentment in interpersonal relationships but also is totally destructive to inner joy and satisfaction over having arrived. The story is always the same. No one can wear the laurel leaves of success in comfort unless he remembers to express his gratitude to those who have helped him along the way.

One final thought: Success is always fleeting and relative. A few weeks ago on the "NBC 50th Anniversary Telecast," they ran again the tape made on that momentous evening when Hank Aaron hit his 715th homer out of the park. On the scoreboard in Atlanta that night was the record of Aaron's success, and beside it the old record set by George Herman "Babe" Ruth. Seldom has the truth been more vividly demonstrated. The old hero always gives way to the new one. The story is the same wherever you look. Centuries ago a great king who was thought to have reached the top was replaced by another king. The new king climbed the ladder too. When the record of the two kings' exploits was written, there came this somber sentence: "Saul slew his thousands but David his tens of thousands." How time tarnishes success. Old idols fall and new ones take their place. The poet was painfully accurate when he wrote these lines:

Time, like an ever-rolling stream,
Bears all its sons away;
They fly, forgotten, as a dream
Dies at the opening day.

Success measured by external approval is too fleeting to be satisfying. *Newsweek* used to have a regular column entitled "Where Are They Now?" In it were named some of the newsmakers of the past—people who were in and out of the headlines of every paper. So often the names mentioned were only barely remembered, and so many of them, although still alive, claimed little or no attention. The conclusion is obvious: Genuine success is not how the world feels about you, but how you feel about yourself. To believe in yourself, to know that what you have done has made the world a little better for someone, is what warms your heart when you stand at the top and look back.

This is the way it adds up. Success for the sake of success always leaves you feeling empty and guilty over the misuse of life. You soon discover that your exploits will be surpassed by those of another. The applause shifts, and another with more spectacular achievements takes your place. When you ride the top, you need to know that what you sought was worth what it cost to get there. Remember, too, when you walk with kings, not to lose the common touch. Above all, never let the crowd decide whether you are a success. Decide that for yourself!

37

Nibbled by the Minnows

On a November day in 1863, the citizens of Gettysburg, Pennsylvania, held a special memorial observance which will long be remembered in American history. Invited to address the gathering were the president of the United States and a statesman from Massachusetts named Edward Everett. Everett preceded the president on the platform. He spoke for an hour and 57 minutes. His address was so eloquent that the crowd cheered with wild enthusiasm. When Everett had finished, the president was introduced. He read a 267-word speech and took his seat.

The following morning, newspapers across the land carried the report of the Gettysburg observance. In most of the papers, Everett was acclaimed as one of America's finest orators. The president, however, was treated far less kindly. One editorial writer was reported to have said, "The president is a cunning clown. He is the original gorilla. Those who seek the ape are fools to go to Africa when he can be found in the White House in Washington." Today the world has a different estimate of those two speakers on that long-ago day in Gettysburg. Few Americans remember Everett's speech, but almost every schoolchild can quote from Lincoln's address.

Seldom has anyone been more severely censured and criticized than was Lincoln in his day. It is true, of course, that not many of us make it through this world without being subjected to the harsh judgment of others. Recently the editor of one of America's most popular magazines declared, "I don't like criticism—constructive or otherwise—but we are getting it more than ever these days. I am being forced to adopt some wholesome attitudes toward it, for it is the most valuable service our readers can render." That editor was making a worthy resolution. The constructive use of even destructive criticism is a marvelous achievement. The question is, "How do we manage to do it?"

The first thing we must learn in using criticism constructively is to expect it. In one of the oldest books in the world, there is a little verse which reads, "Judge not, lest you be judged." If the point of that instruction is to prohibit an evaluation of people, it is obviously impossible. Every time we cast a ballot, embark on a business venture, choose an employer or employee, buy a bag of groceries, or even select a used car, we must sit in judgment on someone else. Our critical faculties are essential to our social existence. Indeed, the failure to exercise these faculties can be devastating. Most of us expect to be subjected to critical examination when the reasons are good and valid.

There are judgments, however, which are unnecessary and not nearly so wholesome. Years ago in a little book there was a sentence which is descriptive of human nature. Someone said, "Mediocrity has a way of resenting excellence." Whoever wrote that sentence was fully aware of our chronic temptation to minimize our own imperfections by maximizing the faults of others. It's the oldest strategy in the world—the attempt to build ourselves up by pulling another down.

Anyone who has been out in the world for any period of time knows about this method of attack. He will be especially aware of it if he attempts to be a front-runner. Lift your head above the crowd, and you can bet someone will shoot at it. The reason is that it's easier to ridicule than to compete. Every person who achieves excellence, whether in his vocation or his avocation, needs to remember this. Excellence inevitably breeds its own resistance. If we expect to live above the level of mediocrity, the thickness of our armor must increase in proportion to our chosen altitude. The failure to remember this leads to troubled times. No one hits the top without feeling the hounds of jealousy and envy nipping at his heels. If it is any consolation, it helps to know that the critic reveals more about himself than about the object of his criticism. It's the little people who nibble at the lives of the great.

It's not enough, of course, to expect criticism when you walk the high road. We must pursue a second principle. If harsh judgment is to serve any good purpose, we must learn from it. A lot of stories have been circulated about Abraham Lincoln. Whether they are fact or legend does not diminish their lessons. You will recall a report that one of the members of Lincoln's cabinet once called the president a fool. Lincoln replied, "If Stanton said I was a fool then I must be one. For he is nearly always right." If that story is true, then one can easily understand Lincoln's greatness.

This is not to suggest that criticism does not hurt. It does, as anyone who has been so victimized fully understands. One of America's great black leaders once stated, "A good many unfair things have been said about my people, and they are inspired by the color of our skin which is solely the accident of birth. We have a right to be angry about these things, and we are. But if a fault is to be found with us—no matter how rudely or maliciously stated—we must not allow our resentment to blind us to that fault." No wonder the man who made that observation is numbered among the greatest of Americans. His advice is sound, but it isn't easy to follow. It is true, however, that the best way to get even with a critic is to learn from him.

The truth is that only through the testing fires of criticism do we grow. It's a foolish leader who surrounds himself with "yes men." I remember a man many years ago who said that everyone should have at least two friends: one who agrees with him and another who does not. They are equally valuable. The friend who is agreeable and supportive will enable us to maintain our balance, and the other friend will keep us from becoming complacent. That's a word of wisdom ignored at great peril. Often it is in the shock of the harsh blast of criticism that we learn most about ourselves.

39

Now and then in professional schools, students are offered a course in public speaking. One of the exercises usually involved in that course is the preparation and delivery of a speech to fellow students. The role of the class is to analyze the speech with the most critical judgment. Those who have undergone such an exercise find it an ego-shattering experience. But when they review that day from some distant vantage point, most will admit it to have been their most profitable training.

It is said that Thomas Edison was often interrupted by well-wishers who came to visit him out of curiosity. Edison found many such visits frustrating and of little value. But his ingenious mind found a way to turn those useless visits into a profit. He attached a pump to the gate, and every visitor who came through pumped water into a reservoir. That's a marvelous way to come at life—using everything that happens to you for something good. The painful barbs of criticism should not be excluded from that list. The truth is that we sometimes learn more about ourselves from our enemies than we do from our friends.

There is a third step in acquiring a positive attitude toward criticism. While we may learn from our critics, we must never allow their criticisms to deflect us from holding to a matter of conscience or pursuing a worthy goal. Down in the deep South many years ago, there was an eccentric minister who had his own quaint way of stating ideas. One of his favorite expressions was, "I don't mind being swallowed by a whale, but I'm not going to be nibbled to death by the minnows." This was his way of saying that if you are going to lose, then lose in a great battle with a worthy foe. Never allow your defeat to result from the nibbles of minor opponents.

Aesop had a fable about a man and his son who were leading a donkey to town. A passer-by laughed at them for walking while the donkey had no load, so the man had the boy ride. Before long they met a man who took the boy to task for riding while his poor tired father walked. The boy got off the donkey, and the man got on. Soon another traveler called the man selfish because he was making the little boy walk. To neutralize this objection, they both got on the donkey, only to be accused of cruelty to animals. In desperation they tied the donkey's feet together, put a pole between them, and began to carry the donkey. But people laughed so much that they let the donkey down. As they did the animal began to kick. He rolled into the river and drowned. There is no need to state the moral of that story. It's perfectly clear.

Hugh Latimer, the famed English cleric, was once invited to speak before the king of England. That Sunday as he was preparing for the appearance, he said later, "I heard an inner voice saying, 'Latimer, be careful what you say today because you will speak before the king.' But after a while, I heard another voice saying, 'Latimer, be careful what you say today because you will be speaking before the King of Kings.' "

We all stand in a higher court than the one where we are judged by our fellow man. It is the verdict of that higher court that really counts. The secret to great living is to have a clear conscience no matter what the judgment of our detractors may be. When you learn to live at that level, you can listen to the nibblers, learn from them, and still be at peace.

Fooling with the Hubcaps

There is a writer in California who tells of a friend he had back in college days. The friend owned a new sports car to which he had attached the finest hubcaps money could buy. The price of the hubcaps far exceeded the lad's budget, so he felt compelled to protect them with his life. Wherever the fellow went when he parked his car, he would take out a screwdriver, remove the hubcaps, and lock them in the trunk. The ritual was always the same. When the car stopped, off would come the hubcaps. When it was time to go, the spinners came out of the trunk and onto the wheels.

One wonders why the fellow went to so much trouble to protect his hubcaps. Surely life would have been far less complex if the boy could have settled for ordinary wheel covers less likely to be stolen. His problem, however, may have had something to do with image—the kind of impression the boy thought he was making as he rolled along the streets. Image seems to be important to most of us. We go to all sorts of extremes to create the impression we want others to have of us. We build our houses, buy our cars, and design our clothes not always the way we want them but to establish our image. We work at jobs we do not enjoy, stand for causes we do not really believe, and even have friends we do not like in order to create what we imagine to be favorable impressions. There is nothing intrinsically wrong with this effort except that it sometimes robs life of its joy and beauty. So often we let ourselves be pushed and shoved around, live lives which drive us into early graves, and discover all too late that the price we paid for the image we wanted just wasn't worth it.

Even more troublesome is the fact that the images we think we have created are transparent and visibly artificial. What we imagine others think of us and what they really see us to be are not the same. Perhaps for this reason something needs to be said about the business of image building. A fruitful insight on this matter was suggested recently by one of America's leading newspaper columnists.

There is a well-known syndicated writer who sometimes devotes his column to word definitions. A while back in that column, he pointed out two words we often use interchangeably but which do not mean the same at all. The two words are *identification* and *identity*. These two words, frequently used as synonyms, really have different meanings. *Identity* is what we really are, and *identification* is what others take us to be. A recent article in a southern newspaper illustrated the distinction between these words. A man wanted for robbery had been photographed at the scene of his crime. His picture was on the front page and underneath was this sentence: "This man has been identified as the thief, but his true identity is unknown." This reporter, whoever he was, used the two words correctly. Identification is what others take us to be, and identity is what we really are.

Now the point of this exercise in semantics has real meaning in life. Most of us spend a lot of our time working on our identification rather than our identity. That was the problem with the boy and his hubcaps. He wanted to be identified as the well-heeled fellow about town when in reality he was living beyond his means. He wanted to appear to be what he was not, and the result was a life of anxiety and concern. That's the way it goes when you try to project an unreal image.

Whenever anyone attempts to project a false image, life becomes a drag. The effort will work itself out in one of two ways. Sometimes we try to appear better than we are. I am a minister and often get letters asking me to recommend someone for a particular position. A letter came the other day with a curious question in it: "Do you know this person's daily habits?" I caught the meaning of that. There is often a difference between our Sunday disposition and the way we live through the week. To put it another way, we usually exhibit our best side when important people are looking. We can cover our bad dispositions with some success at least part of the time.

There are times, however, when we attempt to be worse than we are. A lot of people do wrong things rather than stand out from the crowd. They do and say things contrary to conscience for the purpose of peer acceptance. Young people are particularly susceptible to this pressure. Many teen-agers act completely contrary to what they have been taught and what they believe rather than risk ostracism by their comrades. This isn't to suggest that adults do not play the game, too. They do! They surrender highest ideals in order to run with the pack.

These artificial projections of identity seldom work out. Time has a way of sifting things down to what they really are. No hero remains identified as a coward for long, and no coward will be remembered indefinitely as a hero. In the long run it's a mistake to spend all your time working on identification. Lincoln was right when he said, "You may fool all the people some of the time; you can even fool some of the people all of the time; but you can't fool all of the people all the time."

The real business of life is to concentrate on your identity; and when you do that, identification takes care of itself. The reason is that what we are finally overshadows what we try to make others think we are. A friend reports on a used car he once bought. It was shiny and bright, with chrome in all the right places. It looked like a real "cream puff," so he never bothered to have it checked out. A few months later the real identity of the car came through. It had been a hard-driven taxi in a northern city. The car began to wheeze, smoke and rattle. It's the car that counts and not the hubcaps.

There is a biography of a man contained in one of the world's oldest books. This man stands as one of history's most admired figures. He made no claim to goodness or greatness. Indeed, on one occasion

43

he declared: "I am the chief of sinners, but I want to be different."
One of the reasons we hold this man in such high regard is that he
never engaged in pretense. He was open and unpretentious. He spent
his whole life trying to improve his image by improving himself. That's
the way to build an image. You can't do it with hubcaps only.

Many years ago, a man walked the streets of a little town. It was
early morning, and he had not slept. For some strange reason, his mind
was alive with thoughts. At the time he had no way of knowing that
when he wrote down these thoughts, he would profoundly affect and
influence the lives of people such as Oliver Wendell Holmes, Matthew
Arnold, Abraham Lincoln and Woodrow Wilson. We shall never know
the full impact of Ralph Waldo Emerson's thoughts which resulted
in his widely known essay, "Self-Reliance." In that essay, Emerson said
this: "There is a time in every man's education when he arrives at the
conviction that envy is ignorance; that imitation is suicide . . . My life
is for itself and not for a spectacle . . . What I must do is all that concerns me, not what the people think. This rule . . . may serve as the
whole destination between greatness and meanness."

Emerson's words are profoundly true. We spend too much of our
lives trying to make an impression—projecting an image, protecting
our hubcaps. We spend too little time trying to become a person worthy of respect and admiration. The result is a life of distraction and
anxiety; and in the end, it's all in vain. Images artificially construed
are always shattered, and we are at last known for what we really are.
This is why the words of Shakespeare could well be the motto for every life:

> *This above all: to thine own self be true,*
> *And it must follow, as the night the day,*
> *Thou canst not then be false to any man.*

One Door at a Time

There is an old story about a king who wanted to select the best man in his kingdom to be his prime minister. The selection process continued until only three men were left. They were so equal in their abilities that the king did not know which one to choose. The king decided to devise a test to enable him to make the best choice. The finest locksmiths in the kingdom were called to the palace. They were told to devise the most intricate lock they could imagine and place it on a nearby door. The king then told the three men that the prime minister would be the man who could open the door. Two of the men sat down and with complicated math calculations began to search for the combinations to the lock. The third man simply stared at the lock. Suddenly he crossed the room and turned the handle. The door opened immediately. It had never been locked at all.

There is a lesson about life in that story. Many of the things we seek are not really hidden from us. We only have to take the initiative in seizing them. In this list are friends, beauty and knowledge. These possessions are available to us, and the doors which separate them from us are always unlocked. We often miss a lot through our failure to test the doors.

Some of the things we seek, however, are not so easily found. The doors are really locked, and we have no choice but to struggle with them. Kenneth Wilson, on the editorial page of a national magazine, referred to that well-known story of a farmer who was asked for directions to a certain place. He fumbled for an answer and declared, "You can't get there from here." "Some things are like that," said Wilson. "They are so complicated that we aren't likely to find total solutions, at least in our lifetime." Peace, hunger, poverty and crime are but a few. "But," continued Wilson, "while we may not be able to get anywhere we choose from here, we can get somewhere." That's a thought worth remembering.

One of the great temptations in life is to be overwhelmed by the complexity of it. Many centuries ago a man was quoted as saying, "Oh, that I had the wings of a dove that I might fly away and be at rest." The man who said that was reportedly the ruler of a kingdom in a time of great unrest. The people were rioting; even the king's closest friends were plotting his downfall. It was too much for the man. He wanted off, and he wanted out.

Many of us feel that way at times. We are paralyzed by the sheer immensity of our problems. But a lot of us fail to recognize that big problems are the result of little things which keep piling up until their collective weight is overwhelming. The housewife faces a rainy day; the dryer goes on the blink; a child cuts his finger; another leaves the refrigerator open, and all the frozen foods spoil. At the height of the confusion, the doorbell rings and someone reports that the family dog has bitten a neighbor's boy. A phone call brings news that her husband's car has to have major surgery. Most of the time the big problems are little things which keep adding up toward the proverbial straw on the camel's back. When the budget gets tight, the roof starts to leak; the children need special dental or medical care; and our jobs get shaky. We then understand the thoughts of that long-ago man who wistfully declared, "Oh, that I might fly away."

Escape from such circumstances is impossible. Children may pick up their marbles and go home, but adults have to stay and struggle. There is no place to hide for most of us. We have to confront our problems no matter how immense. The question we ask is, "How do we handle them?"

There is some direction on this matter in the thought, "If you can't get there from here, you can get somewhere." One of America's newspapers sponsors a Father's Day contest. Children write in and nominate their fathers for the top father of the year. One youngster reportedly wrote, "My pop's tops because he lets me take accordion lessons. He lets me practice outside. When I practice outside, he goes inside. He says that he can hear better from a distance." There is a hidden moral to this story. You can do something to relieve every situation. If nothing more, you can stand back and gain perspective.

Samuel Johnson once said, "If a man were to compare the effect of a single stroke of a pickax or of one impression of the spade with the general design and the last result, he would be overwhelmed by the sense of their disproportion; yet those petty operations, incessantly contrived, in time surmount the greatest difficulties and mountains are leveled." Johnson was stating a truth about life. Big things are changed by the constant bombardment of little things.

There was a professor at the University of Glasgow who in a physics class would suspend a heavy bar of steel from the ceiling of the classroom. He would then stand back and throw paper pellets at the steel bar. After a long time the bar would begin to move ever so slightly and finally would swing vigorously back and forth. The point of the exercise was that every action, no matter how slight, has its effect. That's as true in life as it is in physics. Even the largest problems yield to the constant pressure of little things. The most difficult problems change when we apply patience and determination to their solution. We may not be able to get just anywhere from where we are, but we *can* get somewhere.

The trouble with so many of us it that we want to unsnarl everything in one fell swoop. As a minister I find people every day whose lives are totally jumbled. They are at their wits' end. So often these people are looking for the shortcut, the quick way out. Frequently these people have to be reminded that there is no shortcut. The only solution will come from finding one right thing, no matter how insignificant, and then doing it. The curious thing about life is that once you start this process, each right step reveals another one which can be taken until locked doors begin to open.

Cardinal John Henry Newman in his famed poem, "Lead, Kindly Light," wrote these lines:

> ... *I do not ask to see*
> *The distant scene; one step enough for me.*

Newman sensed the nature of life. Providence seldom gives us all the directions at once. Doors open one at a time. Most often that open door only gives us enough light to see the next one.

We are too willing to surrender and throw in the towel. No problem is completely hopeless. Perhaps the full solution can't be found, but we can change the dimension of the problem and make it a little less vexing and difficult. We do that by taking one handle and working with it until another handle comes into focus. We open the one door before us and then look for the next one. Even the most complicated problem yields to this methodology. We may not be able to get just anywhere from where we are, but we can get somewhere. There are no substitutes for patience and perseverance in life. Mountains are moved with tiny shovels. Seemingly insurmountable problems are changed by opening one door at a time. And every problem has at least one door which can be opened if we look for it.

The Value of a Poor Memory

The other day I found an advertisement about a study course designed to help people more effectively utilize their minds. According to the publishers, the course is being widely used. I suppose the reason is that most of us feel the need to increase our brainpower. For a long time, psychologists have told us that we use only a fraction of the potential of our minds. Many of us have vast latent mental resources, if only we could discover ways of harnessing them.

One of the faculties most of us want to strengthen is that of memory. Instant and accurate recall is invaluable both in our jobs and personal lives. A lapse of memory is both frustrating and embarrassing. We lose names, appointments, dates and important facts. The result is usually troublesome. It is little wonder that so many people enroll in memory courses. A retentive mind is a tremendous asset for anyone.

As important as a good memory may be, however, the power to forget is equally valuable. Centuries ago there was a man who wrote a letter to some friends in a faraway corner of the world. In that letter there is this significant sentence: "Forgetting those things which are past, I press on." We do not know precisely what the author had in mind when he wrote those words. We suspect he had learned that in some things and in some places it is better to forget.

One of the places where a poor memory is a blessing is with our past accomplishments. Several years ago Dr. William Fisher wrote a book entitled *Don't Park Here*. He began one of his chapters with this important thought: "More lives have been shriveled by success than failure. Out of the humiliation of failure can come powerful incentives to try again, to prove one's worth, and to verify one's ability. But out of the satisfactions of success too often come a complacency and contentment that lull the mind, erode the will, and cut the nerve of continued effort to achieve."

The truth of Fisher's thought is evident in so many ways. Multitudes of people park by some past accomplishment and thus fail to grow and reach their potential. A few years ago, a famed southern after-dinner speaker spoke to one of the great manufacturing associations of America. His title was "You Can't Do Business Today With Yesterday's Tools and Expect to Be in Business Tomorrow." That point, so apparent in the business world, has wider implications. Many a student, graduating at the top of his class, has never matched performance with possibility simply because he dwelled on what was done rather than what remained to be done. There are artists who could be great but are content to be talented; writers who are masterful but have settled for mediocrity; and students who could be pacesetters but are simply satisfied to pass. It's a terrible waste of life to rest upon one's laurels, no matter how satisfying they may be. It's far better to forget past achievements if in remembering them we become too easily contented.

Consider, too, the importance of forgetting our hurts. We know a great deal about that ancient man who wrote, "Forgetting those things which are past, I press on." Few people, in the long record of history, have tried more diligently to build a better world and have been more rebuffed in their efforts. This man was often beaten, many times jailed; his character was assailed and his sanity questioned. He was tried and convicted in courts where even the judges believed him innocent. No one ever had more cause to reflect upon the past with bitterness and resentment. But here in his letter is his firm resolution: I am forgetting the past and looking to the future.

Sooner or later all of us are the victim of some unjust misfortune. There is more than humor in the story of the fellow who was involved in a traffic accident. His car was badly damaged, while the other person drove away with hardly a scratch. A nearby witness came running up, "You should have that fellow arrested. It was plainly his fault." The man shook his head sadly. "Thanks, but it couldn't possibly have been his fault. His father is the mayor; his uncle is the chief of police; his brother is the judge; and I'm married to his sister." It happens that way at times. Life has its uneven places, and we get hit when it's not our fault. But it's still dangerous to dwell on the past. If nothing else, it siphons off energy and potential which might otherwise be used constructively.

Alongside the Forum in Rome, there is a narrow stairway running down to a dark and dingy room chiseled out of limestone. In that room there are no windows. There is an iron bed, a small table and a hard chair. There are chains anchored in the wall with leg irons attached. Here, it is said, a man named Paul spent his last days. Imagine, if you can, Paul sitting at the rough table with a small lamp flickering near his cold hands. Perhaps he reflects on the days just past. He had come to Rome on a great mission, but strange events had contrived to place him frequently in jail. He had a choice. He could chaff under the inequities that had befallen him and surrender in bitter resentment, or he could chart a new course. Paul chose the latter alternative. The Romans had silenced his voice, but they had not stilled his pen. Paul couldn't speak, but he could write. He wrote, and his writings have become immortal. They constitute a major portion of the most important book in the world—the New Testament. From that faraway day, Paul's life speaks to us: "It's fatal to nurse injuries from the past. It's better to forget and go on to what's still left to do."

A third place where a poor memory is a blessing is at the point of our failures. Several years ago a newspaper reporter interviewed one of the country's better known psychologists. The reporter asked, "What do you try to do for those who come to you for treatment?" The psychologist replied, "Our objective is to free our patients from the tyranny of the past." How important that is. Most of us have a past that is less than satisfying. We often try but miss the target. The alternatives are to accept failure or to rise and try again.

In 1932 an American president suffered the worst political defeat in history. Ridiculed by members of both parties, Herbert Hoover was a colossal failure in the eyes of millions. But with quiet dignity Hoover forgot the past and moved on beyond the blame, beyond defeat and with grace and poise entered new fields of service and duty. By the sheer greatness of his spirit, he began to regain the respect of his fellow Americans. His distinguished service to his country won again for him the admiration of many who in other days had rejected him as a failure.

The past, with its failures, its defeats and unobtained goals, can tyrannize us. The oppression can be so total and brutal that the present seems useless and the future hopeless. But the lives of great people remind us that defeat is not falling down; it is staying down. No one who says "I'll try again" is ever a failure.

A poor memory is not always a liability. If we forget the right things, it can well be our greatest asset. The people who make life what it ought to be are those who never allow past achievements to lure them into complacency. They refuse to let hurts and injustices dampen their spirits. And most of all, they put aside their failures and stand to try again.

We Don't Have the Right to Be Happy

Recently in a widely read professional journal, there was an article about the number of Americans who seek skilled help in dealing with the stresses and strains of contemporary life. According to the editors, the peak load for counselors and psychiatrists is the month of December. They report that many people are glad when the holiday season is over and are thus relieved of the pressure of having to be happy.

How accurate this explanation is may be open to debate. It is fairly evident that many people in our times imagine they are supposed to be happy. A while back a newspaper carried a cartoon of a family on a camping trip. The mother was none too fond of outdoor living. On this trip it had rained constantly. The father and mother were seated in their leaky tent while their disappointed children were creating havoc everywhere. The harassed mother was saying to her husband, "Tell me again about the good time we are having." A lot of us share that feeling. If we are supposed to be having a good time in life, someone has to tell us about it.

Involved in all of this is at least one notion that needs to be challenged. Frequently you will hear the question, "Don't I have the right to be happy?" Implied in this question is the suggestion that first and foremost and at any price some people imagine happiness to be the chief goal and purpose of life. That's an old idea, but one wonders about its accuracy. Is happiness the chief objective of life?

One thing we have learned about living is that the *direct* pursuit of happiness is futile and usually disastrous. Oliver Wendell Holmes once declared, "Repose is not the chief end of man." One suspects Holmes was well aware that what many of us believe to be happiness is not possible in our kind of world. We long for an existence where life is one continuous picnic and the only pressures upon us are those we elect.

Such a dream, of course, is an illusion. Do you recall the story about the little girl who one day asked her mother, "What can I do ?" The mother replied, "Anything you like, my dear." The little lady responded, "But I'm tired of doing that." What the little girl discovered has been the common experience of mankind. There is a saying which contains more than casual wisdom: "The more you do just what you want to do, the less you enjoy doing it."

In one of the oldest books in the world, there is a story of a boy who declared his right to be happy. One day, tired of the rugged discipline of home, he took his leave and journeyed to the inviting streets of a distant city. For a while things went well as he exercised his unrestrained freedom. But the story continues with these solemn words: "When he had spent all, a mighty famine arose in the land and he began to be in want." The crisis which overtook the boy was not just financial. The real poverty he faced was that of the spirit—the emptiness of life which always comes to those whose only pursuit is happiness at any price.

A long time ago an English author penned an essay on the illusion of happiness. He began the essay with the story of a young man who was facing a difficult and momentous decision. The boy asked, "Don't I have the right to happiness?" The author responded, "No, you don't! And if finding happiness is the chief pursuit of your life, you will never find it."

This makes a second observation necessary. Happiness is always the byproduct of another pursuit. There is an interesting word in our language coined 200 years ago by Horace Walpole. The word is *serendipity*. Walpole picked up the word from the story of three princes from Serendip, the ancient name for Ceylon. Wherever these princes went, they never found what they were seeking but always something else. The word *serendipity* came to mean finding something that could not have been found unless one had been seeking something else. Happiness is always a serendipity.

Back in the early days of this country, a rancher hitched his team and wagon to a post in a small western town. Gun-happy cowboys with six-shooters flashing frightened the team. The horses bolted and began to run just as the rancher was leaving the village store. The man raced for his team and managed to catch one bridle. Jerked off balance, the man was trampled by flying hoofs before he could bring the horses to a halt. The rancher was taken to the town doctor, who soon discovered nothing could be done. "Why did you do it?" demanded the doctor. "Why didn't you let the horses run? No team is worth your life." The rancher pointed to the wagon. The villagers looked inside and found three children peacefully sleeping.

There is an important lesson in that old parable. Peace of mind and spirit is not personal tranquillity or repose. It is the byproduct of faithfulness to duty. To put it another way: When you do what you are supposed to do, you feel the way you want to feel. A third observation becomes evident. The chief pursuit of life is not to be happy but to be faithful to responsibility. People who sit at the couselor's desk frequently observe something interesting about nature. When personal happiness is in conflict with duty and responsibility, most people are likely to choose happiness. While this may be a perfectly human reaction, it seldom works. We have not yet devised a way to feel right over the long pull while traveling the wrong road. The schoolboy may play and ignore his lessons, but he is forever haunted by the vague awareness that examination day is inevitable. Duty and responsibility demand attention. To ignore them always mars and tarnishes tranquillity.

The contented heart is never acquired by evading what we ought to do or be.

A part of the reason for the restlessness of modern man is his inclination to ask, "What do I want to do?" rather than "What ought I to do?" It is said that during the Civil War, Lincoln expected action from General McClellan and his army; but for some reason, McClellan failed to carry through. Lincoln in his subtle way sent word to his commander: "General, if you are not using your army, may I borrow it? There is a war on." Lincoln has been remembered in part for his tranquillity of spirit. Most likely the reason for Lincoln's tranquillity is that first and last he was faithful to his duty.

In the publication *Nuggets* the following prayer appeared:

"Lord, don't give me rest.

"Give me tasks to do, O Lord. Big ones, long ones, time-consuming ones, challenging ones.

"Give me jobs that look all but impossible. Give me assignments that others don't think I can handle. Give me projects that I cannot finish in a day but must set aside at evening and sleep on and anticipate for tomorrow.

"Give me work I'm not quite sure how to do, Lord, and give me deadlines and give me people standing there impatiently waiting for the result—discriminating people who expect it to be right, who need it very much.

"Give me all this today, Lord, and then tomorrow give me more tasks just as tough or tougher.

"All this give me, Lord, instead of rest, because I want to learn, to grow, to be of value, to accomplish, to have purpose, to anticipate all my tomorrows. Amen."

The River Never Waits

Someday when you have a moment, pick up a dictionary and look for the definitions of the word *time*. A good dictionary will devote considerable space to the word, but for the most part the definitions seem vague and redundant. This confusion in meaning, of course, is not crucial. There are a few words in our language which really need no definition. By common consent we seem to understand them, perhaps more by intuition than anything else.

Now and then, however, we can give partial definition to some of these words through imagery and symbolism. Long ago Isaac Watts began a stanza of one of his poems with this striking thought: "Time, like an ever-rolling stream, bears all its sons away." Such an analogy seems appropriate when measured against our experience. Time does seem to have the character of an ever-rolling stream, flowing at a relentless pace. Perhaps this is the reason why there are countless references in literature to the "River of Time."

When you examine this analogy, certain things become apparent. All of us are thrust into the river to make life's journey. Sometimes the waters are calm and peaceful; at other times they are restless and turbulent. But whatever may be the circumstances of the journey, time as a river gives life to a special urgency which none of us can afford to ignore. There are at least three things that are important.

First, *the River of Time gives movement to life, but it does not govern the direction.* One of the great rivers of the world spans the South American continent. The Amazon has its headwaters in Peru and then flows for 3,900 miles to the Atlantic. Although the river runs largely through low country, its banks in most places are clearly pronounced. But down near the ocean, the Amazon is 150 miles wide and is divided into countless channels by the silt deposits of the centuries. Navigation on the lower Amazon is not easy. Sometimes a channel will seem clear and inviting. But the unskilled sailor taking that course will find himself at a dead end enmeshed in tropical jungles. It's not a good practice to drift on the Amazon. The currents of the river and the ocean tide pouring in at its mouth can be deadly.

The River of Time is not unlike the Amazon. The currents flow in many directions. Sometimes the channels are throughways by which one may reach intended goals and destinations. But other channels lead nowhere and end in tangled confusion. The current provides movement but not direction.

Several years ago a widely known attorney wrote an article for a southern publication. The article was entitled, "Time Guarantees Movement but Not Progress." That's a fair analysis of the way the River of Time works. If you really want to reach a preselected destination, the river may or may not take you there. Constructive living demands decision. To rely on luck or chance is to court disaster.

There is a second thing evident about the River of Time: *It has a way of deciding for us what we do not decide for ourselves.* In 1836 a messenger left an abandoned church mission in southwest Texas. He skirted through 100 yards of almost certain death and rode away into the darkness. The messenger was bent on finding help for 187 men who had converted the unused mission into a fort. Outside the fort stood an army of 3,000 men determined to crush all resistance within the walls of the mission. The plea of the messenger was urgent. The men in the Alamo were doomed unless help was sent. But the commander of the garrison to which the messenger made his plea was torn with indecision. For two days his army was immobile. Finally, he dispatched a regiment; but the commander's decision was too late. The fate of the Alamo was sealed. Time decided what a man couldn't decide for himself.

Written into that story is a timeless truth, and it has been illustrated over and over. Somewhere there is an account of two men who were drifting on the Niagara River. They fell into an argument over how far above the falls they should put in to shore. The argument continued, but, the river didn't wait. By the time they said "yes" to each other, the river had said "no."

This happens so often on the River of Time. Days come at us one at a time, and each of them presents opportunities for decision. If we fail to make a choice, then the passing of that day will make a decision for us. John R. Mott once said, "Time is the only possession we have which we cannot replace. Wealth can be replaced. Even our health in many instances can be regained. But lost time can never be recalled." That isn't altogether true, but it is true enough to merit attention. Our days are linked together, and the harvests of tomorrow are dependent upon the seeds sown today. Maybe this is the reason a great poet penned into the wisdom literature of the world an important prayer: "Lord, teach us to number our days that we may apply our hearts unto wisdom." The poet knew that the river never waits. What we fail to decide for ourselves, time will decide for us.

All of this leads to a third observation: *In the River of Time, man— not the current—needs to be the deciding agent.* Many years ago William Ernest Henley wrote his famous poem, "Invictus." In that poem he declared, "I am the master of my fate: I am the captain of my soul." These lines raised a storm of controversy. At first glance, they seemed to be defiant and irreverent. But Henley wrote these lines out of two years' confinement to a hospital bed. Since childhood he had suffered an agonizing tubercular infection of the bones. The usual Victorian remedy was amputation. One foot had already been removed, and the other was threatened. It was in the hope of avoiding the second operation that Henley had been confined to the hospital. The treatments went on endlessly. Turning his face to the wall, Henley declared: "I won't give up, no matter what happens. I thank God for my unconquerable soul."

A part of what happens to us in life is programed by circumstances. We don't choose our talents, nor are we always able to choose our environment. But we do have a hand in what we make of life. Within our reach are thousands of opportunities to use the moments allotted us for constructive and important things. This is why we need to take a constant inventory of our priorities. We need to ask ourselves, "Is life bringing to me its finest possessions? Have I become a slave to artificial and trivial things? In my battle for the top, have I missed the joys of my family and friends? Am I running so fast that I've missed the beauty which could have been seen along the way? Have I exchanged the priceless treasures of life for the cheap and worthless?"

It is said that King George V kept a note written in his own hand on his desk. Where the thought originated no one knows. It has been attributed to Victor Hugo, George Eliot and others. Whatever its origin, it has been repeated everywhere.

I shall pass through this world but once. Any good, therefore, that I can do, or any kindness I can show to any human being, let me do it now. Let me not defer nor neglect it, for I shall not pass this way again.

That's an appropriate thought for all of us. We only go around once, and the river never waits.

The Displacement Principle

Several years ago, a Greensboro, North Carolina, newspaper carried a story about a tractor-trailer rolling along on a side street in a southern city. The driver came to a low bridge and misjudged the height of his rig. When the truck came to a stop, it was wedged tightly between the bridge and the street. Wreckers were called to remove the truck, but with all of their skills and equipment they could not budge it. Among the bystanders was a young student. The lad walked over to the men and suggested that the tires on the truck be deflated. As the air screamed from the tires, the great truck began to settle slowly away from the bridge. A wrecker was chained to the truck, and it was pulled gently backward. When the truck was free of the bridge, the tires were reinflated and the trucker was again on his way.

One of our difficulties in this sophisticated world is our unwillingness to believe that complex problems sometimes have simple solutions. We bring together the experts, get out our slide rules and turn on the computers. We write volumes of theories and come up with all sorts of complicated formulas to get at the things that trouble us. Many times this is necessary. We live in a complex world, and anyone who suggests that the answers are always easy isn't aware of the magnitude of our difficulties.

Sometimes, however, in our intricate computations, we overlook some simple ideas that are almost as old as man himself. In one of the oldest books in the world, there is a little parable about a house inhabited by a demon. One day the owner passed the house, found the demon inside and ejected him. The owner then swept and cleaned the house and went on his way. The last two sentences in the parable go like this: "The demon came back and looked in the house. Finding it empty, he went out, found seven other demons, and returned." There is in this little story an important rule for life. You get rid of a bad thing only by replacing it with a good thing. This rule has been called "The Displacement Principle." Consider a few of its applications.

Take the matter of our *thoughts.* Any high-school student in physics will remember an axiom discovered centuries ago: Nature abhors a vacuum. There was a day when many physicists believed that an absolute vacuum was impossible on this earth. Whether this is still true may be open to debate, but it is reasonably clear that when something is moved from a place, nature attempts to put another thing in that place. That's not only true in the physical world, but it also appears to be true in other areas.

The human mind, although strange and mysterious, reflects this tendency. It is capable of all kinds of thoughts: fear, envy, hate, etc. Sometimes our thoughts are so sordid we are ashamed of them. Even more vexing is the way in which the mind can fix itself on some small worry and transform a trifle into a mountain. Medical students, it is said, often encounter this phenomenon. People hear the symptoms of a disease and then by an overactive imagination discover themselves with those very symptoms. Thoughts have a way of feeding on themselves, and little worries can become so immense they paralyze us.

You don't get rid of unwanted thoughts by ordering the mind to shut them out. The more you try, the more you find yourself concentrating on those thoughts. It's difficult to empty the mind; you displace one thought with another. Someone tells the story of a woman who, when she began to worry at night, would get out of bed and bake a cake for a friend. One day one of those friends remarked, "That was a wonderful cake you sent me." "It should have been," said the lady. "I gave up a night's worrying to bake it." The Principle of Displacement is hidden in that story. You get rid of one thing by replacing it with another.

This Principle of Displacement also has application in our *disappointments*. There is a saying that suggests, "Into every life some rain must fall." Few, if any of us, would deny the truth of that. It isn't likely that we will go through life without somewhere, sometime finding ourselves walking in the rain. There are moments of despair when a particular dream or hope is lost. We miss a business opportunity or a promotion in our vocations. An ambition will be unrealized, or a cherished dream will be crushed. Sometimes we can cope easily with the disappointment; at other times we are devastated. Our friends counsel us stoically, saying that in this world you have to "grin and bear it." But if the Displacement Principle is true, then there is another alternative: One hope may be replaced by another hope.

Years ago someone wrote an essay on this very theme. The sense of that essay is this: When something vital is taken out of one's life, the way to handle the situation is to replace the loss with something else. To achieve this we must give all the thought and energy to the new interest or dream that we would have given to the lost or unattainable thing. Don't leave an empty place in your life. Replace it with a new thought or activity. That's sound advice, and it works.

Most people at some point in life have to settle for second-best. Phillips Brooks wanted to be a teacher; Edison intended to be a telegrapher; and Alexander Graham Bell planned to invent a hearing aid. But the business of living is to take what life gives you and handle it. More often than not, our second choices bring us as much or more satisfaction than the dreams we leave behind. Replacing a disappointment with another dream—that's what life is all about.

The Displacement Principle works, too, with our *sorrows*. That old parable about the demon and the empty house has often been used to affirm the proverb, *The idle mind is the devil's workshop*. It's more than that! The lesson of that parable runs across the whole range of life, speaking directly to our problems and troubles. It speaks even to our heartbreaks and our griefs. The best way to forget one's own sorrows is to enter into the sorrows of someone else.

That's a paradox seldom understood by many people. We imagine that our sorrow is enough without assuming the sorrows of another. We sit alone and think; we remember and brood until our grief chokes out all joy and peace. We can't understand that the best way to handle our tragedy is to help someone else handle his. But the verdict of all human experience is clear. It works!

There is a heartwarming story about a little crippled boy. His parents took him to a dog pound to pick out a pet. He looked at all the animals and finally selected a pathetic little puppy with an injured leg. When asked why he did not choose one of the healthy animals, the boy replied: "Me and him will understand each other." What the boy missed in his grammar, he made up with his wisdom and insight. He was working with the Displacement Principle. Your trouble is always easier to handle when you share the troubles of another.

So often it's difficult to accept simple solutions to our problems. We search the world over for joy and serenity. We spend fortunes on gimmicks and rack our brains for complicated answers. In the parable of the demons, however, there is a lot of wisdom. It may not be the total answer, but there is enough truth in the Displacement Principle to make some difference in every life. When we are overloaded with worries, baffled by disappointments, and overwhelmed by tragedies, the principle is worth trying. A lot of people across the centuries have found that it works.

Standing at the Crossroads

He is one of the brightest and most personable young men I have ever known. All things being equal he will make it to the top, and in doing so he will help the world to be a better place. But the other day when he called, I knew he had a problem. Just one year short of his degree in graduate school, he had received a fabulous job offer. "Man, I don't know what to do," he said. "How do you cut it when you stand at the crossroads, and all the signboards are down?"

Talking to young people these days can be a bit confusing. If, however, you listen carefully, you discover that in spite of their mod vocabulary they are asking age-old questions. My young friend had a hard decision to make, and he was looking for direction. His problem placed him in the company of the rest of us. For as long as people have been on this planet, they have been facing the dilemma of difficult decisions. There is no way around that problem for anyone. Whether you run the business or sweep the floor in the factory, you keep coming to the crossroads where you have to make up your mind. More often than not, there are no signboards. You make a decision and go on. Sometimes you are right, and sometimes you are wrong. But it's a tough, nerve-racking process, as the young fellow on the telephone was discovering. Did you ever wonder why we find it so difficult to make up our minds?

I have a friend who suggests that most of us fret too much over decision making. "All you need to do," he says, "is to get things into perspective." This fellow reports, "Each time I have to make a big decision, I take a long walk in the evening. Somewhere along the way, I stop and look up at the stars. I am then reminded that I am a tiny creature on a speck of dust in a remote corner of the universe. There may be a hundred billion worlds like ours out there. In such a universe what difference will my decision make?" That's one way of looking at things, I suppose; but most of us find little comfort in the stargazing process. We may be small and our journey here brief, but we don't want to tangle up what we do have by a wrong choice. It's a real question, therefore—the one the lad was asking on the telephone: "How do you cut it when you stand at the crossroads with the signboards down?" Why is it so difficult for us to make up our minds?

Well, a part of the anxiety in decision making comes from the awareness that our choices can have far-reaching effects on our lives. At the Continental Divide in southwestern Canada, there is a little brook that trickles from beneath the rocks. A few yards down the way, the waters of that brook divide into two small streams. One flows east and the other west. As these streams wind through the mountain passes, they get farther and farther apart. Thousands of miles from their source, one stream flows into the Pacific and the other into the Gulf of Mexico. The waters of those mountain brooks constitute a real parable on the way life works. A slight alteration of course at a given point can have far-reaching effects on what our lives are to be.

It is this awareness that makes us so apprehensive when we stand at the crossroads. We realize that, depending on our choices, our lives may never again be the same. Young people sense that dilemma in deciding on a vocation. People in business wrestle with the same puzzle. What happens if I take the offered promotion? What about the investment opportunity that seems just down the road? Public officials ponder important issues and wonder where the alternatives lead. No wonder decision making is so tough. A lot of times the choice can affect our lives forever.

Add to this awareness the fact that decisions have to be made, and so often made in a hurry. Someone tells a story about Lou Gehrig who one day during his famed baseball career came to bat. He swung at two balls and missed. The third ball passed, and the umpire called him out. Gehrig threw down the bat in disgust, and muttered something to the umpire, all of which was totally out of character for Gehrig. News reporters afterward asked him what he was complaining about. "I didn't complain," said Gehrig. "I simply said to the umpire, 'I'd give a thousand dollars for a chance at that last ball again!'"

One of the great dilemmas of decision making can be observed in that story. Life has a way of coming to us in a hurry, and we have so little time to decide. Edward Fitzgerald in his writings has a somber line about this: "The Moving Finger writes, and, having writ, moves on." It does! Life can't be placed in a holding pattern while we ponder the issues at stake. Living is a moving process where you select your alternative on the run. And the failure to decide has a way of becoming a decision.

Someone has rightly said that man may be free, but he is not autonomous. He has the freedom to say "yes" or "no" but not the freedom to avoid saying one or the other. That's but another way of saying that indecision is an impossible luxury. We have to make up our minds.

There is little wonder that decision making gives life its serious texture. When we remember that choices have to be made and can change the course of our lives forever, standing at the crossroads can be a fearful and troubled time. There is, however, one bright thought that needs to be imposed on this otherwise solemn picture: *A decision may have to be hurried, and it may be final, but it never has to be fatal.*

There is a story told by William George Jordan about a lumber company that years ago was trying to find a way to ship logs from Canada to New York. Someone came up with the ingenious plan of lashing the logs together and floating them to their destination. The decision turned out to be less than profitable. On the first voyage the novel craft hit a storm, and the logs were scattered everywhere. The chief of the Hydrographic Department in Washington heard about the failure of the experiment. He sent word to ship masters all over the world to look for the logs and report any discoveries of them. Hundreds of replies came in. The reports were collated, systematized and tabulated. New discoveries about ocean currents resulted and they have rewritten our geography of the world.

One of the wonderful things about life is the forgiving character which the Creator built into its scheme. No decision can ever be so wrong that something cannot be done to redeem it. If you can't get your logs to port for lumber, they can be used to chart the meandering streams of the ocean. Out of every bad thing, something good can come.

It's a good thing that life is that way. Few if any of us always make the right decision. Sometimes we lack sufficient information to make the wise choice. At other times we will misread the information we do have. Even those choices which seem to be right at the time may turn out to be wrong. Perhaps we can't go back and correct past mistakes. The "Moving Finger" does move on. We can, however, extract from every decision a new opportunity. I do not know what my young friend who called the other day will decide as he stands at the crossroads. But whatever his choice, it need not be fatal. If he looks for them, there will be enough opportunities down either road to make his life an exciting adventure. The Creator made his world that way.

It's the Long Pull That Counts

A generation ago you could find them everywhere—those novels written by Horatio Alger. The stories differed in detail, but the themes were almost always the same. Some unlikely fellow faced the world and made good. Alger always identified the reasons for the success of his heroes. The good guys were honest, thrifty, kind and courteous. Most of all they were persistent. Such stories, of course, are too romantic for this so-called age of realism. We now place the premium on craftiness, shrewdness or political savvy. That's the way to get ahead.

Now while Alger's tales passed too lightly over complex matters, I sometimes wonder if the simple virtues he extolled are really outdated. This is particularly true of persistence—the business of holding steady even in contrary winds. Samuel Miller of Harvard once described us as burned-out shells. At least a part of what he meant was that our exposure to life in these pressurized times has left us listless, shockproof and jaded. Our problems are so complex, and we have struggled so long that we are out of steam. That's a bit exaggerated, of course, but it's near the truth. Sometimes all of us get fed up with things and are tempted to call it quits.

Almost 2,000 years ago a man wrote a letter to some friends. Portions of that letter we still have. The letter was written to people who were working on a cause that did not seem to be going well. In that letter there is this significant sentence: "Let us not be weary in well-doing, for in due season we shall reap if we faint not." There is a lot of truth in this sentence, and it's worth exploring.

Someone has observed a dangerous inclination in our culture to believe in instant everything. Perhaps it has something to do with the nature of the times. We want to believe that all human needs can be met without delay. Ours is a world where everything is precut, precooked, preshrunk, prefrozen, flipped open or nonreturnable. While some problems yield to these kinds of solutions, others do not. Being schooled in the "instant culture," we get up-tight when everything won't follow that pattern. A mother tells about a little girl who was crying about something one day. The girl's father asked her to take a walk with him. "Dry my tears, Mother," she said. "I'll finish crying when I get back." Perhaps the little girl was on to something. Some things can't be cried through instantly. It takes time to work through them properly.

A host of problems fit that category. We struggle with them every day. They are massive and complicated and do not yield easily to our efforts. The worst thing we can do about them, however, is to give up too quickly. So many of our circumstances are like the tides in

63

the ocean. They change by the imperceptible diminishing of momentum, slowly yielding to the tugging of gravitational pull. This principle often operates in life.

A few years ago a government agency conducted a study of school dropouts who later enrolled in adult education classes. The researchers discovered that in many instances the reason for the earlier dropout was not the lack of intelligence but the lack of persistence and endurance. The students had not been willing to take the hard grind and the long pull. They wanted diplomas but no long hours and tedious work. The students who came back to class were those who discovered that there are no shortcuts to a trained mind.

In my work I talk to a lot of people about their marriages. My experience as a counselor suggests that there is no such thing as an instant home. Love is an ever-growing process. A good home is the result of ceaseless effort, and you work at it when the wind is favorable and when it is not. The reason so many marriages come apart is because someone lacks persistence and endurance.

Many of our failures result from our lack of endurance. If we can't reach our objectives by one Herculean effort, we drop out. Perhaps Harvard's Miller was right. We do seem to be burned out, fed up and turned off. The difficulty, however, may not be that our objectives are impossible. It may be that we just lack endurance.

Now and then we need to reread this sentence from that ancient letter: "Let us not be weary in well-doing, for in due season we shall reap if we faint not." The point of it all is the necessity of patience in working at life. Marc Connelly once wrote a play entitled *Green Pastures*. It was a folksy story about God's persistence in his purpose. One scene in that play is memorable. The Lord and Gabriel were having a conference on man's sorry record in building a better world. The Lord had tried everything to persuade man from foolish designs. Gabriel is about to blow his trumpet and put an end to it all. Just as Gabriel lifts his trumpet, the Lord says to him: "Hold it, Gabe. I'm gonna try one more time." Connelly's play may have lacked sophistication, but his point was right. Good things don't often come about easily. You sometimes have to work at them a long, long time.

Patience, of course, is not an easy virtue. We want the glamor of results—to see the task done and go on to something else. It's difficult to work and wait, to keep your cool when things move too slowly. As a result many of us become discouraged. Parents feel that way about their problems, especially when rearing children seems so painfully slow. Young people surrender to despair as they grapple with identity problems, trying to find who they are and what they were intended to be. People battling for good causes often have to battle pessimism when the tide runs against them. This is partly why depression is so common among us. If we could always run with the wind, life would be easy. But a lot of life must be spent with the wind in our faces, holding on silently and steadily when we don't seem to be

64

getting anywhere. That's why this sentence is worth repeating: "Let us not be weary in well-doing, for in due season we shall reap if we faint not."

There is a hard but certain reality about life. It is the steady pressure of little efforts that bring about great changes. Gerald Kennedy tells about the chief of a volunteer fire department who was asked what his crew did first when they got to a fire. "Well," drawled the chief, "we immediately drench the premises with water and break open the windows to get our equipment inside." "What do you do next?" the chief was asked. "We then check to make absolutely certain we have the right address." That might be humorous if it were not so true to life. Like the fabled rider, we jump on our horses and ride off in all directions. We spend vast amounts of energy without much thought as to its effectiveness.

Any history book will reveal interesting studies in the dynamics of great movements that have prevailed. About 2,000 years ago, 12 men set out on a mission. Their work moved so slowly. Their number increased to 70. They moved from a small city in a little country to the eastern rim of an empire. Little by little they traversed rivers and mountains until these men and their successors covered an empire. From that empire the movement these men started has stretched over the world. Few of the gains of this movement were spectacular enough to make the headlines. It took so long and was so gradual that it's difficult to know when it happened. But almost every community in the free world contains a church—a monument to the persistent efforts of countless people who by tireless and ceaseless efforts made their cause prevail.

From this remarkable story there is encouragement for us all. The winds of life blow in all directions—sometimes good, sometimes ill. But the people who prevail are those who can survive the steady push and the long pull. It's not the "fireball" who always makes it. A part of the reason is that the fireball soon burns out. He makes a big splash, but in a short time the still water returns. The people who make it are usually the steady folk who know how to "keep on keeping on."

William Ernest Henley wrote a poem sometimes considered by unwitting people to be profane. But when you recall this man's life, you read that poem with admiration. Henley had been hospitalized in the Edinburgh Infirmary for nearly two years. He had lost one foot and been subjected to at least 20 operations in as many months to save the other. One day, almost in despair, he turned his face to the wall. But he refused to yield. This in part is what he wrote:

> *Out of the night that covers me*
> *Black as the pit from pole to pole,*
> *I thank whatever gods may be*
> *For my unconquerable soul.*

Those lines made Henley immortal, and they should have. Those who refuse to be conquered are usually the people who prevail.

The Runaway Syndrome

On an October day in 1957, from a site near the Caspian Sea, a 184-pound package of highly sensitive instruments was shuttled into outer space. The flight of that small flying laboratory was the culmination of an age-old dream. Men such as Kepler, Copernicus and Jules Verne had dreamed of the day when man would overcome the gravitional pull of the earth. *Sputnik I* proved that it could be done, and with its success the long race to the moon began. Three and one-half years later, Maj. Yuri Gagarin made the first trip into outer space. On the afternoon of July 20, 1969, the world received the now-famed message, "The *Eagle* has landed." The message came from a lonely rock pile a quarter of a million miles away in space.

Scarcely a person in the civilized world heard that message without some emotion. For many it raised the possibility of a new world. Perhaps out there somewhere there is a new planet capable of supporting life. To it, mankind might escape and leave this cluttered, ravaged, strife-ridden planet with all of its complicated problems. That's a dream that lurks in the back of many minds. If we can find a new world, we imagine we might begin again and do a better job.

Across the centuries, countless people have toyed with this solution to their problems. Far back in the dusty records of the past, there is a story of a king who was tempted by the "runaway syndrome." There was strife in the streets of his kingdom. People who had once been loyal to him were in rebellion. Even the royal family was divided. One evening the king walked out onto the roof garden of his palace. Surveying the troubled city below, he cried: "I am as a sparrow alone on the housetop. Oh, that I had wings of a dove that I might fly away." That's the feeling you and I have now and then. We want to run, and it doesn't matter where. We just want to get away. There are two or three things that might be said when we face this temptation.

It may help, for instance, to remember that most people at times want to get away from it all. There is a popular television program that has for its theme song "Those Were the Days." Something about that song touches a responsive chord in many lives. Ours is a complex world, and life is a rough-and-tumble business. When the problems get tough, it is only natural for us to long for simpler and quieter times.

Thirty-four hundred years ago, there were some people who lived as slaves down by the waters of the Nile. For four long centuries, they had dreamed of escaping to another land. One day a man came down from the nearby hill country and led these people in their quest for freedom. The struggle was brief but violent, and the slaves won their battle. They marched out of Egypt and were on their way to the

67

Promised Land. But the moment the march began, the people started to murmur. Listen to what they said to the man who had led them to freedom: "Have you brought us out here in the wilderness to die? It would be better to be slaves in Egypt than to die in the desert. Take us back to the good old days."

The effort to find a different world and better days keeps cropping up in the records of human experience. The Great Teacher told of a boy who one day looked down the road to a far-off country. The place where the lad lived seemed so drab in comparison, so the boy wandered off. Out there in the far country, however, he began to look back. Soon he was wishing he could go home. It's the same old story from the sands of Egypt to the 20th century. Most of us, at least some of the time, wish we were anywhere but where we are.

Sometimes people feel that way about their vocations. "If only I had chosen a different field or applied for a different position . . . . " Housewives wish they could shift their responsibilities; parents wonder if rearing children is worth the effort; and students keep thinking about different schools or perhaps no school at all. No matter who we are or how carefully we have planned, the runaway syndrome gets to most of us once in a while. It's a rare person, indeed, who hasn't been tempted now and then to run rather than stand.

We need to remember, too, that despite this desire the runaway syndrome is not usually a workable solution. Many years ago when Joe Louis was heavyweight champion of the world, he was challenged by a nimble-footed opponent. When the young challenger was asked how he planned to handle the Brown Bomber, he replied, "I'll outrun him." Louis' answer has been remembered: "He can run, but he cannot hide." A lot of life is like that. We can't run away. There are at least two reasons.

For one thing, life often imposes upon us unalterable circumstances. While it is true that *something* can be done about everything, not *everything* can be done about something. An ancient author wrote, "God hath appointed the bounds of our habitation." There are limits placed upon us, and beyond them we cannot go. That long-ago king may have wished for the wings of a dove, but he still couldn't fly. Those far-off slaves could not return to Egypt. We have hardships we cannot change. Some of us have come too far in our vocations to turn back. We can't trade in our children or our parents. Many of the accidents of heredity are like iron chains. Try as we will to break them, we are still bound. "We can run, but we cannot hide."

The other reason the runaway syndrome won't work is because most of us carry our problems with us. Americans, it is said, are always talking about getting away from it all. They build all kinds of exotic hideaways. A few years ago an enterprising reporter visited one of those remote islands where people had fled seeking quieter times. He stayed a few days and then wrote, "Life is as hectic here as it is there. Americans have made it that way." Thomas Kepler was right when he wrote, "People at odds with themselves will be at odds with their world wherever they are." We never solve our problems by changing our geography if we take our problems with us. That wayward boy the Great Teacher told about was as tormented in the far country as he was at home. His problems arrived when he arrived.

The more you know about human experience, the more you understand that the business of living is not running away but finding meaningful existence where you are. A while back a radio station in the Midwest was having one of those evening talk shows. A listener with a quaint accent called in and made an unusual statement. "Everywhere I go," he said, "I find people who are trying to get away from it all. I'm not one of those people. I'm trying to get into it." That's an interesting turn of thought and one worthy of consideration. A lot of energy is wasted trying to hide when there is no hiding place. That energy could be used more constructively if we tried to find the "Promised Land" where we are. It's a real mistake to imagine that happiness is always down the road or just over the next hill. The fact is, if we can't find happiness where we are, we likely will never find it even if we roam the farthest reaches of the universe. This is not to suggest that we shouldn't look for new frontiers. We owe it to ourselves to find the best possible world. But most of us now have the only world we will ever have. The better part of wisdom is to settle down and make the best of it.

There is a proverb reprinted now and then, "Bloom where you are planted." The people who make life work are those who take that instruction seriously. Happiness does not come from finding the easy places. People who live that way soon become dissatisfied, bored and dull. Life is exciting for those who take tough circumstances and wrestle with them until they are different. Almost every football player will tell you that the thrilling games are not those their team should have won, but rather the games where their team pulled an upset. And even to lose in such a game brings a special satisfaction when the players have done their best. That's the way life works. Happiness and satisfaction are always commensurate to the struggle involved.

A long time ago a man lived in a remote corner of the world. His places of work were the tiny villages of a desolate country. He never traveled more than 150 miles from home. He commanded no armies, conquered no lands, and amassed no fortunes. He lived only 33 years. He took what he found and used it as he could. Today he is remembered as no king, past or present, will ever be remembered. A while back from one end of the world to the other, we observed this man's birthday. Why do we remember him? There are many reasons, but at least one of them is because he turned a manger into a palace and a cross into a throne. His life is an eternal example of what happens when you decide not to run but to stand tall where you are.

The Way the Mills Grind

When I was a boy, there was a book in our home entitled *The Wise Sayings of the Ages.* I don't remember who the editor was, but I do remember that the book was packed with proverbs gleaned from around the world. Many of those sayings would be meaningless in our times. They were couched in the language of the culture from which they were derived. I suppose in their day, however, these proverbs conveyed timeless truths.

One of these proverbs seldom heard today was widely used a couple of generations ago: God's mills grind slow but exceedingly sure. This maxim has been attributed to a well-known poet and philosopher, although no one really knows whether it was original with him. We do know that it speaks to an age-old question. For many of us, life seems so unpredictable. We wonder if there is any rhyme or reason to it all. One person wins and another loses; and we observe stoically, "That's the way the cookie crumbles." No one can deny that some of what happens to us is a matter of luck. There is something to be said for being in the right place at the right time, but often we are where we are through no effort or fault of our own.

It's a grave mistake, however, to imagine that we are the helpless victims of the crumbling cookie or the bounce of a ball. That's what the poet was trying to say when he spoke of the slow but sure grinding of the mills. We of the scientific generation should be aware of this. A moment's reflection on the scheme of creation as we now understand it should make this crystal clear. Consider a few ideas.

Begin with the notion that every action has its alternate reaction and consequence. The other day scientists announced the fly-by of a space package near the planet Venus. This remarkable achievement was not the result of chance or luck. It was the careful application of precise laws in existence since the dawn of creation. It's taken a while for us to unravel those laws, but once we understood them and applied them properly the space package behaved exactly as was predicted. This kind of experience is not surprising. We have long since learned that the universe is reliable. Set up the proper action and you get the appropriate reaction.

Every golfer knows this. Now and then you hear someone declare, "That was a lucky shot." Anyone who has played the game for any length of time knows that a good drive is not so much a matter of luck or chance as it is the result of the serious application of the laws of physics. A club of the proper weight and design swung at the proper speed in an appropriate arc will strike a properly designed ball with sufficient force to move it in the desired direction. If you meet those conditions, a good game of golf is inevitable. It's the old story of the

70

mills grinding to their certain conclusion.

In what field of human endeavor does this principle not prevail? The doctor utilizes it every time he treats a disease. The economist sees the same phenomenon when he manipulates the laws of supply and demand. The manufacturer observes it each time he starts a machine. It's a universal principle—this slow but sure grinding of the mills. It prevails in the moral, spiritual and social world with the same precision evident in the physical world.

The famous poet, in his statement of the principle, however, gave us an insight we sometimes miss. *There is often a time lag between causes and results.* There was a story in our paper recently about an 84-year-old woman who was suing her husband of 60 years for divorce. The judge asked the woman why after all these years she was leaving her husband. To this the woman replied, "Well, yer honer, enough is enough!" That's a crude example, but it's not without a point. Sometimes it takes a while for seed to come to harvest.

About 2,000 years ago, a dozen men met in a little room in a faraway city. These men were committed to a cause, and so far as we know they were about the only people in their day who were committed to that cause. From that room they went out on the busy streets of a mighty empire. The movement they espoused was so very slow in gaining momentum. They faced incredible difficulties. Their activities were declared illegal, and as a result they were forced to work underground. Most of these men died violent deaths far short of their life expectancy. But these men planned so carefully and worked so diligently that even after their deaths their work went on. Today in every city of the free world there are buildings marked with the sign of a cross. The seed sown by these 12 men has taken centuries to come to harvest. Indeed, it's still going on. The mills keep grinding even though they grind slowly.

Sometimes the mills grind so slowly that we lose sight of what is happening. Here is a boy whose parents want him to take piano lessons. He does, at least for a while. One day he skips a practice session. Nothing spectacular happens. The difference in his performance is so slight that no one can tell the difference. Consequently, he skips another and another. The mills grind to their inevitable conclusion. Today he can only listen to great music. He cannot participate in making it. The mills grind slow but sure.

So many of us are deceived in life by this time lag. We take a wrong road and nothing seems to happen. We refuse our responsibilities and seem to get by. But the mills are grinding slowly but surely toward their inescapable results. On the other hand, we take a right road and struggle toward a worthy goal. Nothing seems to happen. But that poet is trying to tell us something. The mills may be slow, but they *are* sure.

All of this leads to a final thought. *If life is to be serene, we must set in motion the proper actions and then take the long view.* One of the reasons so many people are depressed and anxious is their chronic tendency to take the short look at life. Ralph Waldo Emerson once described the difference between the truly great people and those who only seem to be great. He declared that great people are those who can take a position of conscience and then have the courage and confidence to wait. About 150 years ago in England, a new member of Parliament gave his support to an unpopular cause. He had looked down the road and knew that somewhere, someday, that cause would have to prevail. One day he stood in the House of Commons to speak to the matter. The halls of that great building came alive as the members of Parliament tried to shout him down. The young man stood quietly at the rostrum until the jeers and shouting ceased. Finally, when the room was quiet, he picked up his manuscript and said softly but clearly, "The time will come when you will hear me." That's the mark of greatness. You take a right position and then have the courage to wait until the mills can grind to the conclusion.

A widely known minister of the past generation tells about a woman who lived through the great London blitz. One night the bombs were raining fire through the streets and the city was ablaze. She began to wonder what would happen if Hitler really did conquer the world. She became so worked up at such a terrifying thought that she couldn't sleep. Then she remembered some words of an old song she had heard somewhere, "He's got the whole world in his hands." She thought about the Caesars and the Napoleons who for a time held the world at bay. But they had come and gone. Their empires had risen and fallen and out of their rubble the world was reborn and went on. She knew then that the red-running sword of Nazism couldn't survive. Muttering to herself, "To hell with Hitler," she turned over and went to sleep.

The business of life is to judge the days by the verdict of the ages. That's worth remembering when life isn't going very well—when you've struggled to do your best and for the moment things seem to be going wrong. God's mills grind slow, but they grind exceedingly sure. If you've done your best and your direction is right, learn to wait. Someday you'll come out where you are supposed to be.

How to Pay Your Debts

Several years ago Dr. Arnold H. Lowe wrote a book entitled *The Worth of Man*. Near the end of the book there was a chapter with the intriguing title, "When Glory Comes Too Late." Lowe told of attending a performance of Mozart's *Don Giovanni* at the Metropolitan Opera in New York City. At the conclusion of the performance, there were numerous curtain calls, great bursts of applause and shouts of "Bravo!" Lowe said that as he left the opera house that evening he could not help but think, "What a shame Mozart himself could not have heard the applause. Most of us forget that the immortal composer's funeral was attended by only a handful of people, and he was laid in a pauper's grave."

What Lowe was getting at in his book was that often there is a kind of injustice built into life. In this world, at least, people do not always get their due. There are those such as Abraham Lincoln and Stephen Foster who were missed when the laurels were passed out during their lifetimes. Foster died in poverty even though he enriched immeasurably the folk traditions of our country. Lincoln died never knowing that his Gettysburg Address would someday be called the "most precious gem of the English language." All Lincoln knew in his day was that his speech was called "falsified history" and that he was accused of using the graves of American soldiers for political oratory. Lowe's thesis is supported by at least some evidence. There *are* times when glory comes too late.

It is true, is it not, that sometimes the people to whom we owe the most we are able to repay the least. It is this very circumstance that often troubles us when we reflect on who we are and what we have. We are schooled in the American tradition that each person is entitled to an honest day's pay for an honest day's work and that everyone should receive a just reward for his contribution. Yet, it is clearly evident that such does not always occur. Many times we have deep feelings of guilt that our benefactors go unpaid. Such feelings of guilt are devastating to our sense of self-respect and serenity. We keep asking the questions, "How do we repay people who deserve far more credit for what they have done for us than they have received?" "How do we pay our debts?"

Any answers to these questions hinge first on the recognition that all of us are debtors. In the South the other day, there was a man who celebrated his 100th birthday. Reporters went out to interview the man, and they asked the usual question: "To what do you attribute your long life?" The man replied, "I have lived a clean life, rested well, and kept my conscience clear!" That pattern of living is conducive to longevity. The old man, however, missed a few things when he listed the reasons for his being able to celebrate a century of birthdays.

A few years ago, a leading health authority made an observation gleaned from a study of selected octogenarians: "Physical life and health are in some measure gifts to us. If we want to live long lives, the best insurance is to pick our parents from families of long-livers." That's absurd, of course. We don't pick our parents, but the point of the observation is clear. In many ways life and health are gifts which we do not necessarily earn. There are places on this earth where 50 percent to 90 percent of the babies die in the first year of their lives. We live in a land where the bequests of science, the sacrificial toil of those who probe the precious secrets of life and death, make it possible for most of us to reach our "threescore and ten."

Much the same is true of our mental equipment. When the *Encyclopaedia Britannica* was first published in 1768, there were three volumes. One of the latest editions has 23 volumes, and at least one new volume is added each year. We draw from that vast wealth of knowledge every day. Each time we go to a doctor, we make a withdrawal on a deposit of information gleaned from the past. No wonder someone has written, "Not a truth has to earth been given but that brows have ached for it and souls striven."

An ancient man once declared, "I am a debtor." We all are! We enjoy the privileges of freedom, the opportunities of this great land, and the rich heritage enabling us to pursue our own ideals of happiness. These gifts we did not earn. There are no self-made people. We owe to someone, at least in part, a debt for every blessing we enjoy. Most of the time we cannot repay those to whom we are indebted.

The reason, of course, is that the movement of time prohibits our returning just payment for benefits received. Lowe was right: Sometimes glory comes too late. For one thing we do not always recognize our blessings at the moment they are received. A few years ago in an address in a southern city, the speaker was reminiscing about his childhood. "My parents," he said, "had so little of this world's goods, but they did have character and integrity. Years later I came to recognize how priceless that legacy was. One dark night I was traveling through the little town where I had lived as a boy. I ran out of gas. When I found a gas station, I discovered I had left my money at home. I explained my predicament and told the attendant my name, but he said: 'No money, no gas!' As I started to leave, the man called to me, 'Are you Mr. Jim's son?' I said that I was. The attendant picked up a can and started for the gas pump. 'If you're Mr. Jim's son, you will be back.' How do you pay for that kind of heritage? Back in my childhood, I didn't recognize how important that heritage would be."

Sometimes we are so long in recognizing our heritage that those to whom we are indebted have been carried away by the "pale rider." Mozart's opera, *Don Giovanni*, is often said to be the greatest ever written. But Mozart's funeral—held in Vienna—was attended by only a handful of people, and they didn't even go to the cemetery. He was buried in a potter's field and his grave is lost. William Penn, who spent a fortune founding the state that bears his name, also spent his last years in a debtor's prison. More often than not we can't repay our debts to the people to whom they are owed. Time and tide prevent that. We sense a need to square accounts, but those who should be paid often are gone. ·

How, then, do we repay our debts? Dean Elbert Russell once said that in pioneer days a man stopped his covered wagon in front of the frontier cabin of Russell's grandfather. The man and his family were exhausted, unable to go farther. Russell's grandfather took in the travelers and cared for them overnight. In the morning the gentleman said that he wanted to pay for the night's lodging, but the host would take no payment. The guest was an independent spirit, and the two men argued. Finally, Russell's grandfather said, "Friend, if thee wilt not feel comfortable unless thee payest for the lodging, the next time thee findest a man in need of a place to stay overnight, take him in, and thee will have squared the account."

A long time ago the Great Teacher said, "Freely ye have received, therefore freely give." Russell's story hammers home that point. We repay our debt to the past by being faithful to the present and future. We can't always repay our parents for the heritage we have received from them. We can, however, be faithful to our children. Sometimes that's the only way we can square accounts.

Robert Schuller tells about a woman in California. She was working as a volunteer, preparing meals for the aged, the disabled and the poor. The woman had a small child who kept pulling at her skirts. The lady appeared harassed and tired. "Why do you do it?" Schuller asked. "Because," she said, "I was sick a while back. The people here came every day, week after week, bringing food for my family and me. This is my way of getting even."

Most of us have been helped somewhere along the way. Perhaps someone believed in us when we were standing alone and going through tough places. Maybe someone opened a door for us when all other doors were closed. It may have been a business associate, a friend, or maybe even a passer-by who took time to say a good word or offer a simple act of kindness. We look back, remember those people, and wonder how we can pay our debt to them. But they are gone. Time and distance have separated them from us forever. There's no way back to them; and we feel a bit of guilt knowing that for them, "Glory has come too late." It's worth remembering, however, that while we may not be able to return the blessings to those from whom they came, we can still pay our debts. We can pass along to someone else a special act of kindness, a good deed or a good word. The people who do that make an amazing discovery. They find a new peace of mind and inner serenity. They know their debts are paid.

The Case of the Unfinished Puzzle

In almost every home where there are small children there is a box that serves as a depository for toys. The box is usually filled with all sorts of treasures, ranging from talking dolls and whistles to popguns and spring-driven rockets. To rummage through that part of the playroom is to risk life and limb. If you don't lose a finger to a toy snapping turtle, you could be surprised to death by an exploding jack-in-the-box. One day in our home, I was looking for my hammer, which had a way of getting into that box. I came across an ugly-shaped piece of cardboard which appeared to be part of a puzzle. I asked the children where the piece belonged. After a moment's reflection, our daughter—who was then small—showed me the incomplete picture of a race horse standing amid the blue grass fields of Kentucky.

The lessons of life are learned in unlikely places, and that toy box was no exception. As I looked at that puzzle that day and slipped the missing piece into place, I recalled a line from one of the oldest books in the world. An ancient author, writing to his friends, remarked: "The wisdom of this world is foolishness." That long-ago man was admonishing his readers to beware of pride in their wisdom. The Creator has ways that the mind of man never understands. That's a thought worth remembering when you stand at certain places in this bewildering world.

How many times have you and I held in our hands an ugly piece of life? Most of us believe that the Creator's intent for us is a life that is satisfying and filled with a reasonable measure of inner joy and peace. It is unthinkable that the purpose for human existence is to endure only hardship and suffering devoid of all satisfaction and happiness. A widely known American has traveled the earth saying, "Something good is going to happen to you." Most of us want to believe that. The trouble is, there are events and circumstances that do not fit the pattern. These circumstances and events when reviewed alone seem completely outside any reasonable plan. We are left to ponder their meaning, and we want some answers.

One thing we might remember as we look for answers is the limitation of human knowledge. It has been said that we have learned more in the past 50 years than man had learned to that point from the dawn of history. There is evidence to support this. Our laboratories have produced incredible things. Sleek airplanes whisk through the skies at breathtaking speeds. Great nuclear-powered ships traverse the trackless oceans of the world. We have computers more accurate than the human brain. We are doing human organ transplants and have cracked the door to the creation of life itself. There is some reason for man's pride in his wisdom. In 1900 the United States Commissioner of Patents wanted to close his office. "All that can be invented," he said, "has been invented." If that man could see us now!

The ancient admonition, "The wisdom of this world is foolishness," is still applicable, however. Our accumulated knowledge has produced an interesting awareness of our limitations. Every field of knowledge, no matter how sophisticated, fades into the unknown. We are left with the distinct impression that the more we know the more there is to know. Strange, isn't it, that we still don't know what electricity is. We have mapped the surface of the moon but do not know for certain what lies at the center of our earth. We can't predict simple weather patterns except by percentages; nor can we know for sure the environmental impact of nuclear radiation. We are pondering "black holes" in space, and our minds are boggled by them. Yet we can't even cure the common cold.

A few years ago, identical twins died only hours apart in two separate western North Carolina towns. All their lives they had been plagued by strange events. Once, while one was hospitalized, the other became violently ill. Although separated by dozens of miles, one claimed to feel the pain of the other. The credibility of these events may be subject to question, but it does make us wonder what strange forces linger about us. That ancient writer was right: The best that we know is foolishness when compared to the unknown. How can we, who know so little, judge the significance or value of any event?

We need to remember, too, that what appears to be an ugly piece of life cannot be so judged until it is seen in its proper context. It is the context of any event that establishes its meaning. There is a church in our land that posts on its bulletin board the pastor's sermon title for the week along with an invitation from the church to attend its services. When seen separately, the two announcements usually seem appropriate. Recently, however, the bulletin board conveyed an interesting impression. "Do You Know How Awful Hell Is?" "Come and Hear Our Pastor." Context *does* establish meaning. It's true on bulletin boards, and it's true in life.

Remember that old story of the shipwrecked sailor marooned on a deserted island? Working with desperation and sometimes in despair, he managed to build a camp and in time provided the necessities for his existence. One day his campfire got out of hand and his camp burned, destroying everything he owned and had worked so diligently to build. Completely hopeless, he thought all was lost. Far out to sea, however, a passing ship's sailor saw the smoke from the fire. Knowing the island to be deserted, the sailor had the ship turn back to investigate. The shipwrecked sailor learned what most people learn after a while. The ugly pieces of life more often than not fit a lovely pattern.

Things are not always what they seem when isolated from their context. Seldom can we see the total picture because the finite mind sees only the past and the present. The future is blocked from our vision. Thus, we cannot see how the ill-shaped pieces of life fit into the total picture.

Anyone who is aware of these things will likely reach a third conclusion. The substitute for comprehension of the total picture is trust. I won't forget the day I found that piece of cardboard. It was ill-shaped and ugly; and from where I saw it, it would always be that. I entrusted it, however, into the hands of a little girl who was wiser at that moment than her father. She had the picture into which the piece fitted. I learned something that day. It's wrong to judge any piece of life to be ugly until you've seen the total picture. And when you can't see the picture, you have to live in faith.

I sometimes ponder what may seem to be a daring thought. I wonder if sincere people who struggle for a right cause for the right motive, earnestly seeking the proper direction, ever have a bad day. Of course, all of us are the potential victims of disaster. There are misfortunes, accidents, failures, disease and even death. We judge these things to be ugly pieces of life primarily because they bring us pain and suffering. But even pain and suffering seen in their total context are not always bad. Lincoln's death, for instance, was a tragedy. Most historians believe, however, that Lincoln's untimely death focused timeless attention on one of the greatest lives in human history. Lincoln may well have accomplished in death a grander victory than he could have in life.

There is a recent book that probes briefly into the lives of a dozen or so widely known Americans—presidents, senators, congressmen, sports celebrities, corporate executives, etc. In every case the stories are about some of our nation's greats who met unexpected reverses and became losers. Many of us have read their stories in the press and wondered how they managed to carry on in the face of such defeats. What most of us did not know is that in each case these are people of great faith. The answers become clear when we know this. These people fought and lost their battles for the sake of conscience. They believed, therefore, that their battles were not in vain. Even in losing, they served a creative purpose. This faith became the source of courage by which they were able to carry on.

That's a faith worth cultivating. Any day in life may appear to be an ugly one. We may feel like a loser or the victim of some cruel misfortune. But learn to wait. Time has a way of fitting ugly pieces into a lovely picture. People who work with diligence and patience some day discover that.

Pay Now and Go Later!

"You need to take a trip around the world!" That was the byline on a folder that came to my desk the other day. The return address on the envelope carried the name of a company I had not heard of before, but I gathered it had a national reputation. The folder was well done from a technical point of view. It was colorful and imaginative. "Nothing," said the authors of the flyer, "affords wider opportunity for learning and excitement than world travel. If you are worried about the money, we can offer you two plans for financing your trip. You can, of course, pay in advance and realize substantial discounts. If, however, it is more convenient, you can do your traveling now and care for the finances later through our easy-payment plan."

The day I read that folder, a thought kept coming to me. Whether the authors of the brochure knew it or not, the proposals they were suggesting for financing world travel are identical to the alternatives we confront in life. Back in one of the world's oldest books, there is a story that sets these alternatives into focus. One day two men set out to build their homes. Tradition suggests that the building sites were located near a dry watercourse. One of the men, a thoughtful builder, dug down to the deep hidden rock. There he anchored the foundation for his home. The other builder, a man in a hurry, built his house on the smooth and inviting sand. One day when the houses were finished, an unexpected storm swept the area. The dry channel, which had seemed so pleasant and secure, became a raging torrent. The two carpenters discovered the relative worth of their buildings. One, who had dug his foundations deep, enjoyed the sturdiness of a well-built house. The other man found himself standing in the rain. If you think about that story, you will discover that in its simplicity it speaks in a profound way to people in every age. Two or three things are apparent.

One lesson inherent in this parable is the clear indication that all of us are creatures of choice. A few weeks ago a distinguished philosopher gave a commencement address at a southern university. In his address the lecturer observed that contemporary man sees himself as the helpless victim of biological and historical determinism. That is to say that you and I believe what we are and what we do are determined in part, if not altogether, by what we have inherited and the circumstances under which we live. The speaker told about a cartoon in which a little boy is seen handing his report card to his father. His grades are all F's, and the boy is saying to his father, "My environment is all right. It must be my heredity." "That's the way we think," said this commencement speaker. "We want to blame our behavior on external factors. It gets us off the hook."

79

Now no one can deny that to some degree our lives are influenced by our surroundings. But to believe that we are helpless victims of fate makes nonsense out of a lot of things in our society. Why have laws, for instance, if everyone does what he has to do? A while back a criminal court judge addressed a youthful offender before his court. The lad came from a fine home with splendid parents. "Young man," said the judge, "there is a better way to live than you are living. Until you decide that and take a new direction, you are on a collision course with trouble." We nod in agreement with that judge. Our contrived theories of determinism do not erase our deep-seated conviction that we do in some measure control our destinies.

That's one of the lessons focused on by the parable of the two builders. Each of us is a builder. Someone has said it well: "Every thought is like a timber; every habit is like a beam; and every imagination is like a window. Well or badly placed, they all fit together in some kind of unity." *That* we shouldn't forget. We are builders and thus must bear responsibility for what we build. We are creatures of choice and have to pay for our decisions. The story of the two carpenters suggests that we can make our payments in one of two ways.

First, we may use the delayed-payment plan. A few years ago, one of the widely known sports figures of our land wrote an article for a national magazine. He said that he remembered the first time he visited a cafeteria. He was just a small boy. "The food looked so inviting that I took some of everything. What I didn't remember was that sooner or later I would come to the cash register. Life is like that. You can take what you want, but after a while you always hit the cash register." There is nothing especially startling about that writer's observation, but it's so easy to forget. Educators report that unprecedented numbers of adults are enrolling in extended education classes. Many of these new enrollees spurned earlier opportunities for training. Interested in quick jobs and instant money, they forewent the rigors of education to get on with the business of exciting living. Much later they discovered the law of the cash register. The quick-and-easy way has its price, even if it is delayed.

We live in a world with an inordinate fascination for the shortcut. The quickest way we imagine to be the best way. We can build our business that way. Attracted by the "fast buck," we lose sight of such fundamental principles as a satisfied customer, a reputation for integrity, fairness and simple honesty. Our enterprises spiral overnight. Then comes that inevitable day of reckoning. What we thought we had built to stay has come and gone. Even in our personal lives we live constantly with the temptation of the quick-and-easy way. We scorn opportunities to build friendships, to share the obligations and relationships of our families, and refuse to "take time to smell the roses." We scramble to the top only to discover that the top lacks the glamour we thought it would have. In the end, we pay a price for everything. The law of the cash register is always operative, and we never set it aside. If we decide to go now, we should never forget that payment has to be made later as well as the interest on the loan.

There is, however, another approach to life. It is the advanced-payment plan. The year Charles Lindbergh flew across the Atlantic, two French flyers left Paris bound for New York City. They didn't arrive. The two men were impatient, impetuous and anxious to set a record. They were depending on good weather for the crossing. Before they could properly equip their plane, there came a hint of clear weather, and the two men decided to risk the journey. The captain of a ship at sea reported hearing a low-flying plane, but the men were never found. Lindbergh, too, was anxious to set a record. But on that May morning in 1927 when he took off, it was after months of work, practice and patience. Thirty-six hours later he arrived in Paris. All three men paid a price: two of them at the end, Lindbergh at the beginning.

In the late 1930s the western part of North Carolina was hit by a violent storm. The rain went on for days, and the streams sweeping down from the hills turned rivers into angry waters. Bridge after bridge was swept away, and much of the debris was pushed along to the churning waters of a small man-made lake. At the foot of the dam that held the lake was a powerhouse. Most of the workmen in that powerhouse fled to higher gound, fearful that the weight of broken bridges and pilings would push the water through. One of the men stayed, however, and kept the lights burning. A passing policeman saw the lights and rushed in to tell the man to leave. "Don't you know we are having the worst storm in 50 years?" asked the policeman. "Yes," replied the man in the powerhouse. "Why don't you leave?" the officer asked. "Because," said the man as he turned back to his work, "I know what's in that dam."

As a minister I spend a lot of time with people in the critical moments of their lives. It doesn't take long to discover the folk who will stand when others go down. These are the people who have taken the time to live their lives well. They have played by the rules and taken no shortcuts. They have left no tracks that have to be covered. They may not own the world, but what they have they wouldn't trade for the world. They are at peace with themselves. They have made the payments and made them in advance. From what I see in these people, I am convinced that in life it's better to pay now and go later. When you travel by the other plan, you not only have the payments to make but you also have to pay the interest.

There Is a Time to Wait

A lot is being said these days about the terrific pace of modern living. Anyone who is aware of what's happening to us knows there is some justification for it. We have surrounded ourselves with machines of mobility. We travel in supersonic planes, build express elevators, and spend millions on instant communication satellites. Even our speech patterns are being affected. In 1830 the average public speaker used about a hundred words a minute. Today it is not unusual for news commentators and other public figures to race along at a 200-word-a-minute clip.

The acceleration of life and events in our world is leaving a lot of psychologists gravely concerned. We are moving so rapidly that many people feel burned out and used up long before their time. If, however, we can believe the specialists, there seems little hope to reversing the trend. Alvin Toffler, in his best-selling book, *Future Shock*, pointed out that the worst is yet to come. High-speed technology feeds on itself. We will be confronted by ever-tightening spirals of change.

The rapid pace of life, of course, is not altogether bad. We like to call ourselves the "now" generation. We seem to mean that we are people in a hurry and determined to rid the world of age-old ills and bring into being the good life now. There is nothing wrong with this, but our haste can have its destructive and devastating side effects. It is possible to run so fast that we forget some age-old facts about living. A lot of things in our world can't or shouldn't be rushed. One of the most important achievements in life is that of striking a proper balance between haste and patience. There are places where being patient is a priceless virtue. Think for a moment about a few of them.

One place patience is important is in our self-development. A part of my work as a minister is spent in counseling. One of the problems often uncovered in troubled people is the lack of endurance. Many of these people can't handle the long pull. They become too easily discouraged and drop out of life.

Anyone who knows anything about life recognizes that many of our most important possessions are not discovered overnight. Russell Conwell had a remarkable parable about this in his famed address, "Acres of Diamonds." Many years ago in California there was a farmer who owned a rough and rocky farm at a place called Sutter's Mill. Tired and discouraged of trying to grow crops where nothing seemed to grow, the farmer sold his place and moved on. You will remember, however, that a while later in the mid-19th century gold was discovered in California. The discovery took place on that rocky farm at Sutter's Mill. Conwell with his gifted imagination suggested that the greatest mistake most of us make is that of giving up too soon.

82

Those of us who enjoy reading biographies are aware of Conwell's point. Great living does not come from finding things easy but from wrestling with impossible things. The greatest achievers are not always the people with the greatest potential. Most often they are ordinary people who have extraordinary staying power. Oliver Goldsmith once said that man's greatest glory is not in never falling down but in rising every time he falls. Exceptional people lose battles just as the rest of us do. Their greatness rests in their refusing to accept defeat.

William Ernest Henley wrote an immortal poem entitled "Invictus." In that poem he talked about his head being "bloody but unbowed." He declared himself the master of his fate and the captain of his soul. To many people the poem seems irreverent; but when we remember the circumstances out of which that poem came, its irreverence seems more palatable. Henley was a patient in an Edinburgh hospital. One foot was gone, and doctors had done 23 operations in as many months to save the other. As Henley lay on his cot, he kept saying, "I won't give up; I won't give up no matter what happens. I thank God for my unconquerable soul." That's a great thought for all of us. Great living comes to those who learn the fine art of hanging on to great dreams.

A second place patience is important is with others. It's so easy to become impatient with people. Thomas Edison's teacher said that he was too dull to learn, and Winston Churchill was once declared an incompetent student. Some people find it difficult to remember that the most beautiful flowers are frequently late in blooming.

Someone once wrote an essay with the intriguing title, "Recycling People." The essay was in part a study of some of the people the world now remembers as saints. The study revealed some interesting facts. Without exception, the people we remember as saints had blemished records. Somewhere all of these folk had a tarnished past. But even though they fell, they stood again to redeem the mistakes they had made. We could well take this lesson as food for thought. Good people occasionally do bad things. Consider our children, for instance. Simply because they make mistakes does not mean they are bad people. A lot of young people have to go down some wrong roads before they find the right one. Our business colleagues constitute another group of people where patience might well be practiced. Anyone who attempts anything will "blow it" sometimes. It's a grave mistake to give up on people too soon. One of the great businesses of our country was put together by a man who was earlier fired by his employer for a rather minor blunder. The employer lived to see the day he received his orders from the man he had fired.

This thought has even wider implications. We are coming through some days in our land when the temptation is to be cynical about human nature. It's easy to become disillusioned about people. We are, however, in for some miserable years until this spirit of trust and confidence is recovered. This does not mean that we must be blind to the faults and failures of others. To do so is an invitation to be swindled. But in most instances, most people deserve a second chance; and the failure to give them that chance can be a colossal waste of human potential. You and I need a second chance now and then. Surely we are under obligation to be as patient with others as we would ask them to be with us.

A third place patience is needed is with the "Hand that governs in the affairs of men." A long time ago a writer admonished us to "wait on the Lord and be of good courage." We know little about the author of this sentence. A bit of imagination suggests, however, that he was living in a day when everything seemed to be going wrong. But this long-ago writer had a magnificent insight: Bad days are inevitably followed by good days.

William Cowper wrote some lines we still remember:

God moves in a mysterious way
His wonders to perform.

What he meant, of course, was that an "unseen hand" is moving in invisible ways to achieve its purpose. Many times we have not known that hand has been working until we get far enough down the road to look back. The discerning eye, however, can see evidences of a plan that sometimes may be delayed but is still working to a fixed and good conclusion.

The thoughtful student of history soon discovers that we don't manage this universe. Abraham Lincoln once said that the important thing is not that angels are on our side but that we are on the side of the angels. Lincoln's wisdom provides us valuable insight. The universe never permanently sides with brutality, cruelty and injustice. After a while the wrong rights itself.

Years ago I had a friend who was well into his 80s. I sensed in his spirit a calmness and tranquillity not present in my own. I would read the morning papers and become mighty troubled about the future. I would talk to my friend about these things, but there was simply no way to get him rattled or discouraged. "It's God's world," he would say. "He has not resigned, nor is he dead." I wondered what he had that I didn't have. I understand it now. He had lived a long time. He had been through two world wars, the Great Depression, and seen empires rise and fall. He had heard all the prophets of doom and seen the world move from the brink of one disaster to another. But he had also seen the sun rise every morning for 80 years. He still found the world beautiful and the remnants of goodness prevailing over the worst of things. He had lived long enough to see justice prevail when it seemed that justice would never come. He would share these things with me and then lean back in his rocker, "Be patient, son. There is still goodness abroad in the world, and it's going to win. Hitler predicted that the Third Reich would last 1,000 years. He missed it by 988."

The years have passed since that old man stated his childlike faith. I'm beginning to believe he was right. The world hasn't come apart. When you remember that, it's a lot easier to be patient.

Running by What You Mean to Catch

"Do you have a price?" That was the question put to a group of people in a northern state recently. Sidney Sowers, in his book *Living Without a Magic Eightball*, tells of a study made by a psychology professor at one of America's well-known graduate schools. The professor asked 652 people this question: "What is the least amount of money you would take to push a button to kill a person inside a black box, providing no one would ever know what you did?" The results of that survey were astounding. From 25 to 45 percent of the people said that they would kill for money, and the asking price ranged from $20,000 to $50,000.

Most of us would have some question about the validity of such a survey. A lot depends on the way the question is asked and the people chosen to respond. But if that psychology professor's survey is to any degree accurate, the results are appalling. It's difficult to imagine that such a sizable portion of our population would be willing to kill for money. Perhaps this helps explain the ever-growing crime rate in our country. We are caught up in an age of materialism where money seems to be king.

Thoughtful people, viewing this trend, are urging Americans to conduct intensive studies in what is called "value clarification." Courses on this theme are being offered in businesses, churches, and in the classrooms of colleges and universities. Many of us believe that such courses are long overdue when we consider the moral climate of our land.

The need for establishing values is age-old. There is an old parable told by the Great Teacher about a man who lived his whole life thinking one thing to be important only to discover at the end he had missed all that really counted. The story reads this way: "And a certain man's lands brought forth plenty. The man said, 'What shall I do? I have nowhere to store my crops. I know what I will do. I will tear down my barns and build larger ones. Then I will say to myself, "Take your ease; you have ample goods stored up for many years. Eat, drink, and be merry!" But that night a voice said to him, 'You fool, this night you will die. Then whose will these things be?'"

No thoughtful person can read this parable without some serious soul-searching. The question raised is this: "Am I finding in life the truly important things?" Many sophisticated methods have been devised to aid people in this quest. There are, however, a few simple questions that could help us establish our values.

The first question is this: "Have I learned to appreciate properly the world about me?" G.K. Chesterton was once asked, if he were marooned on a deserted island and could have only one book, what would it be? Whoever asked the question expected Chesterton to say the Bible. Now no one had a greater appreciation for the Bible than did Chesterton, but he was also a practical man. His reply was this: "If I were marooned on a deserted island and could have only one book, it would be *Taylor's Guide to Home Boat Building.*"

Sometimes the emergencies of life bring important things into focus, but it's tragic to await a crisis situation to force the issue. So often the resulting awareness comes too late. That was the predicament of the ancient landowner who became so preoccupied with his business affairs that he neglected some things he did not intend to miss. By the time he was ready to live, it was time to die.

On the wall of a little country store in the South, there is a plaque with this inscription: "Don't travel too fast. You'll run by more than you will ever catch." We need to remember that when the pace of life gets hurried and hectic. If value clarification does nothing else, it should establish the importance of living in the now. Never get caught in the someday syndrome, postponing the joys we should be having today while waiting for tomorrow. That was the landowner's mistake. Just as he was getting ready to live, he heard the ominous pronouncement, "You fool, tonight you will die."

Perceptive people have long since discovered the things that make for real happiness are not down the road or over the next hill. They are present in the here and now: health, friends, family, the beauty of the earth, etc. The time to enjoy them is today. Tomorrow may never come.

There is a second question: "Have I learned the proper utilization of my resources?" It has often been said that in the creative scheme the Creator intended us to use things and love people. The turmoil of our world results when we attempt to reverse that process by using people and loving things. We are expected to use our resources in service. When we fail to do this and attempt to hoard these resources, we do not become rich. We become poor. Remember the landowner in the parable. He tried to keep everything and discovered he could keep nothing. There came that threatening voice: "You fool, tonight you will die. Then whose will these things be?"

Years ago Edwin Holt Hughes told of visiting a rancher somewhere in the Southwest. That afternoon the rancher took Hughes to a spot far out on the great plains. "Anywhere you look," said the rancher, "you are seeing the land that belongs to me. It's all mine." "That's not quite true," said Hughes. "It's not really yours." "Oh!" said the rancher. "Why isn't it mine? I hold the title to every acre of land you see. I paid for all of it. If it isn't my land, to whom does it belong?" Hughes' eyes twinkled as he said to the rancher, "Let's talk about that a hundred years from now."

No commentary is needed on Hughes' comment. What we call ours does not really belong to us. We only hold it in trust. If that's true, then we are accountable for the use of it. Perhaps this is the reason that timeless saying persists, "You only take with you what you send on ahead." What we leave behind falls into the hands of others.

There is a final question: "Am I properly disposing of the gift of life?" There is an old fable about a king who had in his court a jester who amused him very much. One day the king had a beautiful staff made and presented it to the jester, saying, "You may keep this staff until you find a bigger fool than you." Weeks later the king became seriously ill. He called in the jester and said, "I am going on a journey and will never return." The jester asked the king what provisions he had made for the journey. The king replied, "None." The jester handed the king the staff and said, "If you have made no provisions for a journey that lasts forever, then the staff belongs to you. You are a bigger fool than I."

That fable comes from a time when life expectancy was much less certain than it is in our day. The final journey seems so far away for most of us that we seldom think of it. That's the way it should be. Life is too important to be wasted in morbid reflection on death. There is, however, one thought we should ponder. All of us want to be able to stand at the end of our journey knowing that we have so used our lives that we can now have joy and satisfaction. The only way to achieve that objective is to live each day to the fullest by spending the moments given to us on things that really matter. Someone has wisely said that everyone needs to stop now and then and ask, "If this were my final day, how would I spend it?" When you think about that question, life takes on a new perspective. We discover that many things we so often take for granted are more important than we dreamed.

Knots We Can Not Untie

Recently there was a story on national television about an unusual holiday celebration held in a small North Carolina town. Years ago the people in that community began ushering in the New Year with special festivities coupled with a unique custom. For 18 hours prior to New Year's Day, someone fires a gun every 30 minutes. The purpose of the gunshots, according to the news account, is to drive away the witches. The reporter who covered the story declared, "The custom must work. No one has seen a witch in that part of the country for years."

There are a lot of quaint customs tucked away in the folklore of America. Where these customs began is often difficult to determine. In a more enlightened day, many of these traditions are nonsense, and the continuation of them is more a matter of fun than anything else. No serious person would dare equate the firing of a gun with the absence of witches. The people of that North Carolina town would be the first to admit that the whole idea is an ancient superstition.

It needs to be said, however, that while some things don't hang together there are others that do. They have been put together in the scheme of creation. Back in one of the oldest books in the world, there is a line that reads: "What God has joined together, let not man put asunder." That sentence is more than a gentle reminder that some things are sacred. It also suggests that there are things that are tied together and nothing we can do will untie them. This fact is well worth remembering as we make our way through life. Some things go together. If we have one, we have or soon will have the other.

Take, for instance, freedom and discipline. Several years ago, a well-known minister on the West Coast wrote a book entitled *The Lion and the Lamb.* The theme of the book had to do with the paradoxes we encounter in life. One of the chapter titles in that book suggested that there is no freedom without bondage. Standing alone, that title seems to pose a contradiction. A bit of reflection, however, reveals that this author was on target. Only the bound really become free.

No student of the past is unaware of the impact that Winston Churchill had on world history. Among his greatest talents was the ability to use words to motivate the English-speaking world. Back in the dark days of World War II, this strange-looking man with his gravel voice molded words together with such force that he pulled a despairing world to its feet. We will never forget such phrases as, "I have nothing to offer but blood, toil, tears, and sweat," or "Let us . . . so bear ourselves that, if the British Empire and its Commonwealth last for a thousand years, men will still say: 'This was their finest hour.' " But Churchill's biographies point out that his fluency with words and the ease with which he handled the language did not come readily. Born with a speech impediment almost impossible to handle, Churchill spent hours practicing his diction and the cadence of his voice until his speeches were like bolts of lightning. There is more than passing truth to the timeless saying, "Before you are free to do anything, you must first be a slave."

Every specialist understands this principle. The freedom to handle a basketball comes from the slavery of practice. Only the musicians who wrestle with scales and études are finally free to play great music. The student able to move freely in intricate fields of knowledge has been a slave to study and research. The businessman or -woman who handles gigantic transactions with skill and expertise has first been disciplined in lesser things.

A great inventor of another day once said that genius is 1 percent inspiration and 99 percent perspiration. That's a thought worth remembering as we struggle with life.

Consider, too, the fact that there is no darkness without light. There is an old story about a college student who wrote a letter home to her parents. "Dear Mom and Dad, I'm sorry I have been so long in writing, but all my writing paper was lost the night the dormitory burned. I'm out of the hospital now, and the doctors say my eyesight should finally come back to normal. The wonderful boy, Bill, who rescued me from the fire kindly offered to share his apartment with me. He comes from a wonderful family so you won't be too surprised to learn that we are married and are expecting your first grandchild. Love, Mary. P.S. Please disregard the above practice in English composition. There was no fire. I am not blind. I am not married and don't even have a boyfriend. I did get a 'D' in chemistry and an 'F' in French, and I wanted you to receive this news in the proper perspective."

Beyond whatever humor may be in this story, there is a profound lesson. The bad things that happen to us can take on a different dimension if seen in a different context. It must have been an awareness of this truth that prompted the coining of the phrase, "Every cloud has a silver lining." Things are never quite as bad as they could be, as that college student pointed out to her parents. Even the worst things leave some room for thanksgiving if we examine them carefully enough.

But more than this, the Creator has so arranged things that every hardship contains the seeds of something useful. The world is full of stories of people who have discovered blessings disguised as disaster. Paul Harvey reported recently that the person who invented chewing gum was trying to discover a substitute for rubber. He was a dismal failure on one endeavor, but he succeeded in making a fortune in the other. Beethoven in his deafness heard music that most of us never hear. St. Paul said it centuries ago: "All things work together for good for those who love God." This was his way of saying that those who are sensitive to the Creator's intent can find the light in every dark day and that every disaster contains the seeds of good.

Finally, there is no giving without receiving. The physicist often refers to the balance of nature. He means that everything fits into the give-and-take system inherent in creation. When that balance is upset, there are cataclysmic results. The air we breathe is dependent upon the proper ratio of plant to animal life. When that ratio is disturbed, there is always a penalty. Nature tolerates no long-term robberies. You can't keep on receiving without giving. Creation is committed to balancing the scales.

Most of us accept this principle as operative in the physical world, but we sometimes forget that it holds at other levels as well. An Old Testament writer declared, "Cast your bread upon the water, and after many days it will return." This was his way of saying that what we put out eventually comes back. Hate breeds hate, and selfishness has a way of spawning selfishness. It is also true that generosity engenders generosity, and kindness brings kindness in return. Cheerful people receive a cheerful response from their world if their attitudes are given a chance to germinate. Most of us make our own worlds. What we give, we receive after a while.

As a minister I talk to a lot of people, many of whom are rather discouraged. Often they are despondent over the bad roads they feel forced to travel. Sometimes things are so jumbled that these people live without hope and there seems to be no light at the end of the journey. Among other things I try to say to these people that the forces of creation are at work on their behalf. Some things are inseparably tied together. Choose a right road, follow it long enough, and somewhere you come out at the right place. That's a thought worth remembering when life seems hopeless and the going is tough. What we put out eventually comes back. God made his world that way.

Things Worth Living For

The man had been called to the White House for a visit with the President of the United States. The time was during the Civil War, and the purpose of the visit was to consider enlistment in the intelligence efforts of the Union Army. That visit and the resulting story became the theme of a movie which came out of Hollywood several years ago. Abraham Lincoln was in desperate need of imformation about enemy troop movements. He had called a friend to ask him to consider becoming a secret agent. As the two men visited together, Lincoln said, "Jim, how much do you love your country?" "I reckon I would die for her," said Jim. "I can find 10,000 men who are willing to die for America," replied Lincoln. "I want you to live for her." Lincoln fully understood the risks and dangers of espionage. If caught and exposed, the agent could well suffer a fate worse than death.

A few years ago, a noted American wrote an essay with the title "Things Worth Dying For." The author's effort was to remind us of those values held sacred by most Americans. The list included the usual things: God, freedom, the flag, etc. The essay had an important theme and pointed out that all too often these days we give a low priority to ideals our fathers were willing to die for. That's a matter which needs renewed emphasis. It's so easy to let precious possessions slip away and not miss them until they are gone.

Will Rogers once said, "A lot of people who say they are willing to die for a cause ain't willing to live for it." That's the point Lincoln was making to his friend on that long-ago day. Values worth dying for are also worth living for. That's true not only of our collective heritage but also of certain personal possessions. Some things are worth spending our lives for. Here are a few worth considering.

First, there is the matter of self-esteem. A while back a southern newspaper editorial contained a penetrating question, "If everything that could be taken from us were gone, what would we have left?" That's an interesting area for thought. We hold so few permanent possessions. Health is always subject to unexpected disease; family circles can be broken by death; and wealth can be eroded by economic conditions. Even life itself is held by a slender thread. Only a few things can't be taken from us unless we are willing to give them away. Among these possessions is integrity—that inner sense of rightness which comes from allegiance to principle.

In an old biography of Robert E. Lee written for schoolchildren, there is a little story about the sterling character of that great American. Perhaps the story is romanticized a bit, but it speaks to an important point. Lee was asked to lend his name to a highly lucrative scheme but one of questionable ethics. He is reported to have said,

"I lost everything in the war except my name, and that is not for sale. If I lose that, I have nothing." Whatever may be the facts in this incident, its lesson is worth remembering. No possession is a substitute for integrity. People in every time and place have known that. Long ago the Great Teacher put it candidly and simply when he asked, "What does it profit a person to gain the whole world and lose his own soul?" When we lose respect for ourselves, nothing provides a worthy substitute. This is why people who hold to principles they deem honorable and right are usually content regardless of circumstances. The verdict of human experience is clear. Personal integrity is worth living for. When that is lost, nothing else retained really matters.

Another possession worth living for is inner peace. Somewhere there is an old painting about the final trial of the Nazarene carpenter. The scene is in the palace where the Roman governor Pilate held his court. Pilate is dressed in his royal robes, and the symbol of his authority is in his hand. Before him stood the Nazarene in simple white, completely helpless and without defense. We still remember the story. Pilate attempted to badger his prisoner, but the prisoner stood quietly and confidently. The record reports that Jesus said not a single word. The painting is entitled "Christ Before Pilate." We now know it was the other way around. It was Pilate who was on trial that day. The Nazarene carpenter claims the allegiance of millions, while Pilate's name is only a footnote in history. The man who stood a prisoner in Pilate's court could well afford to be confident. He knew that at last justice, decency and honor prevail in this world and not even the powers of Rome could set them aside.

We can get pretty cynical in these turbulent and disjointed times. So much is wrong that it's easy to fall into cynicism and despair. We have come up with countless expressions to describe our frustrations. Take Murphy's Law, for instance: "If anything can go wrong, it will." The world does seem to react in the worst possible ways. If you don't have some philosophy about life, some deep convictions about what's really happening, you are likely to lead a troubled life.

James Russell Lowell once wrote a poem about those days when truth seemed to be on the scaffold and wrong on the throne. But Lowell saw beyond these things and remembered, "One who stood within the shadows keeping watch over his own." Serene and confident is the person who understands that beneath the troubled waters on the surface there is a strong undercurrent which makes right prevail at its proper time. It's a priceless possession, that sense of inner peace. It's worth living for; and when you have it, it makes life worthwhile.

Finally, the future is worth living for. There is an old fable about a land where the king could rule only one year. At the end of that year, he was banished to an island to spend the rest of his days. Each king who reigned lived in mortal fear of that dreadful day. One king, however, was wise. He chose his island. While he was still king, he took his treasures and established a paradise in which to live when he no longer had his throne.

In the scheme of life, we generally get back tomorrow what we put in today. An ancient writer once admonished his people to cast their bread upon the waters. "After many days," he said, "it will return again." That's a magnificent promise, and it is consistent with the way things work. Security in later years is largely dependent upon careful planning in productive years. A reputation for honesty and integrity is enjoyed by those who build it carefully across a lifetime. Friendships are constructed by diligent attention to care and concern. Even a storehouse of happy memories is the harvest for those who extract from life happy things. Indeed, each of us is a king with limited tenure here. Happy is the person who uses what he has today as an investment in tomorrow. Anyone who lives his life so that he can look back and not be ashamed is rich.

Are there things worth living for? There are! No possessions are greater than a sense of integrity and inner peace coupled with the assurance that you have lived today so that tomorrow may be good. Lose those things and nothing else matters much. Keep them and you have a peace that no one can give you or take away.

Risky to Be a Judge

One hundred and forty years ago, Daniel Webster made a speech before the United States Senate. The Senate was debating the admission of the Western Frontier to the Union. Apparently Webster was opposed to the annexation. "What do we want," asked the senator, "with this region of savages and wild beasts, of deserts, of shifting sands and whirlwinds, of dust, cactus and prairie dogs? What could we do with this western coast of 3,000 miles—rock-bound, cheerless and uninviting?"

It's been a while now since Webster made that speech. We have had time to see the western part of our country in a different perspective. Today, "this region of savages and wild beasts" cradles some of the most important resources in this country. That "rock-bound, cheerless and uninviting coast" has become the land of opportunity for millions. Each year the scenic beauty of Southern California and the great forest of the Northwest attract millions of visitors from all over the world. Webster, were he alive today, would be surprised indeed to discover what has happened to that 3,000 miles of "uninviting" land.

A few years ago, Halford Luccock of the Yale Divinity School cited Webster's speech as a reminder that our judgments can come back to haunt us. Webster's speech on the worthlessness of the Western Frontier was not so much a commentary on the value of that land as it was a revelation of the senator's lack of vision and foresight. "Be careful in your judgments," said Luccock. "You may reveal far more than you intend."

A long time ago, an ancient author wrote a sentence we still remember: "Be careful in passing judgment on one another; for in passing judgment, you really condemn yourself." The instruction here, of course, is not against the use of our critical faculties. Judgments in life are essential. Every time we stand before a ballot box, we must make some evaluation on candidates and issues. Each time a jury deliberates, decisions must be made if justice is to be carried out. We can't go shopping, allocate our time, or establish friendships without utilizing evaluative processes. Judgments are necessary in life, and the failure to exercise them would be fatal. Luccock, however, was right. Every judgment we make has an alternate consequence. It opens windows into our lives through which our innermost beings can be viewed.

As we make our judgments, for instance, we reveal our estimate of the important. There is an old parable about a tourist who was visiting a British art gallery. The lady passed a famous painting and paused for a moment. She then turned to the curator standing nearby, "Why so much fuss about that painting? It doesn't look so great to me." "Madam," said the curator coldly, "it's not the painting that's on trial!" The curator was right, of course. History had already turned in its verdict on the masterpiece. It was the viewer who was on trial that day.

Every time we make a judgment, we run a risk. As the tourist revealed her lack of appreciation for important art forms, so do we reveal ourselves as our judgments are made. Our choices in music and literature, even the movies and television programs we watch, reveal our concerns and interests. The way we spend our resources, time and money constitutes an index into what we think is important. The Great Teacher once said, "Show me where a person puts his treasures, and I'll show you where his heart is." Even our choices in friends and associates suggest more than we dream about our own characters and personalities. No wonder that ancient writer declared, "Be careful as you make your judgments; for as you make them, you may condemn yourself."

It is true, also, that in making our judgments we reveal our estimate of self-worth. In the folklore of the Southland, there is a story about a farmer who took a wagon of cotton to the cotton gin to be sold. While the gin owner was busy with the scales, the farmer stepped on the scales and fraudulently added his weight to that of his cotton. The gin owner saw him but said nothing until he paid the farmer. The check was made for all that the scales measured. "John," said the gin owner to the farmer, "you sold yourself today for a dollar and thirty-seven cents."

There is something penetrating and disturbing in that old story. George Bernard Shaw with his caustic humor once said, "It is easy to be respectable when no one is offering you a chance to be otherwise." That's true, of course, but respectability without an alternate choice is not a likely luxury for most of us. We are forced every day to make choices that reveal our estimate of self-worth. We face them in our businesses and professions, in our fidelity to friends and loved ones.

It was Al Capone who gave notoriety to an old, old saying: "Everyone has his price." That's a debatable premise, to say the least. There are some people who refuse to sell at any price. In any event, however, the point at which we surrender principles is a dead giveaway on our estimate of self. That southern farmer sold himself for $1.37, which is mighty cheap. Perhaps that ancient writer had this in mind as he wrote to his friends. He might have put it this way: "Be careful how you set your price. In doing so, you could condemn yourself."

Finally, through our judgments we determine the response of others toward us. That's not completely true, but it's accurate enough to establish this timeless axiom: "Judge not that you be not judged. For with what judgment you mete out, it will be measured to you again." Judgments can boomerang.

A long time ago there was a carpenter from Nazareth who found a way to enlist the best from others. He picked out nondescript people, the nobodies of his day, and inspired them to undreamed heights. They let him down at crucial moments and in some ways passively participated in his death. They didn't even protest when he was executed by Roman soldiers. But remember that many of those who helped to crucify this carpenter became his most devoted followers. The methodology of that carpenter is outlined in the New Testament. He sought out the best in others and challenged them with it. As a result, that weak little band of followers—erratic in loyalties, unsteady and undependable—became the movers of history. They changed the world.

Wise is the person who heeds the instruction of that long-ago writer, "Be careful in your judgments; for in your judgments, you may condemn yourself." Daniel Webster said a lot about himself when he judged the West Coast to be worthless. His mistake should remind all of us that it's risky to be a judge, for in our judgments we really reveal ourselves.

Running in the Middle

"We need a real fireball!" That was the conclusion of the corporation's directors who were meeting to select the executive officer for their floundering company. For months the entire operation had been on the verge of bankruptcy. The existing leadership just didn't have the imagination and skill to turn the business around. Over in the corner of the board room, however, was an old, weatherbeaten director. "No fireball for me," he muttered. "Fireballs burn out too quickly. Give me a strong and steady leader who knows how to handle the ups and downs."

That director, whoever he was, said something worth remembering. The people who hold the world together are not the "fireballs," who are far too erratic to handle the complex problems in today's business community. The "fireballs" may give off a lot of heat and light, but they usually go out in a hurry. It's the people who are geared for the long pull that keep this unpredictable world from coming apart. These people hold their direction in good and bad times and are not discouraged by momentary events. They have learned how to manage their affairs because they have learned how to manage themselves.

Nothing in life is quite so valuable as the ability to hold one's course while everything else is bouncing between extremes. There is an old folk song which begins, "I'm sometimes up, and I'm sometimes down." That's an accurate description of the way many of us live. We are exhilarated and active when things are going well. We are paralyzed with depression when they are not. We swing between a sense of belonging and total insecurity, elation and despair, calm reason and uncontrollable anger. We can't hold the center or run in the middle. We are either red-hot or stone-cold.

Nothing can be quite so destructive to us and those around us as these radical mood swings. Our behavior becomes irrational and thus devastating to our entire existence. We alienate friends, damage our careers, and even destroy ourselves emotionally and physically. This happens not only in moments of discouragement. There are also people who have equal difficulty handling prosperity. They become intensely excited and overelated, and in their dream world of false security make bad judgments and poor decisions. The real secret to successful living is to hold the middle ground with steadfast and persistent purpose. That's not an easy task, but there are people who know how to do it.

One essential thing to keeping in balance is maintaining perspective. Many years ago a visitor to western North Carolina decided that a part of that mountain country was ideally suited for growing grapes.

Determined to open a business, he tried to get the people of that community involved in his venture. He met with resistance and a singular lack of interest. Finally in desperation he called these mountain people together and made a slick sales pitch. "Join me," he pleaded with the natives. "In three or four years you'll be so well fixed you will never have to worry again." There was a long and heavy silence among these folk. Then one old-timer drawled, "I ain't worrying none now."

All of us know people like that. They remain tranquil and poised despite the pressures of the moment. Other people may become excited and stampede into unwise decisions, but these folk take the longer look and make their judgments accordingly. They refuse to sacrifice their future for the momentary gains of the present. They look way down the road and try to determine where the proposed course will take them. If you "ain't worrying none now," why risk a direction that might or might not work?

It's the people who take the long view who manage to live life at its best. From such a vantage point, they discover certain unfailing principles at work in the world. They know, for instance, that time tolerates no unpaid debts. You sow good seeds, and you will somewhere reap a good harvest. After a while, the tide brings back what you send out.

Students of history are acutely aware of this. There are times when the world has been knocked to its knees and people of selfish designs have held it at bay. But after a while the stubborn forces of what ought to be struggle to the surface again. Napeoleon *did* eventually get to Waterloo; Socrates *has* been exonerated, despite the condemnation of his judges; and the Roman Empire finally *had* to yield to the forces of the Nazarene carpenter whom it had tried to eliminate. Time has its own way of meting out justice and getting things to their just and proper conclusion. People who know this find it a lot easier to manage their moods. It's the people who take the long view who cope best with the events of the moment.

Another thing helpful in keeping one's balance is a deep faith. Many years ago in a tiny village nestled among the Great Smokies, there lived a grand old man who was well into his 80s. He had come through the storms and stresses of a lifetime, but his spirit was strong and unbroken. Each Sunday he went down to the neighborhood church to teach a class of young adults. One Sunday the title of his lesson was, "What I Have Learned Thus Far." He talked of his experiences and ticked off the lessons life had taught him. "One thing I have learned," he said, "is the truth of an old proverb: 'Never forget in the dark what God has told you in the light.' "

Anyone who catches the meaning of that sentence is bound to find it easier to hold the middle ground. One of the reasons we become so easily discouraged in life is because we imagine that the trends of the moment are permanent directions. We believe one failure to be a lasting defeat and one bad day to represent the nature of all days. In the hurt of the moment, we forget that underneath there is an "Unseen Hand" working in our behalf.

A long time ago an author wrote a line which has been preserved in the New Testament. "All things work together for good for those who love God." This writer did not mean that everything that happens to us would be good. Some of the inevitabilities of life bring to us immeasurable pain and suffering. By no stretch of the imagination do these things contribute to our joy and happiness. What this author was trying to help us see is that even in the crucial moments of bad times the Creator's benevolent hand is at work to bring us something good. If we can learn to trust this benevolent hand, after awhile we discover that even our hardships can become our steppingstones. It is this sort of faith that keeps us steady when we are tempted to throw in the towel. It will keep us running down the middle when the "fireballs" have all burned out and dropped out of the race.

Handling the 'Night Shift'

There is an old song tucked away in the folk music of the South which begins with the mournful line, "I'm sometimes up and I'm sometimes down." Nowhere is there a more apt description of the way life works for many of us. There are days when everything goes well and it seems, as the poet said, "God's in his heaven—All's right with the world!" There are other days, however, when it all goes wrong, and everything we touch gets tangled. Sometimes this happens to us in our businesses and professions; it happens in our families or even in our personal lives. The deep, dark valleys are hard realities for multitudes of people. We move from exhilaration to despair and live a lot of days in "quiet desperation."

Not long ago Robert Goodrich in one of his books made reference to what he called the "night shift." He pointed out that there are times when we live in the dark, unable to sense direction or to find the way. The world seems to come apart, and our dreams and hopes go astray. This, of course, doesn't happen to all of us. Some people manage to keep their bearings no matter what. More often than not, however, the "night shift" is a common human experience. When it happens, we wonder how we will ever get through.

The answer to that question is not easy. Across the centuries, however, there are those who have discovered a few simple rules that help them to deal with the "night shift." About 300 years ago, Sir Isaac Newton stated some principles that seem to be true in the world of nature. He labeled these rules the laws of motion, and one of them went something like this: An object set in motion will tend to move in the given direction unless acted upon by a contrary force. In its simplest form, this rule is known as the "law of momentum."

Near our home in Winston-Salem, North Carolina there are a couple of hills just right for sledding on snowy days. When the icy flakes begin to fall, the children can be seen tugging their sleds toward those hills. They have learned that if they gain enough speed on the first hill, they can coast up the second one and down the other side. It's a simple matter of gaining sufficient momentum. They can then get two hills for the price of one. These children are using a principle which has many sophisticated applications.

Scientists probing outer space use the law of momentum. Their rockets are built in stages, each igniting in sequence to set the rocket on its way. The engines run only briefly, and then the machine begins to coast. If the speed is great enough, the rocket will climb the long, long hill of gravity to the moon. It's a bit more complicated than running a sled, but the principle is exactly the same.

Doctors practice this principle in a different way. Each day we are subject to bacteria and viruses that threaten our lives. Doctors know, however, that if we use appropriate health practices we can build an immunity to such threats. Figuratively speaking, when we hit the dangerous places, if the speed is great enough, we can come through. Newton probably didn't have this in mind when he stated his laws of motion. But it's the same principle, and we have been using it a long, long time.

It would be strange, indeed, if a principle so useful in other places did not work in our emotional, mental and spiritual lives. A long time ago a man came down from the little town of Nazareth to change the course of the world. He knew that his work was so revolutionary that his life expectancy would be short. He gathered about him a dozen followers with the full intent that they would carry on his work when his voice was silent. He sat with these men, taught them, always working with feverish intensity. Sure enough, the life of that man was brief. He lived only three years from the day he started to speak out. Roman soldiers crucified the Nazarene, and for a while his handful of followers floundered, not knowing what to do. But the momentum of those years was too great. When the man's followers stood with their backs to the wall, they came through. They carried on their teacher's work and did change the world. Newton's principle of momentum was at work 2,000 years ago in Palestine. Get a thing started, and it tends to move in the appointed direction. This is why those followers of the carpenter from Nazareth were able to endure so many hardships and bad days. They had their direction and sufficient speed and thus made it through. There is something to be said for momentum when you are facing the "night shift."

A lot of people, for instance, have discovered the importance of this principle when they are forced to make hard ethical decisions. There are times for all of us when integrity is at stake. To sell out is the strong temptation. It's the way to quick profits and easy living. Sometimes in those moments our values are distorted. The "bad guys" seem to get the long end of everything while the "good guys" are always shortchanged. At such times, we are living on the "night shift" where it's easy to surrender. When we get to this place without momentum, we are likely to go down.

The people who make it through such places are those who have prepared themselves. On the hilltops they have established their values and fixed their convictions. They have decided in their sanest moments that families are more important than possessions; that a clear conscience is of greater value than quick profits; and friends are worth more than dishonest glory. They know that a right road always comes to a right end, and a wrong one never does. They have learned that in the end it's what they have done for others that really warms the heart. Such people have established and tested these convictions during the best of days. When the "night shift" comes, the momentum of those convictions pulls them through. Fortunate, indeed, are those who have convictions planted deeply enough to make it through the night.

There is another place where the principle of momentum is so important. A while back, a small boy was brought into the emergency room of a hospital. He had been struck by a car. A hush came over the waiting room as the parents received the solemn news. They had hit the "night shift." Most parents in that room wondered what they would have done if they had been where that child's parents were. Life, for a while at least, would have lost its meaning. Every dream and hope would have gone out of focus. The temptation could well be to cash in one's chips and get out of life's game.

Every counselor learns at least one thing. The people who make it through that kind of night are those who possess a faith that can be trusted when the evidence is to the contrary. This doesn't mean that they never have doubts. All of us do at times. But there is a difference between honest doubt and total confusion.

A lot of bewildering things happen in this topsy-turvy world. Viewed in isolation, these events can put you on the "night shift." But the people who stand in the dark valley and don't go down have decided long before what they believe. Propelled by the momentum of that faith, they make it through the "night shift."

As an old and oft-told story goes, a little boy found his grandmother reading her Bible. "Look," he said to his brother, "Granny is cramming for her finals." That story is not without point. After a while, the "finals" come up for all of us—disaster, disease, misfortune, disappointments and even death. These are the kinds of storms most of us must weather somewhere down the road. The people who survive are usually those who have done their "cramming" beforehand. They have faced their doubts, raised their questions and searched for honest answers. When the "night shift" comes, Newton's law of momentum takes over. If their direction has been right, the speed great enough and the convictions planted deeply enough, they get through. It's a good question, then, for all of us: "Are we getting ready for the 'night shift'?"

Never Buy Land on a Hot, Dry Day

There is a college in a southern state which a few years ago offered its students a course in practical logic. One of the purposes of the course was to aid the student in the art of decision making. Vocational guidance counselors at the college had discovered that prospective employers were seeking personnel who could make intelligent decisions. One of the sections of the course was meant to teach the student how to gather the necessary information, and from that information to make appropriate decisions.

Intelligent decisions are not only necessary in business, they are also necessary in life. One of the secrets of Napoleon's success as a military leader was the quick, firm and sometimes terrible decisions which marked the early years of his campaigns. In later years Napoleon was indecisive. The battle of Waterloo may have been lost because the Great Conquerer couldn't make up his mind. Learning how to make decisions is an absolute essential for successful living.

It needs to be said, however, that most courses on decision making neglect one very human element. It is important not only to know *how* to decide but also *when* to decide. In the New Testament there are a couple of passages that should be studied by most of us. "Don't be carried about by every wind that blows." "Be sober in your thinking." Decisions must be made within the proper context. When these ancient writers admonish us to "sober thinking," they may be reminding us of some very important considerations.

It is possible, for instance, to lose perspective in the glow of enthusiasm. Several years ago a man in the Southwest told of buying a small tract of land in the lowlands of a southern state. A land developer had spent an evening with him talking about the security of owning real estate. The next day the two men went out to look at some property. It was a hot, dry August day. The land was level and well marked with tall stakes. The developer was so convincing that a deal was made on the spot. "I went out about once a week," said the man, "to walk over my part of this good earth." When winter came the visits ceased. Then one fine spring day the man went out to survey his land again. The spring rains had come. It took him a while to locate his property. It was accessible only by boat, and all he could see were the tops of the stakes. "You don't buy land on a hot, dry day in southern Louisiana," exclaimed the gentleman. "All you may own is the bottom of a lake."

A lot of wrong decisions have been made in moments of false emotions. A couple of years ago one of the world's greatest tragedies occurred in Jonestown, Guyana. Keyed to a frenzy by a deranged man, hundreds of people took their lives. It's possible to be intoxicated by runaway emotions until reason is completely lost.

Twenty centuries ago King Herod decided to build some monuments to his reign. He set out to build towers all across his kingdom to remind posterity of his greatness. Unfortunately, Herod's money ran out before his towers were completed. His unfinished towers became the subject of jeers and mockery throughout the kingdom. The world is filled with unfinished towers—people making serious choices in frivolous moments. The Great Teacher had this in mind when he said to his followers, "Don't set out to build a tower until you count the cost." That man in the South was saying the same thing. "Don't buy land on a hot, dry day in southern Louisiana. All you may own is the bottom of a lake."

It is possible, too, to make bad choices in moments of anger. There is an interesting verse in the parable of the prodigal son. The wayward boy had come home, and he and his father were celebrating. The prodigal had an older brother who became enraged over what he thought was the unjust generosity of his father. The father went over to talk to his older son, trying to persuade him to go in and join the festivities. There is this somber sentence in the parable, "But the elder brother was angry and would not go in." That's a pathetic line, is it not? It's the story of a boy who cut himself out in a moment of anger.

Mark Twain used to say, "When angry, count to four; when very angry, swear." The first part of Twain's advice bears merit, and the latter part is a strong temptation. In either case, however, never decide anything in moments of rage. Robert Ingersoll, who may have been wrong about many things, was right when he said: "Anger blows out the lamp of the mind. In the examination of a great and important question, everyone should be serene, slow pulsed, and calm."

There is a world of wisdom in some of the slang of our times. Our young people often say, "Don't blow your cool," "Hang loose" or "Don't get bent out of shape." That's good advice, but advice not easily followed. Easy or not, nonetheless, this much is clear: Never make up your mind in a moment of rage. You can lock yourself out forever.

Remember, too, that perspective can be lost when we are discouraged. Most of us are susceptible to mood swings. A lot of study has gone into the causes of these temperament changes. Some people insist that we are victims of as yet unknown cosmic forces that push us into depression. Others insist that the cause is a chemical imbalance in the brain. Still others declare the problem to be genetic. It may be a long time before all the secrets of this problem are unraveled. But there is one thing most of us know. There are days when it all goes wrong and nothing is right.

I am a minister, and I talk to people in every conceivable circumstance. They come to see me when life has knocked them down, and they are trying to find direction. I try to say two things to these people. First, bewilderment always follows a crisis. Don't make any decision you don't have to make. Give yourself time to sort things out. The other thing I try to say is contained in a sentence written by someone a long time ago. "Never forget in the dark what God has told you in the light." I have found on dark and troubled days that instead of dwelling on the adversity, it's better to try to recall some great promises. "All things work together for good for those who love *him*," or, "Cast your burden on the Lord; he will sustain you." Some things you can't handle alone. You must entrust them to a higher power. If you hold to his promises, light has a way of following darkness; and the sun finally overcomes the clouds.

It is important to know when to make decisions. At best we may not always make the right one. This, however, is certain: we have a better chance of being right when our feet are on the ground, our heads are cool, and we are not walking in the dark. It's a thought worth remembering: "Never buy land on a hot, dry day. All you may own is the bottom of a lake."

Learning to Read the News

A few years ago there was a story in the news about a publishing company that bought a computer to send out subscription notices to its customers. One day something went wrong with the machine. Before the error was discovered, a rancher in Colorado received 9,374 notices that his subscription had expired. The company did get the rancher's attention, however. According to the story the man walked ten miles to the nearest post office and mailed in his money with the note: "Send me the magazine. I give up."

If has been said, with some accuracy, that the people of the 20th century are suffering from "sensory overload." It is becoming increasingly difficult to get our attention. We are bombarded with advertising, news flashes and "junk" mail. Our senses have been dulled by a barrage of voices, all clamoring for our attention. Only the spectacular and the colossal seem to get through to us. When our hard shells are finally penetrated, we are likely to accept without question the information received.

One of the side effects of this phenomenon is the mind-set created by whatever breaks into our circle of awareness. Have you observed how different our attitudes can be? Some people dwell on the edge of despair, filled with pessimism and hopelessness. Others are vibrant and hopeful, always optimistic about people and events. Have you ever wondered why there are such differences among us? There can be, of course, many complex reasons. Often, however, there are simple things involved, and they have to do with the way we read the events that happen to us and about us.

We live in a world, for instance, that is full of contradictions. There is an old story about a boy who bought a new sports car. He ordered it painted red on one side and blue on the other. The salesman was extremely curious and asked about the unusual request. "Well," said the lad, "the way I drive, I'm always getting into trouble. I like to hear the witnesses contradict one another." That's a silly story but not without point. There are many signs in our world, and they are not always consistent.

Twenty centuries ago there was a carpenter from Nazareth about whom many things were said. Some declared that he went about doing good, while others insisted that he was a disreputable man associating with people of unsavory character. Both estimates of this man were partially valid. According to the record he did heal the sick, feed the hungry and help those who were in trouble. But he also called about him people considered to be sinners. The evidence that surrounded the man was inconsistent and contradictory.

Such inconsistencies are still apparent. Anywhere you look, you can see indications of the best and the worst. A lovely sunset makes us feel that the Creator is close and friendly. But a world where people starve and natural disasters take countless lives makes us wonder. Newspapers remind us constantly of crime and criminals, leaving us to expect the worst of human nature. Yet every day thousands of volunteers give countless hours to aid the down and out. There are courts of law designed to mete out justice, making us feel serene and secure. Yet a child with a birth defect makes us wonder if there is any justice anywhere. It's a world of mixed signals. Some point to the best, while others suggest the worst.

Knowing this to be true, there is another thought that becomes important. We must choose what we see and hear. James Savage tells about a woman who was passing along a bit of choice news to a neighbor. The woman's daughter chided her, "Mother, you shouldn't repeat such stories. You are nothing but a gossip." "I'm not a gossip," snapped the mother. "I'm a news analyst." To a degree the mother was right. We are all analysts, choosing what we report depending on what we see and hear.

The biographer of Dr. William Barclay revealed an interesting insight into the brilliant scholar's life. Barclay suffered a serious hearing impairment requiring a hearing aid. "But it's no handicap," said Barclay. "When the conversation gets dull, I turn off my hearing aid and think my own thoughts." All of us practice selective hearing to a degree. After a long, tiring day, it's easy to hear, "Dinner is ready." But a request to take out the garbage can fall on deaf ears. We choose what we want to hear, and we also choose what we want to believe.

Did you ever listen to two people report the same event? Both can be equally honest and yet have entirely different stories. It's all a matter of perception—the things that get our attention. The poet's lines are profoundly true:

> Two men looked out from prison bars,
> One saw mud, the other saw stars.

We choose what we see and hear, and what we choose has an important bearing on our mental outlook.

The paramount task in life is to learn to select those things that contribute to a healthy outlook on life. This means that we have to cut through a lot of noises—a multitude of voices clamoring for attention. Out in California there is a museum that contains a cross section cut from a giant redwood tree. Beside the block of wood, there is an explanation of what the naturalist has learned from the tree. He counted the rings and discovered that the tree dates back almost to the time of Moses. The spacing of the rings enables the naturalist to date forest fires, drought and other natural disasters that happened centuries ago. It's as if nature wrote a book on natural history. When we learn to read her handwriting, we can determine a lot about what has happened in bygone days.

Most often the things we need to see and hear come to us in gentle and unobtrusive ways. They aren't written in countless form letters so voluminous that they demand attention. The real news is not always on the front page or blasted at us through radio and television. So often these messages are handed to us so quietly we miss them unless we learn to listen to soft voices and see things that almost go unnoticed.

Much of the pessimism and despair of our times is born of a steady diet of bad news that seems so often to make the headlines. If these headlines are all we see and hear, we are likely to be a hopeless and depressed people. Every once in a while we need to look behind the news and take a reading on more positive things. The world has faced natural disasters and calamities before. Black Death wiped out countless thousands in the Middle Ages, yet somehow out of that unprecedented tragedy came the Renaissance, and a new world was born. In this century we came through the Great Depression and two world wars. Yet somehow mankind not only survived but also prevailed. If history says anything to us, it reminds us not to throw in the towel. Out of the darkest of days, there always comes new light.

It's so easy to see the bad things that befall us. We remember vividly the injustices that happen to us and the people who have tried to do us in. A bit of reflection, however, can reveal another picture. There are still more honest people in the world than the news reports would have us believe. Despite our misfortunes we are having it better than many, many people we know. The devoted father was right when he wrote his thoughts the day his son started to school. "Teach my son, world, that for every dishonest politician, there is a dedicated leader." To learn the truth of this observation, however, requires a conscious effort. We have to learn to look for the good. Those who look for it find it, and life becomes for them a thrilling adventure.

Staying on the Walls

There is a story about a monument that stands in Fort Benton, Montana, overlooking the Burlington Northern Railroad. This monument pays tribute to a collie dog that came down to the train station in the summer of 1936. According to the story, the dog's master died, and his body was being shipped back East for burial. The dog followed the procession to the station and watched as the train rolled slowly down the tracks. When the dog could follow no farther, he dug a spot under the depot and waited.

The dog never left the station. Summer and winter, snow or shine, he met each train and scanned the passengers, tail wagging in hope. He would search up and down the platform, looking for someone special who never came. One January day in 1942, the dog was struck by a train and killed. The railroaders who had befriended the dog buried him high on a hill and marked his grave. Trains do not stop in Fort Benton now, but the townspeople are not about to let the faithful dog be forgotten. They have rebuilt the monument to remind the town of a heartwarming story of love and fidelity.

There is a mountain man in the South who said recently, "The more I see of some dogs, the less I think of some people." I suppose he was saying that there are animals who exhibit qualities of character all of us could afford to emulate. We live in a rough-and-tumble world where the roads we travel are tough and rocky. We are tempted to forsake ideals and duties that should claim our tireless loyalty. It's a rare person, indeed, who hasn't pondered the notion of giving up. Sometimes we are tired of daily routines, the business of making a living and providing for our families. Even more often we are tempted to forsake ideals and the need to be loyal to principles. All of us somewhere, sometime, ask the question, "What's the point of it all?"

There's an old story about a man who kept in his office the pictures of his family. One day a visitor who knew nothing about the portraits asked who the people were. "That's the jury," said the man. "These are the pictures of my family. Every once in a while I have to ask the question, 'What would they expect of me?' " That's a parable worth remembering. Most of us have people who believe in us and expect us not to turn back.

Paul Tournier, the Swiss psychiatrist, once declared that a lot of our behavior is determination by imputation—we tend to conform to what is expected of us. If that's true, then we can have no greater asset than that of people who trust and believe in us. Often the memory of those people can give us new energy and keep us from turning back at crucial times. Such people keep our ideals alive and our loyalties in focus. That's a good thing to remember when the going is tough.

When you do, it's easier to keep going and to avoid the temptation to surrender. After all, it's better to try and fail than to betray a trust. At least we can walk in the "proud company of our self-respect."

There is one other thing. Persistence has a direct correlation to the depth of our faith. Clarence Darrow used to tell a story about Eugene V. Debs, who in the early days of this century, earned a lot of fame and notoriety across our land. In many ways Debs was out of step with American traditions. He was, however, a man of deep conviction. Debs was in jail for civil disorder. Darrow went to see him. "I can't get you out," said Darrow. "Never mind," said Debs. "If we don't win this time, then next time!" Debs' political convictions and activities are open to question, but one must admire a person who believed that if he was right, then somewhere, sometime he would come out at the right place.

There is one question everyone needs to answer, and it has to do with the basic structures of this universe. Is there any rhyme or reason to human existence, or is life meaningless and all effort in vain? Once we make up our minds about that, then life takes on a different dimension.

There are people who have established that faith, and their lives have been transformed. Fear and apprehension lose their paralyzing power. They find the courage to take a right direction in the abiding faith that no right road ever comes to a bad end. Such people become living examples of some folk once described by a long-ago writer: "They shall mount up with wings as eagles; they shall run, and not be weary; and they shall walk, and not faint." That's a great way to live, and it's within the reach of everyone. There's nothing better than the "proud company of one's self-respect."

The temptation suggested here is age-old. Twenty-five centuries ago there was a man named Nehemiah who lived in a far corner of the world. Years before, his home city had been destroyed. Nehemiah decided it needed to be rebuilt. Most creative people discover that their plans meet with resistance. This man was no exception. His efforts were greeted with ridicule, even his life was threatened. Nehemiah's friends tried to persuade him to forsake his venture. But that long-ago builder was determined. His answer to his critics has been recorded in the Bible. "Shall such a man as I flee?" He refused to turn back. Think about this man for a moment, and you can understand some of his reasons.

One secret of that ancient builder's persistence was the recognition of who he was. Gov. David Boren of Oklahoma tells a story about Senator John Tyler, who later became president of the United States. One day in the Senate, he couldn't decide how to vote on a certain bill. His conscience called him in one direction, while political expediency dictated another. When the roll was called, Tyler voted his conscience. Thinking his career ruined, Tyler at first slumped in his seat. Someone wrote this magnificent sentence about him: "He then arose

111

and walked out of the Senate in the proud company of his own self-respect." Said Boren, "What better company can we have than that?"

From Nehemiah and John Tyler to the present, the pressures to turn back persist. More often than not the road of surrender appears to be the easy one. Our lives can be controlled by external forces and our convictions subject to prevailing winds and currents, but the price of surrender comes high. Life without self-respect and integrity is a miserable way to live. Wallace Hamilton was to the point when he said, "It's worth asking once in a while, 'When you get where you are going, will you be where you want to be?' " It helps to remember that question when you are tempted to turn in your chips and throw in the towel.

Another aid to persistence is the memory of those who believe in us. That ancient builder stood on the wall of the city he was rebuilding. Beside him were a handful of sturdy fellows who depended on him for leadership. His critics, however, were brutal and heartless. "We'll get you," they said. "You'd better come down from the walls." But Nehemiah held to his task. "Shall such a man as I flee? I won't come down." He could not betray the confidence of those who trusted him. He couldn't turn back.

It's All Right to Look Back

"Don't look back, something might be gaining on you." These words of wisdom from the famed Satchel Paige are, for the most part, good advice. Counselors discover that many of the people they see are wrestling with the failure and mistakes of the past. In most instances, concern over the misdeeds of yesterday is futile. Remember those words from Omar Khayyám:

The Moving Finger writes; and, having writ,
Moves on: nor all your Piety nor Wit
Shall lure it back to cancel half a Line,
Nor all your Tears wash out a Word of it.

The record generally stands as it is written. We can't go back and undo the past.

People with their eyes on the future are usually happy and healthy. They don't waste precious time "crying over spilled milk." It is not quite right, however, to say that we should never look back. Sometimes a glance over the shoulder can give us a valuable insight into our lives.

Think, for instance, how the backward look can help us get a measure of our progress. A few years ago, one of America's most motivated and successful salesmen addressed a group of his colleagues. In that address he advised his friends not to run with the pack but to be winners. "No one remembers," he said, "who built the second airplane, the second person to fly the Atlantic solo, or the second man to find the North Pole." Most of us would agree with that. We admire winners. The people who run in second place are forgotten. Not all of us, however, can win all of the races and to try to do so can be dangerous to our physical and emotional health. Sometimes, too, the real winners come in second.

We don't all start from the same place in life. Some people by talent, skills and opportunity are half through the race before the rest of us can begin. Two thousand years ago, there was a brilliant orator by the name of Apollos. Endowed with tremendous native talent, his silver-tongued speech charmed the towns and cities he visited. Traveling on the same circuit with Apollos was a man named Paul. In many ways Paul was far less gifted than Apollos. Many historians believe that Paul was half blind, and unsightly in appearance. When Apollos came to town, Paul always took second place. History has finally balanced the scales, and Paul has been given his due. In their lifetimes Apollos may have been the winner. But we remember Paul because he came farther, struggled harder and ran longer to get where he did.

113

The trouble with our ideas of success is that we measure where people are and not how far they have come. Someone has said that there will be only one question asked of us on Judgment Day: "What did you do with what *you* had?" We don't all live under the same circumstances. Some of us have greater opportunities and greater resources. A lot of people are going to make it through the Pearly Gates who came in second—not because of their achievements but because of the struggle they endured. It's a good thing now and then to ask the question, "Have I done what I can?" The only way to answer that is to look back and take a measure on where we started.

We need to remember, too, that a backward look can remind us of forgotten dreams. In one of the world's oldest books there is a story about a man named Abraham. Abraham left home one day and went down to a strange country. There he became involved in some pretty sordid things. The years passed and Abraham decided to return home. The author of the story wrote this into the record: "And Abraham went back to the place he had been at the first, and there he built an altar." There is an important lesson in this story. Abraham realized that in the strange country he had lost something he needed to keep; therefore, he returned to the home place to remember his old loyalties and revitalize his highest dreams.

All of us need to do this now and then. Back during the Revolutionary War there was a man named John Callender, an officer under George Washington. A man of great dreams, Callender failed one day and was dismissed from the army for cowardice at the Battle of Bunker Hill. Washington wrote this on Callender's papers: "Cowardice—a crime of all others, the most infamous in a soldier, the most injurious, and the last to be forgiven." Upon his discharge, however, Callender remembered his old dreams. He reenlisted in the army as a private, and at the Battle of Long Island exhibited such courage that Washington reinstated him as a captain and revoked his sentence. That's more than a story of record. It's a faithful reflection of the way life goes for a lot us. Few people live without stumbling or falling. The winners, however, are those who refuse to stay down when they go down. More often than not, those who get up are those who look back and remember their dreams and ideals.

Finally, a look back helps us to establish a sense of self-worth. Someone tells about a little boy who said to a friend, "Something is wrong with me. If I am noisy, they paddle me. If I'm quiet, they take my temperature." A lot of us share the feeling that something is wrong with us. A part of our problem is our vantage point. We have a low estimate of ourselves, and that sense of inferiority is born from measuring our race against the race of others. Our mental outlook could be changed if we stopped thinking about the achievements of others and started thinking about how well we have done with what we had.

Centuries ago Paul wrote a letter to a friend. In that letter he said, "I have fought a good fight, and I have kept the faith." When Paul wrote

114

that sentence he was nearing the end of his life. He was looking back and thinking about the race he had run. He compared himself with no one. He looked only at himself and how he had made out. He sensed deep satisfaction. He had done what he could.

If there is any serenity to be found in life, it must be found just this way. Spending life worrying about being a winner is a sure way to be miserable. Every champion finally loses his championship. Someone comes along to break his record. There was once an old warrior thought by his people to be the champion. But one day the soldier fell and a new champion ascended the throne. They wrote the story in a single sentence: "Saul slew his thousands, but David his tens of thousands." It always happens that way. The only way to be a lasting winner is to play against yourself. After all, the only judgment that counts is the one you pass on your own life. If you can look in the mirror and be at peace, not much else matters. Spend a while now and then looking back, measuring where you are against where you have been. If you have done what you could, you will find a peace which no one can give or take away.

Standing Tall

The storm came roaring in from the Atlantic, and it left the city of New York paralyzed. Ordinarily such a snowfall causes little inconvenience in that city. Snowplows are assembled, and crews are at work even as the first flakes begin to fall. The weather forecasters do a good job, and because they do the city is kept moving and New Yorkers can continue on their way. But on that cold day a few years back, the weatherman missed it. His mistake was understandable. Weather systems in this country usually move west to east. This storm slipped in from the east, taking New York City by surprise.

This sort of thing happens not only to cities but also to people. An ancient writer once declared, "Let him who standeth take heed lest he fall!" There are many implications of this sentence, but at least one of them has to do with the unexpected events that come crowding in upon us. Those of us who work at the counselor's desk find examples of this every day among the people we meet. Life seems to be going along at an even pace when suddenly the whole world tumbles in. The storms that hit us are varied. Sometimes it's a husband or wife whose marriage is falling apart. It can be a parent who is troubled about a child. It might be a business problem involving serious financial reverses. Or it may be the temptation to surrender a principle or a cause for which one stands. The list can be extended almost infinitely, but such storms have one thing in common. They take us unawares. The question, then, is always the same: "How do we continue to stand when the storm comes?" How do we hang on when everything around us is going down? The quest for stability in an unstable world is a serious one for many people. No one has discovered all the answers, but there are a few simple things that a lot of people have found helpful.

First, stability is a function of planning. In 1904 Ivan Petrovich Pavlov boarded a train in St. Petersburg, Russia, bound for Stockholm. In Stockholm he was to receive the highest tribute for a contribution to knowledge—the Nobel Prize. This Russian physiologist had turned a chance observation into one of the major psychological discoveries of our time—the laws of conditioning. He coined a phrase now commonly used in psychology, "conditioned responses." "The human organism," Pavlov said, "can be so programed that reflexes become automatic."

While Pavlov's law has many applications, at least one of them suggests that life can be arranged so that some responses do not require debate or decision each time a given circumstance arises. No experienced driver in this country, for instance, stands beside his car in the morning and debates which side of the road he will use that

116

day. That decision has been made and reflexes conditioned accordingly. That's true with a lot of our behavior, isn't it?

Someone has rightly said that one way to handle the unpredictable is to get ready for the predictable. A lot of us go down when we might otherwise stand if we only exercised a bit of foresight. Some storms are reasonably predictable. Illness, for instance, knows no strangers. A bit of planning in simple things such as insurance, preselected medical procedures and the like could make that storm easier. Hard times come to most of us. It's a foolish person, indeed, who does not set aside something for a rainy day. Temptations to surrender one's integrity are everywhere. Somewhere we need to decide on the line beyond which we will not go. Standing tall and steady is easier for those who dare to look ahead.

Second, stability is a function of patience. Sometime before John Fitzgerald Kennedy became president, he wrote a book entitled *Profiles in Courage.* He had a chapter in that book about the man who saved a president. The House of Representatives had drawn the articles of impeachment against Andrew Johnson. The vote was being taken in the Senate. The crucial ballot rested with a senator from Kansas, Edmund G. Ross. If Ross voted "aye," Johnson would be removed from the presidency, the results of which no one dared to predict. Ross knew full well that a vote of "not guilty" would be political suicide for him. That day as the roll call moved toward him, Ross said, "I looked down into my own grave." But Ross refused to surrender. When his name was called, his voice was clear and firm, "Not guilty." The president was saved. Ross' vote that day did cost him his political career. For years he lived in obscurity. It took a long time for the scales to right themselves. Today, however, Ross is remembered as one of our greatest Americans.

Sometimes it takes a while for seed to come to harvest. People who do not understand the time lag between cause and effect lead frantic and troubled lives. Abraham Lincoln once said that if he were right in his cause, then nothing could defeat him in his purpose. If he were wrong, then all the angels of heaven saying he was right would not help him. Thus, the Great Emancipator held his course with confidence. All of us need to think about that. So often we do all we can and the storm comes anyway. In such times it helps to remember that the race is not always to the swift or the battle to the strong. More often than we dream, it is persistence that gets us to the finish line. The next time the storm comes and you feel yourself wavering, try remembering this: When you have done what you can and your course is as right as you can make it, then wait for the mills to grind to their just conclusion. The people who work diligently and learn to wait are the people who are standing when the rest of us are going down.

Finally, stability is a function of faith. In the Old Testament, there is a story about three young men who had been kidnapped and taken into Babylonian slavery. Down in Babylon they were told that the best way "to get along was to get along." "You can't lick us," they were told, "why not join us!" But these Babylonian captors asked for behavior the three young men could never tolerate. When told that unless they capitulated, they would be thrown into a fiery furnace, their answer to the king was clear: "O King, our God is able to deliver us from your hand, but if not, let it be known to you that we will never yield." They didn't yield, and the record contains the outcome. The young men stood tall, and they won.

All of us believe in something. The question is, "In what do we believe?" It is worth the effort to spend some time deciding what we will trust. Is life a matter of chance and the Creator not dependable, or is there rhyme and reason to existence? A lot of people have run that question down and decided on an answer. They have concluded that if life makes any sense at all, there is something in the universe that stands behind the honorable and just. Given time, a right cause will prevail. Such people concern themselves not with the outcome but with the effort they put forth. They ask themselves only if they are taking the right road. Once that question has been answered, they settle back and depend on the highest power to bring the proper outcome. These are the people who stand tall when others fall. Their faith gives them stamina and courage even in unexpected storms.

Standing tall! That's what most of us want to do even when life tumbles in. The people who manage to do that are those who spend a lot of time planning, learning to wait and deciding what they believe.

A Selective Memory

"A Backup Brain!" That's the way it was advertised in a southern newspaper recently. The age of the home computer is here, and we are just beginning to discover its possible uses. The new home systems can be plugged into banks, offices and mail-order houses. We can handle our checking accounts by pushing a button and order our groceries with the flick of a switch. The home computer will be a storehouse for countless bits of information. Appointments, tax records, family birthdays and wedding anniversaries can be recorded or retrieved almost instantaneously.

Most of us will welcome such assistance. Sometimes the human memory seems pretty fickle. Our minds go blank at the most inconvenient moments. We misplace our prized possessions, forget needed words and lose names just when we want them most. Who among us has not been embarrassed by a faulty memory and longed for a backup system? We are now being told that such systems are just around the corner.

Despite the incredible advances in computer technology, the present-day equipment is still pretty crude. The human brain is an awesome mechanism. In a few cubic inches it stores more than could be put in the largest computer. One researcher calculated the brain's storage capacity to be one quadrillion bits of information. The power to remember is a consummate wonder. Without this recall ability, life as we know it would be impossible. There is, however, one function of the memory that is often overlooked. A few things need to be said about this function.

How many of us realize that the content of our memories often conditions our moods? In the Old Testament there is a story of a man named Elijah. An advisor and counselor to kings and queens, he cast a long shadow across his time. One day, however, in the midst of a great cause Elijah lost his courage and retreated to a remote hiding place. Despondent almost to the point of suicide, he actually asked to die. The reason for his despair was a manhunt instigated by the infamous Queen Jezebel. The search involved so many people that Elijah assumed he was all alone in his efforts. He was wrong, of course. The story reports that there were still 7,000 people in Elijah's homeland who had not surrendered to the wicked queen. But Elijah had lost sight of those loyal supporters. He remembered only his enemies and those memories led him to despair.

A few hundred years later there was another man locked in a Roman jail. Behind him were the most unpleasant and terrifying experiences. He had been stoned and beaten, hunted as a criminal, and finally jailed. But St. Paul put those terrible experiences in the background and recalled the countless people who had befriended and helped him. He remembered, too, that out of the worst of times there comes the seed of good. Paul wrote a letter to his friends from his cell that contained this magnificent affirmation: "I have learned in whatever state I find myself to be happy."

People who study the human mind remind us that our mental outlook is conditioned in part by what we recall from the past. Christina Rossetti once wrote:

> I have a room where into no one enters
> Save I myself alone.
> There sits a blessed memory on a throne
> There my life centers.

Not all of our memories are blessed, but it is true that our lives center on what gets our attention. People who dwell on the disappointing experiences of life tend to become bitter and cynical. Those who recall the positive and encouraging things remain bright and optimistic. The memory is a window through which life is viewed. The color of that window determines the color of our world.

The trouble is, most of us remember the wrong things. Many years ago a small community in the southern mountains was torn apart by a family feud. The amazing thing about the feud was that no one could recall what the original argument was about. But the people involved in that bitter quarrel could remember every injury inflicted upon them. Each time violence flared in that tiny town, the bitter memories grew. The feud stayed alive, and the community was in constant turmoil.

What happened in that mountain town can happen to individuals. We let our minds wallow in past hurts and injuries. Little by little the bitterness and resentment grow until our lives have splintered with discord, and we become blind to everything else. How often we hear someone who is reflecting over some tragic circumstance ask, "Why did this happen to me?" Seldom, however, does anyone ask that same question when recalling some good fortune. We have a way of dredging up our troubles and forgetting our blessings. As a consequence our whole world seems wrong. If only we could reverse the process and recall our good fortunes, our lives could be different.

What many of us do not understand is that the content of memory can be controlled by conscious discipline. An ancient writer once declared, "Bless the Lord, O my soul, and forget not his benefits." Whoever this writer was, he understood the operation of the human mind. There is an old story about a man who was recalling the hardships of his early life. He exaggerated to such an extent that his wife felt constrained to correct him. "Be quiet," he said to her. "Half of the fun in remembering the good old days is rearranging them." We are capable of doing just that. The memory can be manipulated. Samuel Johnson had this in mind when he wrote, "The true art of memory is the art of attention." What we give to our minds will eventually determine what they contain. This is why the ancient writer reminded us to count our blessings. Feed the mind on the right things and life takes on the right complexion.

Will Rogers once said that he was often tempted to believe life would be better if he lived in a different place. He said, however, that he conquered that temptation by an interesting method. He would subscribe to the leading newspaper from the place where he thought life would be better. "I always find," he said, "things are a lot worse there than they are here." That's worth remembering. The mind feeds on the food that is placed at its disposal.

The next time you find yourself in a season of despair and gloom, try a simple exercise. Take a pencil and jot down a few of the good things that have happened to you. You will discover that this little process will go a long way toward lifting the shades and letting in the light. You will understand what Earl Musselman was thinking when he wrote the following lines:

The sun was shining in my eyes
*   and I could hardly see*
To do the necessary task
*   that was allotted me.*
Resentment of the vivid glow
*   I started to complain*
When all at once upon the air
*   I heard the blind man's cane.*

It works that way. If we train our minds to do so, we can see our blessings. Our memories will then become pleasant. And pleasant memories from yesterday will go a long way toward helping us have a good tomorrow.

A $40,000 Golf Shot

When Alan Shepherd made his historic trip to the moon, we were told he carried a golf ball for a tee shot on the lunar surface. A statistician toying with the numbers came up with a bit of information that made the news. Analyzing the weight of the golf ball against the total cost of the mission, the statistician calculated the cost of transporting the ball to the moon to be $40,000.

The accuracy of this figure may be open to debate, but it does point to an interesting idea. A little weight in a strategic place can be of considerable consequence. That's a thought worth remembering in a day when the significance of the individual seems to be diminishing. Many of us feel that in a society as complex as ours, our lives simply do not count. Perhaps people have always felt this way, but in our time it seems more acute. If nothing else, the immense increases in the world's population add to our feeling of aloneness. Now and then there is need for reflection on the meaning and importance of our lives as individuals.

One factor we often forget is the interrelatedness of people. There is a principle in nature which is persistent and certain. Creation will sustain nothing that attempts to stand alone. We become more and more aware of this as we explore the delicate balance in nature. A few years back when the Aswan Dam was built on the Nile River, ecologists soon discovered the effect of the dam on the rest of the river, all the way to its delta. Rich silt deposits once brought by rampaging floods are now diminishing. Marshlands that were cleaned by the river's overflow are becoming stagnant mires. Fishing grounds that have been fertile for centuries are now becoming barren. The Aswan project proves again what we have known for a long, long time: We do not gain anything in nature without sacrificing something else.

Interpersonal relationships are not greatly different. Minton Johnson tells about a bridge game that resulted in cruelty to animals. A company president's wife had a bad evening at bridge. The next morning she vented her anger on her husband. When the husband arrived at work, he snapped at the vice president for some minor offense. The vice president took it out on the office manager who turned on his secretary. The secretary took it out on the office boy. The office boy had no one left, so on the way home he kicked a stray cat. Something like that often happens in the world of human affairs. Like the waves of the sea, our influences move on and on.

We do not live in a vacuum. Every action produces its reaction. A golf ball carried to the moon runs up an astonishing bill even though the ball's weight is minimal. A change in river currents affects its channel, and the attitudes of people move through the social structure with a domino effect. Nothing can be isolated so that it stands alone.

If this be true, then another thought follows. Each of us has an influence on someone or something. That's easy to believe when you think of people who, by position or circumstance, have great power. Big names alter times and events, but the little known and the unremembered have their impact, too.

Consider an example. We owe most of the New Testament to one man, and for the most part that man's name is unremembered. There was once a young fellow named John Mark, who in his earlier years must have been pretty erratic and undependable. John Mark had a friend named Barnabas who saw great potential in the young man. Barnabas stayed with Mark, encouraged him, and urged him to use his talents. The day came when Mark was to write one of the most important books in history—the biography of a carpenter from Nazareth. The biography which Mark wrote is considered by many to be the cornerstone of the New Testament. Few people, however, remember the name of Barnabas.

Henry Ward Beecher once declared, "The humblest individual exerts some influence, either for good or evil, upon others." This is true, and so often the unnamed people never know what they have done. It was in the news somewhere recently. Five of the greatest physicists in the world came from the same little town in Germany. Someone traced the record and discovered a high-school physics teacher who caught the imagination of the five men when they were boys. Beecher was right. All of us touch someone. We can't help it.

The startling thing about it is that we do not always know the far-reaching impact of our lives. A little over a hundred years ago, Horace Bushnell wrote an essay that has become a classic. He entitled it "Unconscious Influence." Bushnell pointed out that there are two forces radiating from every person. One, of course, is the result of conscious effort when by direct action a person sets out to change a given circumstance. The other is the unconscious force which moves out from us. Bushnell contended, with some merit, that of the two forces, the latter is the more powerful. "Indeed," said Bushnell, "involuntary communication is the strongest force on earth."

Think about that in your own life. Who are the people who have guided and directed your steps? For many of us there are parents who by conscious effort helped us find direction. But more often than not the most powerful forces they exerted upon us came not from what they said but from who they were and the examples they set. Too, many of us can remember a teacher or friend who caught our attention and gave us invaluable insights into life. Perhaps it was a business associate who gave us a break at the right time and place. So often, at the time, these folk did not know fully what they were doing or the significance of it in our lives. To these people, however, we owe an incalculable debt.

A long time ago a man wrote a line the world still remembers: "No one lives alone, and no one dies alone." The author of that sentence had something different in mind from what is being considered here. His thought, however, is profoundly true in many ways. We don't live alone or die alone. We do count for something—although often we do not know where or how. There are no insignificant people. What we do and say touches someone directly or indirectly. Sometimes a small word or deed can have a profound effect on the world. The next time life seems rather useless to you try remembering that. Tomorrow's harvests come from today's seeds. You may be sowing one that could make the world a different place.

How to Choose a Drum

"If a man does not keep pace with his companions, perhaps it is because he hears a different drummer. Let him step to the music which he hears however measured or far away." That's the way Henry David Thoreau put it in one of his books written more than 100 years ago. In 1845 Thoreau staked out a little cabin near Walden Pond, and for two years lived a nearly hermitlike existence. During those years he thought his own thoughts, which were later published and widely read. His influence on American life is indelible. "March to your own drummer" has achieved almost proverbial status in our land.

No thinking person can accept Thoreau's advice without question. Newspapers recently had a story about a California man accused of several brutal murders. He gave as his reason the "torment of inner voices." A jury will not likely accept that as valid reason for this man's inhuman behavior. Yet the man's claim is not altogether preposterous. Long ago St. Paul referred to the conflicting voices in his own inner life. He suggested that we all struggle with the tension between our higher and lower selves. An anonymous writer once described that conflict in a vivid way:

Within this temple there's a crowd.
There's one of us that's humble; one that's proud.
There's one of us that's sorry for his sins;
Another, unrepentant sits and grins.
From much earthly care, I could be free
If I could just determine which is me.

That's a problem for most of us, and the solution to it is not easily accomplished. There does come a time, however, when we have to make up our minds about the voices we will heed—the drummer we will follow. Indeed, the central question of human existence is the drum to which we march.

One thing is clear about this. *Whatever drum we choose, it must preserve our integrity.* Several years ago someone wrote some brief character studies on a half-dozen or so great living Americans. In one of those studies, there was a sentence worth remembering. The person involved had risen to a place of great prestige in his profession. Suddenly he suffered a series of reverses that left him near the bottom of the heap. Amazingly enough, the man carried on with spectacular calm and inner peace. The secret to his serenity was a thought which he said he considered every day. "Each morning as I entered my chauffeured limousine and made my way to my office—an apex of power and importance—I said to myself, 'Don't get used to this. If it is ever taken away, you'll have nothing left.' " Harry Emerson

125

Fosdick put it another way, but with equal thoughtfulness. "It's a good thing to stop once in a while and ask, 'If everything were taken from you that could be taken, what would you have left?' "

That must have been what Edgar A. Guest had in mind when he wrote:

I have to live with myself; and so,
I want to be fit for myself to know.
I want to be able as the days go by
Always to look myself straight in the eye.

That's a drum worth marching to. *It's important, too, to listen to a drum which keeps life focused on important things.* Samuel Johnson once described a friend, "She was always in the thick of thin things." It is possible to live our lives for things that do not really matter. The Great Teacher once said to his disciples, "I must do the works of him who sent me while it is yet day, for the night comes and no one can work." Counselors often talk with people who are laden with guilt. Contrary to what most people would expect, the guilt feelings arise not so much from things they have done but from things they have left undone.

Years ago one of baseball's all-time great players stood at home plate while the pitcher threw two strikes by him. When the third pitch came, the player stood waiting; but his bat never moved. When the umpire called, "Strike three," the batter turned to the umpire, muttered something, and walked away. Newsmen present had never known Lou Gehrig to protest a call. They cornered Gehrig and asked him what he had said to the umpire. "Oh," said Gehrig, "that was no protest. I just said that I'd give a thousand dollars to have another chance at that last pitch." Life doesn't often work that way, however. You have to work at the right things while it is yet day. The night does come, and the final strike is called.

Price tags can get pretty mixed up in our world. A lovely house is far less important than a loving home. Friends count for more than personal gain made at their expense. A place in the social register is never worth one's physical or emotional health. And it's always a bad deal to exchange an honest reputation for power or prestige. It's a good drum to listen to if it helps us focus on important things.

A third drum worth hearing is the one that gives life an extended meaning. All of us hear it now and then: "Don't worry about it. You won't know the difference a hundred years from now." That sentence suggests another thought. Perhaps we should give ourselves to things that will make a difference a hundred years from now. There are ways to do just that.

In 1723, the body of Sir Christopher Wren was laid to rest in London's St. Paul's Cathedral. Wren had designed the cathedral following the destruction of it in the Great Fire of London in 1666. Wren's well-known epitaph appears in that cathedral: "If you would see his

126

monument look around." Wren's masterpiece still stands as a memorial to one who lived beyond his years.

Most of us will have no opportunity to design great buildings, construct temples or pyramids. Even so, we can live beyond our days. There is a proverb which reads: "If you want to plant for a season, sow a garden; for a century, plant a tree; but if you want to plant for eternity, touch a life for good." That latter door is open to everyone. Frank Laubach's influence will survive infinity. Albert Schweitzer's skilled and talented hands will reach down countless centuries. Abraham Lincoln's gallant and courageous spirit will forever tug at the tides of time. And the Nazarene carpenter changed the world so that it will never be the same. The impact of our lives will not be nearly so great, but in some small way all of us can give something good to the world that will survive us. It may be by supporting some noble and worthy cause, or a word of encouragement or help to a talented person, or perhaps through the lives of our children. All of us can do something that will make a difference a hundred years from now if we listen for the proper drummer. It's the people who march to such music who are able to look back from the end of life and not be ashamed.

The Happiest Place on Earth

At the world-famous amusement park in Anaheim, California, there is a large sign near the entrance which reads "Disneyland—the Happiest Place on Earth." Each year thousands of people come from all over the world to visit this fairyland and find it to be a happy place, indeed. It is difficult to walk along the streets and paths of Disneyland and be sad or melancholy. This make-believe world catches the imagination of the most somber person.

A lot of people never make it to Disneyland and yet find life happy and satisfying. When you first observe the lives of these folks, you are likely to believe they are the recipients of some good fortune not afforded the rest of us. Closer examination, however, reveals that the happy people are not always the lucky ones. They have been the victims of the toughest breaks in life; they live in the hardest places and under the roughest circumstances. You can't help but wonder how they manage to remain cheerful and bright.

A few years ago someone writing about this paradox penned a thoughtful sentence: "If you have a happy life, it is not because you found it that way; it's because you made it that way." That sentence suggests that happiness is self-made, a do-it-yourself project. If that's true, the question arises, "How do we achieve happiness?" What are the ingredients of a happy life? A few years back William Barclay, a prolific British author, suggested three essentials in achieving happiness. Those essentials are : (1) something to hope for; (2) something to do; and (3) someone to love. Those thoughts are worth exploring.

First, happiness depends on something to hope for. Dr. Karl Menninger, in his book *The Vital Balance,* tells of a visit to the Buchenwald prison camp a few days after it was liberated during World War II. Thousands had died in the brutal camps from beatings, starvation and overwork. One group survived. It was a group of doctors who got together and organized a medical society. They prepared papers and presented them to one another. They treated sick prisoners and made plans for improving health conditions. They even made medical instruments, including an X-ray machine. Said Menninger, "These doctors suffered the same difficulties others faced, but they survived. They were *kept alive by hope!*"

The function of hope in meaningful life has often been demonstrated in psychobiological laboratories. Mice placed in certain situations with no chance for escape rapidly succumbed to death. If the hopelessness was eliminated, from the situation, the mice survived. People are not greatly different from mice in this regard. We are "kept alive by hope."

Hope does give vitality to living. It is of such strategic importance that none of us can afford to be without it. But hope is not so much something we find as it is something we cultivate. We acquire hope by searching for the potentials in every situation—by looking for the possibilities in even the worst circumstances. Happy people are not those who get the breaks but those who look for opportunities.

Second, happiness depends on having something to do. A lot is being said these days about the stress and strain of contemporary life. Overwork does take its toll. If anything is worse than overwork, however, it is having nothing to do. Recently a church bulletin contained an article about a woman who had spent long years caring for her family. Time had taken the woman's children beyond the need for her care. Death had claimed her husband. He had left her well fixed, with no responsibilities. The woman assessed her predicament as follows: "Hell is when the work is done. When there is no longer anything to do, life is no longer anything." When people lose their zest for active participation, their next loss will be their zest for living.

A proper appreciation of work is essential for happiness. Kenneth Hildebrand reports that the widow of the famed auto maker, the 100-year-old multimillionairess, said that she was happiest when she used to pack Mr. Dodge's lunch box every day. St. Paul must have been among the world's happiest people. But Paul never allowed himself to lead an idle life. Even when he was stopped in his travels and jailed for his faith, he used the prison cell as a place to write the letters which make up much of the New Testament. We could learn from these people. Happiness is having something to do. Most often work finds us. If it doesn't, we need to find it. "Hell is when the work is done."

Third, happiness is having someone to love. Do you remember this verse?

I sought God, and he evaded me;
I sought my soul, but myself I could not see.
I sought my brother, and I found all three.

When you are young, to be encumbered in a caring relationship seems a dreadful drag. It curbs freedom and limits independence. As the years go by, however, the novelty of independence loses its luster. To be alone in later years is a dreadful thing. In my work as a minister, I find people like that every day. They reach out for attention, for someone to care about and for someone with whom they can share life's experiences.

Happy is the person who has cultivated ties and relationships with others. No one is rich enough to afford being without a friend. It takes a little work, of course, and requires some inconvenience and investment of effort, but the dividends are priceless. The poet is right. When you reach out to someone else, you find yourself.

Essentials for happiness: something to hope for, something to do and someone to love. These may not be all the ingredients of happiness, but they are important. If life is not what we want it to be, we could well ask ourselves if one of these essentials is missing. It's amazing how any place can become "the happiest place on earth" when you follow these rules.

Why Do You Work?

They bought his books by the thousands—this famed writer who carved his name into America's literary hall of fame. Horatio Alger died in 1899, leaving behind a legacy of 136 books. With such titles as *Tattered Tom* and *Luck and Pluck,* Alger's stories dealt with penniless heroes who gained success by honesty and courage. Alger believed that America was a land of limitless opportunity and anyone who wanted to could make it all the way to the top. Apparently, these books touched a responsive chord among the youth of Alger's day. Hundreds of thousands of copies were sold in bookstores everywhere.

It's been nearly a century since Alger caught the attention of America's youth. Today the theme which Alger championed has fallen on troubled times. A part of the reason, of course, is that Alger's formula for success was much too simplistic. Ours is a complex world. It takes more than courage to make it to the top. It is true, however, that Alger's dream is still around. Most people want to believe that their lives are successful and that they count for something. A sense of worthlessness is the most dreadful of all human emotions.

A few years ago a management consulting firm did a study for a large manufacturing company in the Northeast. Among the questions they asked of employees was, "Why do you work?" To their surprise, the first answer given was not money. The people responded with such replies as, "To feel useful," "To have a sense of accomplishment" or "To lead a productive life." The consulting firm concluded that the primary motivation for most people in their work is not money. They want to believe they count for something. The employees of that business are not greatly different from the rest of us. We like to believe that our lives have meaning. The question is, how do we acquire that sense of self-esteem?

One thing is clear: To be alive does not guarantee that life has meaning. A few years ago a prominent Canadian minister wrote a book entitled *The Illusions of Our Culture.* In that book he pointed out that many of us believe happiness is an inherent human right. "That," said he, "is an illusion." This minister was on solid ground in that claim. When our forefathers framed the Declaration of Independence, they identified what they believed to be our inalienable rights. They named three: life, liberty and the *pursuit* of happiness. Our founding fathers did not say that we are guaranteed happiness. We have only the right to pursue it. If that's true, then it is possible to go all the way through this world and find no meaning to life.

A lot of people do just that. They lead drab, dull and monotonous lives and tragically enough, they blame it on circumstances. In the

Old Testament, there is an account of Adam and Eve's fall in the Garden of Eden. Adam was accused of eating the forbidden fruit. When asked why he did it, Adam replied: "The woman tempted me." That, of course, was his way of saying, "It's not my fault. Someone got in the way." Adam's alibi is still around. A lot of us believe we are losers because of someone or something else. "If I had only been at the right place at the right time," we often say. We believe ourselves to be failures but imagine it is not our fault.

The real trouble, however, is that many of us ask the wrong question. The problem isn't, "Does life have meaning?" but "How can I *make* my life meaningful?" A few years ago an insurance company distributed a little poster with this sentence on it: "Don't expect anyone to make you happy; it's a do-it-yourself project." The truth of that should be apparent. Place, position and circumstances don't guarantee much of anything. Some of the most miserable people appear to have everything, and some of the happiest people live in the most unlikely circumstances. That's always been true. St. Paul once wrote, "I have learned in whatever state I am, therewith to be content." One translation of that verse reads, "I have learned wherever I am to be content." Paul seemed to have little reason to be happy. He spent most of his life in jail, accused of civil treason. He was stoned and beaten, and suffered terrible physical handicaps. He was turned back from most of his greatest dreams. Paul, however, had learned a timeless truth. If we find happiness, we have to find it where we are. We don't stumble into a meaningful life. We have to make it that way.

The people who achieve peace and contentment always come at life along the road. Twenty centuries ago a carpenter came out of a little town in a faraway corner of the world. He never traveled more than 150 miles from home; he held no college degrees; he presided over no great business ventures; he never wrote a book; he didn't even own a burial plot in the local cemetery. Almost every person in the social register was angry with him. Yet he said it himself, "My soul is satisfied." The example of Jesus suggests to us the only way we can find meaning to life. We must give ourselves to something that counts.

The world owes to one man much of the credit for ridding this planet of slavery. William Wilberforce was a wretched, ailing little man. He was so unsightly that the first time he stood before the British House of Commons, the people broke into embarrassed smiles. But as he began to speak, the great audience was caught up in his cause and became strangely still. They wrote of him, "The little minnow became a whale."

The story of Wilberforce is worth reading. Many of us spend too much time wishing for talents we don't have and for opportunities that will never come. We need to learn to see what we have where we are. That's the secret to great living. Horatio Alger's theme is still important. Not all of us can make it to the top, but not one of us lives without an opportunity to do something worthwhile. When we do what we can where we can, life then becomes worthwhile.

Leaning on the Wind

One morning in Providence, Rhode Island, the editor of a national magazine was walking near a construction site. As he passed a half-completed building, he found a crowd gathered on the edge of the street. A man had fallen from a steel girder several stories above. The foreman of the construction crew told the editor that a near gale was blowing in from the sea that morning. The fallen workman had been walking along the girder leaning into the wind. Suddenly the wind shifted; the man lost his balance and fell. "This near the ocean," said the foreman, "construction work is dangerous. You learn in a hurry never to lean against the wind."

The point of that story is timeless. Twenty-seven hundred years ago, a little country on the eastern edge of the Mediterranean Sea was under siege. The armies of the Assyrian Empire were threatening to annihilate the tiny nation. The people, sensing certain defeat, had turned to the Egyptians for help. There was in that little land a states-man named Isaiah. Isaiah knew that his people were exchanging one danger for another. He said something like this: "Woe to those who go down to Egypt for help and look not to the Holy One. The Egyptians are men not gods, and their horses are flesh not spirit. You are lean-ing on the wind." Isaiah's words are worth a bit of thought even for those of us who live in a different age. Consider three things.

First, remember that we are compulsive seekers. Recently, one of America's eminent psychologists addressed the graduating class of a Southern medical school. In his address he stated that the human organism is equipped with certain basic and native impulses. The labels given these impulses vary according to the particular bias of those who supply them. All are in agreement, however, that in body, soul and mind we are hungry creatures in restless pursuit of satisfaction.

The objects of our pursuit differ from person to person. For some the search is for security. In a recent study of college students the question was asked, "What do you want out of life?" The majority of respondents replied in terms of the right to work with adequate compensation to enjoy life without being anxious about the future. For other people the quest is for significance. This explains our spirit of competitiveness and our search for power. Few of us are complete-ly immune to the longing to be "somebody." For still other folk, the quest of life is the gratification of animal impulses. We want to satis-fy these impulses without discipline or restraint. Regardless of our particular pursuit, however, it is clear that all of us are seekers. We are hungry people.

This suggests a second thought. Some of our pursuits are for things that ultimately fail. The late Fred Allen once defined a celebrity as a person who works hard all his life to become known and then wears dark glasses to avoid being recognized. That's a perceptive comment, is it not? Notoriety never seems to live up to its advance billing. A Hollywood actress stated it well: "Fame is the greatest whitewash there is." Some things are like that. They ultimately fail. It's like leaning on the wind.

It's so easy to be confused about the roads that lead to life—real life. The prodigal son thought that if he overthrew all restraints and gave free expression to his impulses, he could find life. He discovered that the undisciplined life finally destroys itself. People who believe that the secret to life is the security of possessions discover what at last becomes clear to everyone: You can't take it with you. Augustus Caesar thought the answer was power. If, however, he had not been associated with the story of Jesus we might hardly be aware of who he was. So many of our pursuits are failures. It's like leaning on the wind.

There is a final thought. The great possessions of life are not those things we discover on the outside but what we have within. There is a song tucked away in the folk music of our land entitled, "That Old-Time Religion." One verse in that song begins, "It will do when I am dying." The point of that line is worth remembering. In the storms of life, it's not what we have on the outside that counts, it's what we have on the inside.

As a minister I often work with people who are walking through tough places. One thing I have learned is that the difference between those who handle life and those who do not is at the point of inner faith. I have long since concluded that the most important question we can ask ourselves is, "What do I really believe?" There are really only two alternatives. We can believe that destiny is a matter of luck and what happens to us is the result of fate. If that position is true, however, then all effort is useless; and our struggles are in vain. It means, too, that Adolf Hitler and Abraham Lincoln come out at the same place. I can't believe that. There is another position I hold to be true. I believe the creative structures of this universe are so arranged that good seed finally brings a good harvest and the right road somewhere, sometime, comes out at the right place.

A long time ago, a man stood in the British Parliament to plead a cause. The man's cause was right, but it was far from popular. As he began to speak, shouts of anger rang through the hall. The man tried to continue his speech, but the opposition was too great. Finally he closed his notebook and waited until the booing ceased and the hall was quiet. Then with absolute confidence he said softly, "The time will come when you will hear me." It is this sort of faith that sustains us when unfavorable winds blow about us. If we have made up our minds that there is "something" in this world that supports a right cause, we can stand and not go down. The real quest of life, therefore, is the quest for a faith. That's what Isaiah was saying to his people and to us. Don't lean on the wind. Learn to trust the "Unseen Hand."

The Needless Battle

Most American history books tell the story of the strange Battle of New Orleans, which occurred on January 8, 1815. That day more than 2,000 British soldiers died in an attempt to take New Orleans, which was being held under the leadership of Gen. Andrew Jackson. Jackson had arrived in New Orleans in early December. He found the city almost demoralized. In a frenzy of effort, he inspired the townspeople to make preparations for defense. At dawn on the morning of January 8, the British launched a full-scale attack on the city. The battle ended in total defeat for the British. It cost them the lives of some 2,000 men.

The terrible thing about the Battle of New Orleans is that it occurred after the war was over. Fifteen days before the British marched on the city, a peace treaty was signed in Belgium bringing the War of 1812 to a close. Inadequate communications delayed the news of that treaty. Before word reached New Orleans, the tragedy of January 8 had happened. Most historians refer to this conflict as "The Needless Battle." It is the sad and tragic story of a valiant struggle to sustain a cause already lost.

The useless expenditure of human life is always sad. It happens not only on the battlefield but also in daily life. There is an old expression: "You can't fight city hall." That expression is not nearly as true as we sometimes think. A lot of changes for good could be brought about in our world if we were determined to make them. But sometimes we waste a lot of our energies fighting causes already lost. Life would be better for many of us if we kept in mind two or three things.

We need to remember, for instance, that *some things have been decided regardless of the battles fought.* We live in a dependable world. There is a cathedral in Italy built more than 500 years ago. On the floor of that cathedral there is a brass plate upon which the sun shines for a brief moment each June 22. The light reaches that small plate through an opening high in the vaulted towers of the building. The purpose of that rather strange arrangement is to determine whether the cathedral has shifted on its foundations. The builders of that structure were sure of at least one thing. The movement of creation is so precise and certain that they could depend on the sun being at the appointed place at the appointed time. The building might change, but the architects knew the sun would be on schedule.

The laws governing our emotional, spiritual and mental selves seem no less precise. It is said that the most coveted possession of human existence is peace of mind. Peace of mind is not an accidental happening. It comes about through the application of certain unfailing principles. We have long since identified these principles. They can

137

be stated in various ways. In general, however, the people who find inner peace are those who live with integrity, treat others fairly, and trust God for the rest. The folk who follow these principles find them to be dependable and certain. They constitute the only road to peace of mind that we have ever found.

Because this is true, a second thought is important. *To seek inner peace in conflict with these principles is futile.* People who do woodwork often talk about "working with the grain." They mean, of course, that smoothing a surface requires working *with* the fibers of the wood and not *against* them. Sanding with the grain is essential if you intend to have smooth wood.

We understand this lesson in a cabinet shop, but we sometimes miss it in other arenas. Wallace Hamilton once wrote an essay entitled "Shortcuts to Paradise." In that essay Hamilton said that the constant temptation confronting us is the effort to find the good life without being willing to pay the price for it. We try to make new rules, establish new ways to get to "Paradise." We always discover that our self-centered plans won't work. The reason is obvious. The way to inner peace was laid out in the scheme of creation. We can't change that way, and any effort to do so is a "needless battle." Working against the grain is self-defeating.

This makes a concluding thought apparent. *The way to peace is through acceptance of the prevailing plan.* We often say, "If you can't lick 'em, join 'em." Sometimes this advice can have bad results, but not always. There are places when the way to power, strength and peace is through surrender.

There is an old story about a truck that was a bit too high to pass under a bridge. The truck became wedged between the bridge and the street. Every effort to dislodge it failed. Wreckers tugged and pulled, but nothing moved. A schoolboy came skipping down the street. He suggested that the workmen let the air out of the tires on the truck. They did, and the truck rolled free. That's a parable worthy of thought. What we can't manage through struggle, we can sometimes accomplish by surrendering to the prevailing laws of creation.

We don't create power; we only utilize it. We put ourselves into nature's plan, and nature works for us. A river generates power because we harness it. An atom gives off energy because we follow the laws necessary to divide it. The way to strength is by surrendering to laws that are intended to prevail.

Is not this same process essential in our quest for inner peace? There are certain principles, when applied, that always bring peace of mind. When we live with integrity by being true to the best we know, when we treat others as we would expect to be treated, and when we are willing to leave to Providence the final results, there comes to us a kind of peace that no one can give us or take away. This road to peace was established when the Creator made his world. Any effort to change that road is a "needless battle." There comes a time when those who seek peace of mind must surrender to the inevitable plan. If we go the way the Creator intended, we will come out where we want to be.

Bound and Free

On May 9, 1980, a Liberian freighter on its way into the Tampa Bay struck the Sunshine Skyway Bridge, tumbling 1,300 feet of roadway into the water. A large bus and several cars plunged into the bay. It is believed that only one person survived the 150-foot fall. At least 35 people died in the mishap. Dozens of others missed the accident by minutes. One car skidded to a halt just inches from the gaping hole. Moments after the tragedy, newspeople were on the scene to interview those who had come close to death. During the interview, one man declared, "God was extremely good to me. I guess it just wasn't my time to go."

It is easy to understand this man's feelings of relief. To come within inches of death is a frightening experience. Only the most callous person would fail to breathe prayers of gratitude. The man's comment, however, does raise an interesting question that most of us have asked. We wonder if our lives are determined for us. Are we nothing more than the victims of blind fate ? We, of course, are not the first to raise such a question. People have been grappling with it as far back as there is a record. Countless books have been written on this subject, but to date no one has ever come up with a final answer. It is an interesting question to consider, however. There are two or three things that might be said.

It is possible, for instance, to make a case for *determinism*. In 1985 a giant comet will brush through our skies on its long journey around the sun. That comet left the vicinity of the earth in 1910. So far as we know that comet has been coming this way every 75 years. In 1682 an English astronomer spotted the comet. After extensive study he predicted that the comet would appear again in 1759, 1835, and in 1910. Those predictions have been accurate. Halley's comet has always arrived on schedule.

We live in a world of precise laws. The whole universe functions much like a gigantic clock. Each star and planet follows a prescribed course and every piece seems to fit into a total pattern. Apparently these components of creation have no choice in the matter. They simply follow the course laid down for them at the beginning of time.

It requires only a small step in logic to believe that human beings fit into that plan. If the stars and planets follow a prearranged path, is it not reasonable to expect the same to be true for us? There are people who believe this. They tell us that our lives are determined for us. Everyone has a number; and when that number is called, our time is up.

It must be said, however, that such a position leaves a lot of unanswered questions. If we are the victims of blind fate, there are no such things as guilt for crimes committed or fault in any act of negligence. There are no accidents for which we can be blamed. We are simply following the course prescribed for us. We are nothing but actors in a drama we did not write and cannot change. Not many of us are willing to believe that we are robots being manipulated in all that we do and say. We like to believe we have the power to choose.

It is because of these problems that some people hold an alternate position. They suggest that we are *completely free.* In the Old Testament there is an interesting little sentence in the story of creation. The author reports the Creator as saying to humankind, "Have dominion over all that I have made." The implications of that sentence are clear. It suggests that we are creatures of choice. We do have the freedom to decide what happens to us. Such a position seems reasonable enough. We possess faculties for thinking. We are able to take raw materials and produce finished products. We can use the resources of the earth to feed and clothe ourselves, or we can use those same resources to build weapons of war. We *do* have the power to make decisions.

Is it not true, however, that unlimited freedom is also an untenable position? We are not free to do anything we choose. We do not have the freedom, for instance, to repeal the laws of nature. The laws of gravity seem to be permanent despite any effort we might make to change them. In legal circles, attorneys often refer to "an act of God." While the exact meaning of this phrase is debatable, the phrase is generally used to describe a circumstance over which there is no human control. Apparently there are things over which we have no control. It has been said that human beings do not create or destroy matter. We only change its form. We can convert matter into energy and energy into matter, but the sum total remains the same.

What, then, is the answer? Are we the victims of blind fate, or can we determine what happens to us? A long time ago a philosopher, whose name has been lost, wrote an interesting sentence: "We are free to choose, but we are not free to choose the consequences of our choice." This philosopher was trying to tell us that when we choose a direction, we also choose the consequences involved in that direction. A schoolboy, for example, is given an opportunity to study piano, but he decides that playing ball is much more fun. So he refuses to practice his lessons. The result is the inability to play the piano.

We make our choices, and as we do, certain consequences become inevitable. We choose, for instance, to move about in automobiles, and the consequence is the risk of death and injury. We choose to live near other people and, thus, suffer sometimes innocently from their mistakes. We choose a vocation and receive both the rewards and penalties of that choice. "We are free to choose, but not free to choose the consequences of our choice."

Many years ago, a British writer used a parable about a ship which set out for a distant port. As the vessel got under way, the captain said to his passengers: "You may make of this voyage what you will. You can work together and enjoy the journey, or you can live in strife and turmoil and be miserable. That choice is yours. There is one choice you do not have. You will not destroy this ship. We will arrive at our destination."

There are many problems inherent in this analogy, but it does suggest an important lesson for living. Our freedom to choose is limited. We do, however, have the power to make certain decisions. We can choose many things that enhance life and give it meaning—love, beauty, honesty, integrity, etc. We can decide, too, that we are going to be happy regardless of our circumstances. We may not be completely free to determine everything—where we live, how we look, the talents we have, or the misfortunes that overtake us. But what we do with these things is largely up to us. The question, therefore, is not whether our lives are directed for us, but "How can we so direct our lives that we enjoy the journey?"

Life Has a Layaway Plan

On a rainy evening in 1891 an 18-year-old student at Stanford University scheduled a concert for the university community. The boy had enrolled at the university with little money. Orphaned at the age of eight, he was forced to do odd jobs to pay his tuition. On that rainy evening the lad had scheduled the famed pianist, Ignace Paderewski, for a performance. So few people attended that the boy was unable to meet expenses. When the pianist discovered the boy's predicament, the musician refused his fee.

Years later, according to Norman Beasley, Paderewski was serving as the premier of Poland. He came to his post of duty in one of the difficult hours of European history. The world was binding up the wounds of the First World War. Europe was at the point of starvation. Three thousand miles away in the United States a man was collecting food for distribution across the world. "One day," says Beasley, "this man arrived in Poland and went straight to the home of the premier." "Mr. Premier," said the man, "I have come to assist the starving people of Poland. Consider this as partial payment for the fee you canceled for me more than 30 years ago at Stanford University."

This remarkable story from the life of Herbert Hoover reflects something of the romanticism of a novel. All too often this lesson has been used as the motivation for philanthropy. But within this parable there is a truth that runs all the way to the center of creation. There is a principle here that needs to be kept in focus.

Science has taught us, for instance, that the law of cause and effect is basic in the scheme of things. There is an old question running back to the beginning of time: Are we the masters or the slaves of our environment? That question has had many interesting answers. For the most part, however, we have believed that to some degree we are the "masters of our fate."

The earliest attempts to master our environment were mostly magical. People tried to control their destinies by actions which we now know had no direct bearing on their circumstances. The ancient Egyptians, Assyrians, Greeks and Romans followed countless magical formulas, all designed to compel nature to follow their direction. Later generations, however, have abandoned such superstitions. Scientists probed the heart of the universe, listening to its heartbeat, endeavoring to unravel its mysteries. Somewhere along the way, someone discovered something that changed the plan of attack. Creation is governed by a reign of law. This is a world of cause and effect; for every action there is a consequent reaction. This principle operates all the way from the planting of a garden to the movement of the stars.

143

Every field of study is dedicated to the validity of this law. The physics book is filled with examples of it. Even history books suggest that great movements begin with a small seed sown somewhere along the shores of time. Sometimes there is a time lag between cause and effect. Indeed, the action and reaction may be separated by centuries. We need to remember, too, that the law of cause and effect operates at every level of life. Stated in the simplest form, this law suggests that life is usually the sum total of all the seeds that are sown.

Think about the mind and its power to remember. Memory by definition is that process by which the mind preserves the impressions it receives. Suppose for a moment this process were taken from us. We could not remember who we were, the work we were engaged in, the car we drove, where we parked it or how we drove it. Families would not recognize one another. Husbands and wives would be total strangers. Most of us, of course, would like to forget some things. There are some people we would like to forget, and some people who would like to forget us! But memory is more than a facility necessary for identification. It is a storehouse, a filing cabinet for good and bad things as the case may be. This is what modern psychiatry is all about. If we fill our minds with cheap and destructive thoughts, then life comes out the same way. What we put into the filing cabinet determines to some degree our destinies. It's the law of cause and effect, and it operates everywhere.

What we are tomorrow is determined by the choices we make today. The future is rooted in the present, and the present is rooted in the past. There is an old story about a Nobel Prize winner who was asked how it felt to wake up one morning and find oneself famous. "Lady," said the novelist, "no one wakes up suddenly and finds himself famous. I've been at work night and day for years." The law of cause and effect works this way. We are *now* becoming what we eventually will be.

Remember, too, that the law of cause and effect is neutral. One of America's greatest orators made a speech a few years ago in which he quoted a verse from the Bible: "Whatever you sow, you will also reap." " That's a terrible thought," said the man, "if it turns out to be true. Imagine reaping a harvest on every seed you sow." We know, of course, that the law quoted from the Bible is true. We have tested it across countless centuries. It is not, however, a terrible law. As a matter of fact, it is because of this law that we can make sense of life. If we sow the wrong seeds, we get the wrong harvest. But the alternate fact is also true. The law of cause and effect is neither good nor bad. It is neutral.

It must be among the oldest parables in the world—that story about a Chinese landowner who one day called in his foreman and gave him instructions to lay out the finest cattle ranch money could afford. "I shall be traveling for a while," said the landowner. "When I return, I shall retire. I want this project to be our best." The foreman set out to work, but as he went along he began to think, "Soon I shall be without employment. I must make plans to save some money." So he began to cut corners in the workmanship on the new ranch. Wherever he could hide it, he put in the worst materials and the poorest craftsmanship possible. One day the landowner returned and called his foreman. "You have been a faithful servant for many years. I want to show you my appreciation. I have just asked you to build the finest ranch money can buy. Here is the deed. This ranch is yours."

That parable, told so often, probably never really happened. But something like it happens every day. Life does have a layaway plan. Somewhere, sometime, the seeds we sow come to harvest. There may be occasions when what we are and where we are depends on our being in the right place at the right time. Years ago, however, a widely known American made an astute observation: "It may be that life will never present us the real opportunity we seek or desire. But I am determined to so prepare myself that if such an opportunity does come, I shall be ready. I shall have my homework done, the seeds sown and the foundations laid." That's wisdom of the first order. Real living is not reached by the easy road. You can climb the stormy heights only if stamina is built during days when the sun is shining. Those who finally reach the heights are those who remember that life has a layaway plan. The artist is at work long before the day of the great concert. The businessperson achieves success not so much by fate or luck as by sound planning and thorough preparation. People with great religious faith hammer out their creeds long before that faith is needed.

Wise, indeed, is the person who has learned that the contents of the storehouses of mind, heart and muscle can be set aside for future use. Life does have a layaway plan. Have you considered lately what your storehouses really contain?

The Delicate Art of Compromise

Forty years ago on a side street in Berlin, the stillness of the night was shattered by the scuffling feet of the Gestapo as they made their way from house to house. At each door they banged incessantly until the door was opened. When the door was unlocked, the soldiers sprang inside and marched from room to room, peering in every closet and searching every corner. The object of their search was a skillful underground agent who had been responsible for hiding hundreds of helpless Jews considered to be enemies of the Third Reich. In one of the houses there was an attic reached by a secret stairway. In that attic, the hunted agent lay huddled beneath a false floor. The Gestapo believed the agent was in the house, but they were unable to find him. Enraged by their fruitless search, they ordered the family into the street. Once in the street, the soldiers threatened to shoot one family member each minute until they were given the whereabouts of the underground agent.

That story was told, a few years ago, to a group of students in a southern university. Each student was then asked to write the ending to the story. There is here, of course, a question in values. How do you make decisions when no completely right choice is available? While the story about the enemy agent is hypothetical, the circumstance it suggests is not. Those of us who work behind the counselor's desk are often confronted with similar problems. Most of the people who come to see us are searching for a course of action. The other day in one such session, a young lady put it this way: "Does it ever appear to you that regardless of what we do, it turns out to be wrong?" How do you choose the right direction when no right choice seems available? "Is it ever proper for an honest person to compromise?" That's a tough question, but it deserves attention. Sooner or later all of us must find an answer to it. Think about it for a moment.

One thing is clear. Life is a constant confrontation with alternatives. About 2,000 years ago, a traveler was passing through the streets of an ancient city. Somewhere along the way he met a man with a crippled hand. The presence of that crippled man constituted a dilemma. There were strict laws in that city about desecrating holy days. To help the crippled man was to violate sacred laws. Yet here was someone who needed help, and the man who was passing through knew he had the power to help him.

We have come a long way from that far-off day, but in some respects the world has not substantially changed. The roads we travel are jammed with intersections, and decisions have to be made. When Mark Twain penned his immortal story *Huckleberry Finn*, he described a striking scene. Huck was trying to decide whether to help a runaway slave. Remember how Huck put it: "I was a-trembling because I got to decide forever betwixt two things, and I knowed it." That's a universal circumstance for people in every age. Life is a series of decisions. Some prove to be of little consequence—the choice of clothing, the color of a new car or the direction of an evening walk. Some choices are life-changing—our vocations, our marriage partners, the place where we live and so forth. But no day passes without alternatives, and decision is mandatory.

Now and then you hear someone say: "I can't make up my mind." The fact is, we do. Indecision has a way of becoming a decision. We either decide, or time will make the decision for us. To live is to choose.

The problem is that often the choices are not clear-cut. There was an article in a national magazine about a label which appeared on a bottle of air freshener. The label stated, "Bring inside the clean, natural freshness of a meadow. Freshen your home with a scent as fragrant as summer grass. Warning! Inhaling the contents of this container can be harmful or fatal." Aren't those interesting alternatives: Living with stale air or dying with the fragrance of summer grass? But more often than not, this type of choice is our predicament. We seldom choose between absolute rights or wrongs.

This situation was the problem faced by that man 2,000 years ago. On the one hand were sacred laws, and laws are necessary for an orderly society. On the other hand was a cripple who needed help. If he stayed loyal to tradition, he could not help the crippled man. If he helped the crippled man, he could not remain true to his heritage. There could be no completely right choice. Compromise, no matter how unpalatable, was a forced direction.

This sort of circumstance has given rise to some well-known proverbs: "The art of politics is the art of the possible." "The way to get along is to go along." Such proverbs have been used often to justify despicable behavior. In their best sense, however, these proverbs suggest that we often have to accept some bad things to get some good things done.

Countless decisions have to be made at that level. Sometimes we have to accept things that are unacceptable in order to achieve things that are acceptable. Once someone wrote a widely known marriage counselor: "I'm thinking of leaving my husband because he snores." The counselor replied, "I know some lonely people for whom snoring would be heavenly music." We do take the bad with the good. Almost every choice involves some of both.

The question is: If compromise is essential, by what rule or standard is the compromise made? Long ago that man made his decision. He decided to help the suffering cripple. The surrounding crowd mur-

mured, "You have desecrated our holy day. Is that lawful?" The reply to that question has been preserved for us in the New Testament. "It is always lawful to do good, even on holy days."

Looking for the Pattern

Several years ago in a small southern town, an elderly lady died, leaving behind a wonderful family. As her children gathered to plan their mother's funeral, they found her Bible opened at the front page. On that page there was a short verse inscribed in their mother's handwriting. The verse had been taken from a poem published many years before.

> *Not until the loom is silent and the shuttles cease to fly,*
> *Will the Lord unfold the canvas and reveal the reasons why.*
> *The dark threads are as needful in the skillful weaver's hand*
> *As the threads of gold and silver in the pattern he has planned.*

No one really knew why this woman had copied that verse into her Bible. But it was clear that her life had not been easy. Widowed when her children were small, she had reared her family alone. Perhaps on one of those dark days she was wrestling with some misfortune she didn't understand. Despite her questions, however, there was her strong faith that even the dark days can serve a purpose.

Most people want to believe that life makes sense; the trouble is that things often happen to us without any rhyme or reason. We are victims of senseless accidents, untimely illnesses and strange misfortunes. We try to understand these events and determine why they have happened to us. Despite our efforts, these mysteries go unexplained. Somehow we must learn to live with such things if life is to continue. There are two or three thoughts on this matter that are worthy of reflection.

First, we need to remember that *we live in a world where every event can be made to serve a purpose.* A few years ago, a distinguished biologist spoke in a southern city. Quoting an Old Testament writer who said, "We are fearfully and wonderfully made," the biologist declared that this is a description of our whole world. "There is a delicate balance in nature," the biologist continued. "Everything fits into a composite scheme."

This biologist cited numerous examples: The bee, for instance, pollinates the flower from which it steals its honey. Too, when water freezes into ice, it expands. If this process did not occur, then ice would sink, and, thus insulated by surrounding water, would never melt to fill our streams and rivers. The earth would soon be an iceberg. Or again, when water evaporates it leaves much of its mineral content behind. Were this not true, our water supplies would be undrinkable, contaminated with such things as unbearable quantities of salt. It is an awesome and wonderful world in which every event can be used to serve a good purpose.

It would be strange indeed if the events in one facet of creation were so precise, while in another the events were without rhyme or reason. It seems reasonable to believe that all of the circumstances of life can be fitted into a pattern. That pattern may not always be evident, but it is there. Otherwise, life is without meaning, and we are the helpless victims of fate and fortune.

There is a second thought: *The significance of any event, when examined at any given time in our lives, cannot always be determined.* In her book *A Man Called Peter*, Catherine Marshall said that after the death of his mother, Peter was unhappy at home. He decided to escape to the sea. At that time the enlistment age in the British Navy was 15 years and nine months. Peter was only 14, so he lied about his age, and told his friends that he was leaving to join the navy. Two days after his enlistment, Peter's true age was discovered. He was sent home. Bitterly disappointed, he cried himself to sleep for many nights afterward. Peter Marshall might have become an admiral in the British Navy, but think how much poorer the world would have been had we missed his eloquent voice of hope during those dark days of World War II.

Life is filled with deceptive events. That's partly because we measure their worth by whether they bring us pain or pleasure. If an event is pleasing, we say it is good. If it causes hardship, suffering or pain, we say it is bad. But such designations are inaccurate. Often the most unpleasant things are richest in their compensations.

The truth is, we never know when we have had a good day. Sometimes our worst days turn out to be our best. This is why the poet declared:

The dark threads are as needful in the skillful weaver's hand
As the threads of gold and silver in the pattern he has planned.

There is a third consideration: *It helps to keep the longer view of life.* It is said that when John Tyler was a member of the US Senate—it was later that he became president—a crucial issue came up for vote. The political pressures were tremendous, and they were contrary to Tyler's conscience. When the roll call came, Tyler voted his conscience. As someone later wrote, "Tyler slumped into his seat for a long moment. He then arose and walked out of the Senate in the proud company of his own self-respect." What Tyler did not know that day was that the world would remember this dark moment in his life as one of his finest hours.

There is a marked tendency among us to judge too much of life by too little. Often the hard places give our lives their richest textures. Haven't we often heard people say, "I didn't know it at the time, but it has turned out to be the best day of my life." All of us have our moments of struggle, disappointments and difficulty, but the people who stand up to life are those who take whatever happens and use it for constructive purposes. Sometimes it takes a long time to see the pattern, to know where the road leads. Sometimes the full picture may be seen only when our journey in this world is complete. But people of faith believe the pattern is there. Somewhere, sometime, all of the events of life will be put together into a beautiful design by the "skillful weaver's hand."

Taming the Horses

Centuries ago an ancient philosopher told a story about a chariot driver with a team of wild horses. His task was to hold the team together and keep it from wrecking the chariot. The point of the parable was intended to describe human nature. Each person is a bundle of charging impulses, pulling in countless and contrary directions. This parable has survived through the ages primarily because it is an accurate description of a circumstance most of us face.

The problem that troubles so many of us is the disharmony we find within ourselves. Psychologists talk about schizophrenia, or the dual personality. This term may well be an overly modest description. We are not single personalities, not even dual personalities; we are many personalities. There is the social self, the business self, the family self and the personal self. We want to be good parents, good friends, good businessmen or businesswomen, good wives or husbands, good community leaders, well-read intellectually, strong physically, and socially acceptable.

All of these are worthy objectives, but so often the implementation of them leaves us frantic and perplexed. The reason, of course, is that these objectives are not mutually compatible. At times, for instance, we must neglect our business obligations to honor our family commitments. Our allegiance to principles can make us socially unacceptable. The discipline of acquiring knowledge can leave us little time to excel in athletics. If we attempt to pursue all of these goals with equal intensity, we discover that the joy and peace we expected to find in life passes us by.

Thomas Kelly once described our predicament in this fashion: "Each of us tends to be not a single self, but a whole committee of selves. Each of these selves is a rank individualist, not cooperative, but shouting out his vote when voting time comes. And even when consensus is taken, the disgruntled minority agitates on the streets of our souls." St. Paul put it another way: "Sometimes," he said, "I seem to be two people. Who can deliver me from this awful contradiction?"

It has been said that the central pursuit of life is to bring the many selves together. We have to find a way to tame the wild horses, stop the fragmentation of life, if there is to be any peace. The experience of the centuries suggests only *two* possibilities.

First, there is the external solution, the reorganization of the outside structure.

There is an old story about a king who had a dream. Believing the dream had implications for the future, he called his prophets for interpretation. Observing the conflicting opinions among them, he killed off the prophets until they were unanimous. It is possible to approach life that way. We can attempt to simplify our world until all conflict is gone.

There is a scene in the Old Testament about a man believed to be King David. David was under the pressure of conflicting loyalties. He was being pulled by his self-interest in one direction, his concern for his family in another direction and the needs of his people in still another way. One day while lamenting his problem, he declared: "O that I had the wings that I might fly away and be at rest." Isn't that the desire of most of us when we wrestle with the complexities of life? We yearn to get away from it all, find a deserted island or return to the simple days of yesterday. But those who choose that course discover it seldom, if ever, works.

Someone made a study of a group of people who deserted the rigors of city life and moved to a small island off the Florida coast. Life began, simple and easy. Everything was casual and "laid back." Before long, however, the pace began to quicken, and soon the people were struggling with the same maddening and feverish pace they had known before. The problems of those people were not external or environmental. The outer distractions only reflected their inner conflicts. The people had simply carried their problems with them. If the conflict is on the inside, then rearranging the environment provides only temporary relief. The conclusions of that study must be accurate. Today we are able to manipulate our environment to almost ideal conditions. Yet we still lack the sense of inner peace we so earnestly seek. Changing the outside doesn't help much if the problems are on the inside.

The other solution is the integration of the inner life.

Most of us are intrigued by the life of Winston Churchill. In early years, he was a problem child. One of his teachers called him the worst boy in class. Indeed, he was dismissed from school at least once. He was often not on good terms with his parents. He spent much longer than necessary to get out of lower school. He had to take remedial reading and was unpopular with teachers and students alike. His political enemies said he was erratic, without purpose and deficient in staying power. Then on May 10, 1940, England called Winston Churchill to direct its defenses. Suddenly this uncertain and inconsistent man became the Rock of Britain. He fused together the scattered potential of his life and became one of the stalwart giants of history. Churchill's story is an example of a person who tamed the wild horses and put life together.

Isn't the business of successful living a matter of establishing prime allegiances? That's a concern worthy of reflection for all of us. Once we establish what is important in life and give ourselves to it, then contrary impulses can be brought under control. Life must have a single purpose, and to that purpose we must dedicate our energies. Thus the wild horses are pulled together and work as a team. It is this integration of life that makes for peace.

The question, of course, is how to establish that central allegiance. Years ago a clergyman wrote a provocative sentence: "Now and then all of us need to ask: 'If everything the world could take from us were taken, what would we have left?' " That question puts the matter into focus. Business reverses can take our jobs, disease can take our health, calamities can eradicate our wealth, and death can take our family and friends. The one possession we have that is beyond the reach of all eventualities is a sense of inner integrity. Reputation can be destroyed but not character. What we own can be confiscated; what we really are, no one can take away.

The people who live at peace are those who decide who they are and what they will be. Success then is measured not by external standards but by how well they hold to their own ideals. Their chief objective is not making a living but building a life. Those who build a life based on the highest and best they know are those who stand at the end, look back and are not ashamed.

Too Much for a Whistle

Benjamin Franklin said that when he was seven years old, his friends and relatives gave him a pocketful of small coins for his birthday. Young Ben started to the store to spend his newly acquired fortune. On the way he met a boy who charmed him with a toy whistle. Ben offered the lad all his money, and the offer was accepted. That evening when the seven-year-old boy returned to his home, proudly blowing his whistle, his brothers and sisters told him he had paid four times what the whistle was worth. Franklin was so embarrassed that he cried. "In later years," said Franklin, "I think I have met many people who have paid too much for a whistle."

It takes little imagination to move the lesson of this story from its colonial origins into other times and places. Twenty centuries ago, the Great Teacher raised a pointed question: "What does it profit a person to gain the whole world and lose his soul?" Most often this question has been used as a springboard for religious sermonizing, but its true meaning is far deeper than that. The real message implied here has to do with the matter of sensible living. The story suggests some thoughts worthy of serious reflection.

Often people who quote this sentence from the Great Teacher seem to suggest that there is something inherently evil about material possessions. The bookstores of our land are filled with countless volumes denouncing the materialism of our culture. While such books are important, many of them miss the point. There is nothing demonic about possessing wealth. A few years ago a widely known American wrote a few sentences all of us need to hear: "It's no sin to be rich, and there is no virtue in being poor. Rags can result from laziness as easily as riches can be stolen. A pauper may be even more selfish than the person who has great resources." The author of those lines could support his thought from countless sources. In the Old Testament a writer declared that Adam and Eve were placed in a lovely garden called Eden. They were given this instruction: "You are to have dominion over the earth. Subdue the earth, and make it fruitful." While this creation story may be filled with imagery and symbolism, the point of it is unmistakably clear. The Creator intended us to generate out of the earth those things necessary for our welfare and comfort. Indeed it is the accumulation of materials that makes life possible. It takes wealth to provide food for hungry people, to provide shelter and clothing for our families, and to teach children to read and write. For many of us the problem is not too much money but rather the absence of it.

The real point of Franklin's story has to do with the importance of proper values. Someone translating this question from the Great Teacher put it this way: "Do not lose the things that matter most for the things that matter least." That's a chronic temptation among us. It is so easy to lose perspective and fail to keep things in their right relationship.

A few years ago there was a story in the news about a man who beat his child to death because the boy could not remember his evening prayers. While such a father must have been deranged, something of this man's terrible deed often is reenacted in real life. For instance, we sometimes harm our children in pressing them to reach over their heads to satisfy our own standards of success. Or again, we yield to the pressure of our peers and surrender our own ethical principles. It has been rightly said that many of us spend our lives trying to impress people we do not like, doing things we do not enjoy, on budgets we cannot afford. This is the real lesson in Franklin's story. Never make the mistake of spending too much for a whistle. We can lose our best for things that simply do not count.

This message becomes of paramount importance when we remember how priceless our lives really are. Is it not true that we have never been able to put a price tag on human life? If we ask an insurance agent to place a value on a car, a house or a fur coat, he can do that in a matter of minutes. He can even tell us how much a horse or any other animal is worth. There would be a limit on how much insurance we could purchase on such items. But if we ask that agent how much insurance we could carry on our lives, the only limits would be our ability to pay the premiums and the ability of his company to handle the risk. Human life is of infinite worth. If that's true, it is far too precious to be squandered on trifles.

Every once in a while, all of us should take a moment to consider how we are spending our lives. It's so easy to waste precious time on things that in the long run are of little value. I have a friend who makes this observation: "I am trying to remember that to go home at the end of the day and be with people who really care is more important than the job I hold. I am also trying to remember that the admiration and respect of my loved ones are worth more than any honor I can receive elsewhere. I want to keep in mind that a friend is of greater value than winning an argument. I want to be concerned about big things, not trifles." This was what Franklin meant when he advised us not to pay too much for a whistle.

William Temple once told about some pranksters who one night broke into a store and rearranged the price tags. They placed the highest values on the worthless items, and the cheapest tags on the articles of greatest worth. Temple suggested that the world is full of such pranksters. The business of life is to put the right prices in the right places. Life is too precious to be wasted. Happy is the person who takes the time and effort to discover what a whistle is really worth.

Rules for the Race

Recently one of the national television networks devoted a segment of a program to the rash of how-to books flooding the publishing industry these days. Bookstores are jammed with publications designed to help people in the management of their lives. Many of these books make the best-seller lists. Their subject matter ranges all the way from diet control to methods of accumulating personal fortunes. Apparently Americans feel the need for such assistance. They spend millions each year to acquire this "expert" advice.

We, of course, are not the first people to sense such needs. Centuries ago, an ancient author wrote a letter to some friends. In that letter this author declared, "Every runner in a race exercises self-control in all things. So run that you may obtain the prize." This long-ago writer was certain that the race of life is never casual. Living has its disciplines, and the business of life is to discover what the rules really are.

A few years ago an English scholar, reflecting on this problem, wrote an interesting sentence. "There are three important rules for life: Never be self-righteous in goodness, self-centered in happiness or selfish in success." The thoughts in this sentence do not cover the whole matter, but they are worthy of consideration for those who intend to "run a good race." Take a moment to examine them.

Never be self-righteous in goodness. The Great Teacher once met some people who troubled him greatly. He said that one day one of those people went to his temple for prayers. During his prayers the man said, "I'm glad I'm not like the rest of the folk here. They are such wretched sinners." In this sentence the worshipper revealed his true nature. He was good, and he knew it. It was this holier-than-thou attitude that made him a disliked person.

Such people are still around. They parade their virtues and put their goodness on display. But such folk are not attractive. There is an old story about two boys. One of them took his father's fortune, ran away and wasted everything. The other boy stayed at home, did his work, but always complained about his brother's misdeeds. We still remember those two boys. We feel sympathetic with the lad who squandered his wealth. We like him because he had the courage to return and admit his mistake. But we dislike the other boy. He was too smug, too proud and too self-righteous.

Self-righteous people are always miserable beause their lives are masquerades. Personal virtues require no trumpets. Such traits of character are always self-evident. No one needs to make a pretense of goodness. Goodness always reveals itself. People who spend their lives pretending never really live.

157

Never be selfish in success. In his later years Albert Einstein often said he stood on the shoulders of other people. Imagine a person with the greatest intellect of modern times confessing his dependence on others. Perhaps this is but additional evidence that there are no self-made people. No one stands alone. When Charles Kingsley was asked how he accomplished so much during his life he replied, "I had a friend." Such friends need to be remembered. It has been rightly said that those who forget the people who helped them on the way up are likely to meet the same people on their way back down.

One of the distressing phenomena of our times is the number of *miserable* people who appear to have everything. We know a part of their problem. In their scramble for the top, they use, abuse and misuse people. When they reach the pinnacle of success they are friendless, lonely and filled with guilt. No wonder Abraham Lincoln declared, "You never feel right until you've made things right."

There is an old southern saying, "Don't ever get above your raisin'." This is to say that the people who are serene and at peace are those who remain genuine and have a grateful heart. We have few possessions we have earned alone. Indeed for most of our blessings someone has sacrificed greatly. Happy people remember that. They are not selfish in their success.

Never be self-centered in happiness. That recent telecast on the how-to books suggested that a few current authors are advocating a new thesis. These authors are saying that concern for others is a rip-off propagated by romantic idealists. The way to happiness, these writers declare, is by self-assertion—by looking out for number one. That thesis is *not* new. It's as old as history, and no one has ever made it work.

Self-centeredness and happiness are incompatible. There is a timeless instruction from one who knew more about life than anyone who has ever lived. "He who would be first among you, let him be the servant of all, for he who saves his life shall lose it." That's always been true. One of America's richest men once said, "There isn't enough wealth in the whole world to keep a selfish person happy for more than 20 minutes." The reason is obvious. Self-centered people are insatiable. They always want just a little more. Preoccupation with one's self is self-destructive.

The rules suggested by that British writer are important. If we are looking for happiness, we must remember to be ourselves, cultivate a grateful heart and discover interests beyond our own little worlds. People who do these things find life wonderfully different. They are the winners in life's race.

158

Why Me?

The recording industry is a multibillion-dollar business in our land. Each year thousands of songs are recorded, but only a handful become hit records. What constitutes a hit record no one seems able to predict. Most experts argue that either the tune or the lyrics must strike a responsive chord in the mood of the times.

A few years ago Kris Kristofferson had a record that made it to the top. The song was entitled, "Why Me?" The lyrics began, "Why me, Lord; what have I done to deserve all the pleasures I've known?" The question raised by that song reflects our quest for the meaning of existence in a world where things do not always make sense. Life is filled with mysteries, and we are forever probing them. The question "Why me?" is asked in many times and places. Now and then all of us find ourselves wondering about the things that happen to us.

Sometimes, for instance, we ask "Why me?" in awe and wonder. A few years ago a noted American observed that the greatest mystery of his life was his unmerited good fortune. He had splendid health, a fine family and a successful career. "What have I done to deserve these things?" asked this man. Here is the same question Kristofferson asked: "Why me?"

It is refreshing to hear that question in such circumstances. Frequently in calamity and misfortune we ask, "Why?" Seldom do we reflect on the reasons for our *good* fortune. The people in Alcoholics Anonymous have a phrase they often use in their world: "There, but for the grace of God, go I." So many times our good fortune is not merited. It comes to us as a gift.

Have you ever watched a tramp shuffling along the street? We usually imagine that the plight of that tramp is self-imposed—the lack of discipline, bad habits, carelessness, etc. The temptation is to say, "You asked for what has happened to you." We should remember, however, that our failure to be in the tramp's shoes is not necessarily to our credit. Suppose no one had taught us personal responsibility or helped us establish good habits. Suppose in the crucial moments of life no one had assisted us. It's a good question to ask in times of good fortune: "Why me?"

There are no answers here, but we should remember that our good fortune imposes upon us great responsibilities. We may not know why we have received unmerited blessings, but we can express our gratitude by helping those who are less fortunate.

Sometimes, too, we ask, "Why me?" in despair. Where is the person who has not been perplexed over the senseless attacks of ill fortune? At a hospital emergency room recently, a six-year-old child was brought in for medical treatment. A careless driver had missed a traffic light and hit the youngster as he crossed the street. As the doctors tried in vain to help the child, one could sense the question in every mind, "Why him?"

A lot of our misfortunes can be explained. We simply reap the harvests resulting from our own misdeeds. But not everything can be explained in that way. Sometimes we are innocent. Yet we suffer, while the guilty go free. In such moments we are likely to ask, "Why me?"

Here again there are no answers. It does help to remember that time has a way of balancing the scales. Lincoln achieved an immortality in death that he could not have achieved in life. Jesus of Nazareth claims a kingdom today infinitely larger than the empire of those who put him to death. After a while, justice and truth prevail in our world, our suffering notwithstanding.

Finally, we ask the question, "Why me?" in apprehension. In the Old Testament there is a story about a man named Moses. One day Moses was called to go down to Egypt and free his people who were being held as slaves. Moses asked, "Who am I that I should go to the Pharoah and bring the sons of Israel out of Egypt?"

All of us have shared the feeling Moses had that day. We see something that someone needs to do. We find a cause that someone needs to support. Often we ask, "Why me? Why should I be called upon to make the sacrifice. Why should I take the risks? How can what I have to offer be useful in so great a cause?"

There is an old parable about a note on a piano keyboard. The note said to itself, "I am only one of 88. I am not needed." So the note refused to play. On the night of a great recital, the pianist was handicapped by that one silent note. In this children's story there is a lesson. Could it be that we are all keys on the cosmic piano? Perhaps we are one of the little-used notes on the far end of the keyboard. If the melody is to be complete, however, we must remember that our contribution is important. It's a mistake to ask, "Why me?" The better question is, "Why not?" It is in using what we have, where we are, that we find the greatest meaning for our lives.

Reading Your Own Epitaph

One morning, according to an old story, Alfred Nobel picked up a paper and read an account of his death. It seems that a relative had died and the reporter mistakenly assumed that it was the famed inventor. As Nobel read the article, he was disturbed about the way he was being remembered. He resolved to use the remainder of his days to change that record. Apparently he was successful. Not many people remember Nobel as the inventor of dynamite, but any schoolchild can tell you about the Nobel Peace Prize and related awards.

A few years ago in a newspaper editorial, the editor referred to this story and asked a pointed question. "If you were asked to predict your epitaph, can you imagine what it would be ?" There may be something morbid about that question. Life is too important to be spent thinking about its end. Now and then, however, most of us wonder how we will be remembered. When the clock of life has run its course, will our lives have counted for something? That's a question worthy of serious thought. There seem to be only three possibilities.

First, it is possible for our lives to have a negative effect on the world.

About 2,000 years ago, there was a king who reigned in a faraway corner of the world. In many ways he was a brilliant man. While a genius at political scheming, he was in reality sadistic and cruel. Shortly before he died, he decreed that 300 prominent citizens in his kingdom be executed on the day of his death. Knowing that his subjects would never mourn his passing, he hoped that this wretched plot would deceive history as to his importance. His plan didn't work. King Herod died, and the world was glad.

In a New England cemetery there is an inscription on a tombstone. The stone was erected to a Benjamin Wood. The lines read:

Here lies one Wood enclosed in wood,
One Wood with another.
The outer wood is very good;
We cannot praise the other.

So it is with some of us. The world is made poorer because we passed through it.

There is a spirit of individualism in our day, and for the most part that spirit is commendable. We are advised to "do our own thing." That counsel can be pressed too far. It can become a philosophy of thievery. A widely known American minister once preached a famous sermon entitled "Hitchhikers in the Road to Glory." His point was that some of us go through the world as "users" only. We never get involved in anything unless we can profit from it. Like scavengers, we live off the toils and labors of others. But people who refuse to pull their own weight are never really happy. They live and die, and when they are gone, the world is glad.

Second, it is possible to have a neutral effect upon the world. In the New Testament there is a story about some people who lived in the ancient city of Laodicea. About these people the author said, "I know your works. You are neither hot nor cold." These people lived in perilous times—a time when positions needed to be taken. But these folk took no stand. They held the middle ground. It is entirely possible to live life that way.

There are people who are always scheming and calculating. They protect their own interests. They are not cruel in that they bear little responsibility for the hurts of others. They just don't see how they can be concerned about others and still look after themselves. There are the folk who have no convictions. They change sides at a moment's notice. They tell their associates exactly what their associates want to hear. One day they are on one side. The next day they are on the other. Such people are usually well liked, but seldom respected. They are popular, but not trustworthy.

Happiness is never found down this road. For people who always seek neutrality, life is a charade. They spend their days acting out whatever part is in their best interest. When they are gone, no one really cares.

Third, our lives can have a positive effect upon the world. A doctor had just finished examining a patient who looked unusually tired. "My problem," said the patient, "is that I've never learned to say *no!*" That can be a problem. Life is extremely complicated when we try to travel too many roads. But the difficulty isn't the ability to say *no.* The task is to be selective. The people who have a constructive effect on the world are those who learn to say *yes* to things that count.

You will find people like this everywhere, and upon them the world depends. These folk are the leaders. They live at an astounding pace and accomplish incredible things.

Someone asked a famous American how he managed to do so much. The reply was interesting. "The happiest people are those who are too busy to know whether they're happy or not." That's worth remembering. There is no better way to forget your own problems than to become involved in the problems of others.

Lincoln was once asked how he would like to be remembered. It is interesting that he did not ask history to recall him as president or as the leader of his country in troubled times. He said he hoped it would be said of him, "He plucked a thistle and planted a flower where a flower would grow." It is little wonder that Lincoln is remembered with great fondness and appreciation. People who plant flowers where thorns have grown can be sure their epitaph will read: *Gone, but not forgotten.* Because they lived, the world is a better place.

Frozen to the Log

There is an old parable about an eagle that landed one day on a log floating down a slow-moving river. It was a cold day, but the sun was shining and the eagle seemed to be enjoying an easy ride on the gentle stream. After a while, the peaceful waters became restless. The eagle must have known from the noise there were waterfalls ahead. The bird waited, however, until the log reach the precipice. At the last moment the eagle spread its wings to fly. It was too late! The bird's feet had frozen to the log.

The moral of that fable has to do with making decisions. For many people that's the toughest part of living. All of us have encountered those who can't make up their minds. They are always trying to hold the middle ground. These people seldom get along well anywhere. They create problems in their businesses, in their homes and in their personal lives. The reason, of course, is that indecision eventually becomes a decision, and it's often the wrong one.

How to make up our minds is a process everyone needs to consider. It's a tremendously complex problem, but there are a few simple thoughts that can be helpful.

The most obvious one is that life demands decisions. In the Old Testament there is a story about a king standing on the roof of his palace, watching a battle in the streets below. There is turmoil and insurrection everywhere. The king was confronting fateful choices. The words of that king have been remembered: "Oh, that I had the wings of a dove, that I might fly away and be at rest." Almost everyone has had that yearning at some point. The easiest thing would be to run away.

Unfortunately, that's not a privilege we are granted. If we live we confront alternatives, wrestle with choices and choose directions. Even more distressing is that the ever-tightening spiral of change brings these choices to us with increasing speed. Any grocery shopper is aware of that. It almost takes a computer to buy a loaf of bread. There are long loaves, short loaves, thin-sliced, thick-sliced, enriched, whole wheat, bubble-free, oven-fresh, and more. And bread buying is one of our simple decisions. It's a difficult, complicated and intricate world. There are matters related to vocation, family, health, personal business and the like. There are choices that have to be made or we can get frozen to the log.

It also helps to remember that a few major decisions can eliminate a lot of minor choices. An ancient writer once asked, "Can a leopard change its spots?" This reference has to do with behavior patterns. Psychologists often speak of "conditioned reflexes." They are reminding us that life can be arranged so that some responses do not require debate each time the question arises. No driver stands beside a car and debates which side of the road will be used that day. The decision has already been made and our reflexes conditioned accordingly.

We burden ourselves with many decisions we don't have to make. If, for instance, personal integrity is a chosen direction, then we play by the rules no matter who is watching. There is a saying attributed to Abraham Lincoln: "No one is smart enough to be a successful liar." Lincoln was right, of course. If we change our answers, it's terribly difficult to remember which person was given which answer. If one answer is given, then a lot of decisions are eliminated. Making up our mind about some things will make other choices unnecessary.

The important thing about decisions, therefore, is to establish a proper framework against which to make them. The Great Teacher once said, "Seek ye first my kingdom and these other things will be given to you." That's a thought worth remembering. It's foolish to decide every morning what our values will be for that day. If we have established some basic ideals, then many of our decisions are already made.

The utilization of this principle is imperative in building a sense of inner peace. I knew a man who died a while back at the age of 83. In his later years, he developed a kind of security everyone envied. He read the headlines and listened to the news as did everyone else. Other people became jittery and apprehensive. He had come through two world wars and the Great Depression. He had seen sunshine and rain, nations rise and fall, and tyrants come and go. But he had established some basic beliefs. He believed, for instance, that a good direction never comes to a bad end. He had learned, too, that if we do what we should do, then we ultimately come out where we should be. This man didn't spend his life hanging onto the log. He made his choices as best he knew how as they came to him, and he let time handle the rest. That's a good way to live.

Pictures in the Mind

There is a story told by J.K. Jerome about a man who went to the library to read in a medical encyclopedia about hay fever. As the man thumbed through the book, he began glancing at the various diseases listed there. Suddenly he froze with fear. He read the symptoms of typhoid fever and realized he had had it for months. A bit later he came across something called St. Vitus' dance, and, to his surprise, found he had those symptoms, too. Greatly troubled, he sat down to read the book alphabetically. He found he had Bright's disease in a mild form and cholera with severe complications. He also concluded he had had diphtheria from birth. Said the man, "When I went into the library, I was a healthy man. When I came out, I was a physical wreck."

The point of that story is completely serious. People who work in medical schools say this phenomenon is not unusual. It is entirely possible for a person to become genuinely sick by misreading symptoms or by manufacturing them. All of this suggests that the human mind is a mysterious mechanism. The content of it is determinative in our lives. We become what we think about.

McNeile Dixon once said, "The human mind is not [as philosophers would have you think] a debating hall, but rather a picture gallery." The mind may be more than that, but the faculty of memory is a kind of gallery where impressions are stored. The pictures we put there have an effect on our lives. They guide us in mysterious ways.

For one thing, our mental pictures form anchors for our lives.

Someone has said that the ability to handle change depends on having something to hold to that never changes. There is a lot of sense to that. We live in an unstable world, and life is lived at a dizzy pace. The business world is undergoing radical changes in its techniques and practices. The worldwide political climate is in a state of flux. The moral world is in revolution. We live in a culture that doesn't know where it is going or what it wants. In such a world it's so easy to get lost and allow our values to become confused.

Because of this chaotic world there is a need in people for some basic convictions about the meaning and purpose of life. The essential question is whether we are the victims of blind circumstance or whether we have some control over what happens to us. There is an old story about a man who had been taken captive during a military conquest of his homeland. Transported to a strange land, he was being pressured to adopt customs contrary to his conscience. In his story there is this striking observation. "And Daniel purposed in his own heart not to yield to the king's demands." That resolution had its roots in the impressions deeply embedded in Daniel's life. Back in early childhood someone had put some pictures in his mind. In moments of crisis those pictures flashed to the front, holding him steady and keeping him dedicated to his old commitments. Fortunate is the person who has established values and convictions that do not change with the morning headlines.

The pictures in the mind also motivate our behavior.

In one of the world's oldest books there is a story about a man named Ezekiel. Ezekiel was a leader among his people, offering them encouragement and hope in desperate times. In Ezekiel's story there is this sentence: "I sat where they sat." You can understand why this man was able to share in remarkable ways the burdens of his people. He had walked in their shoes and identified with their problems. With their pictures in his mind, he could understand their needs.

One of America's leading charitable organizations made a study of those who had contributed most in helping people. The study revealed that the most compassionate and concerned people were those who had faced hard times themselves. There is nothing surprising about that. The person who has known hunger can identify best with hungry people. Someone tells about a small boy who was the victim of a crippling disease. He was taken to a dog pound to select a pet. He passed by the strong and healthy puppies and chose a little dog with a limp. When asked why he chose that puppy, he replied, "We will understand each other."

A lot of tensions in our world could be eased if we could get a mental picture of the world in which other people live. How would it feel to be the parent of a child in a place where children are starving? How would it feel to be a young person in a world where the pressure is on to conform? What's it like to live in a land where people are not free? How would it feel to be a policeman, a teacher, or a public official in these troubled days? How would it feel to be seriously ill, or to face the loss of a loved one? If we could fit a few of these pictures in our minds, we would be far more understanding and the world a better place.

Mental pictures aid us in remembering our loyalties.

One of America's most distinguished leaders was asked who had influenced his life most. He mentioned a name no one had ever heard. When asked for further identification, the man referred to a schoolteacher he had had years before. He said he turned in some homework one day that had been haphazardly done. The teacher took the student aside, and with a hand on his shoulder said quietly, "You can do better than this." "Countless times," said this famed leader, "I have been pressed to accomplish better things because I remembered those quiet words: 'You can do better than this.'"

Charles Spurgeon, the distinguished British minister, was once told by a parishioner that once a child leaves the home there is nothing more that can be done to direct the child. Spurgeon replied that it is possible, while the child is still at home, to leave in mind an impression that will be with the child forever. Many of us can understand that. Often when we are tempted to take a wrong road, we have been prevented from doing so because of images from the past—people who believed in us and who expected better things of us.

There were four pictures on his desk—a woman and two fine-looking young people. Someone asked the man who they were. The response was interesting. "They constitute the jury. They are my wife and my children. Each time I make a decision, I ask myself, 'Would they be proud of me for taking this course?'" Pictures in the mind . . . Fortunate is the person who has those to whom the finest loyalties are due.

The mind always has its pictures. Our lives are governed by them. How important, then, are these images. We need to be careful about the things we allow to occupy our attention. Some day these pictures will determine how we handle life's troubled places.

Talking to Yourself
A Normal Process of Introspection

During my childhood, there was an elderly man who always passed our home on his way to and from the community store. My parents told me the man had been a casualty of the war and had never fully recovered. There were many strange things about this man. Among them was his constant habit of talking to himself.

Psychologists have never fully understood the phenomenon of self-dialogue. Whatever may be the cause, talking to yourself is not considered normal behavior. There are times, however, when such a conversation can be helpful. In one of the oldest books in the world there is a story of a young man who had a talk with himself. One day, according to the story, the young man got tired of the discipline of his father's farm. Gathering all he owned, he ran away to a distant land where he thought life would free and easy. Things didn't go well for the boy. His money ran out, and he found himself in the fields, eating with the swine. In the story, there is this sentence: "And when the boy came to himself, he said, 'How many servants in my father's house have bread to spare and I perish from hunger. I will arise and return to my father.'" Perhaps the boy didn't have a verbal conversation with himself, but he did a lot of soul-searching. In doing so he made some interesting discoveries.

He learned, for instance, that he did not have to accept his rock-bottom status.

The phrase "self-acceptance" is widely used these days. When properly understood, self-acceptance is psychologically sound. Emerson once said, "There must be a time in everyone's education when one reaches the conviction that envy is ignorance, and imitation is suicide; that one must take one's self for better or worse." Fortunate is the person who has decided that. Life can be squandered aspiring for goals beyond our reach. We do not all have the same gifts. It's a wise person who has established self-identity—who knows what can be achieved and what cannot.

Self-acceptance, however, does not mean self-satisfaction. Self-satisfaction can dull our aspirations and stifle our potential. It's a bad thing to be totally satisfied. We may not be able to run at the head of the pack. Sometimes we are limited by circumstances that cannot be changed. But within those circumstances there is always room for excellence. The boy in that ancient story discovered this. He was broke, but he did not have to accept complete defeat. There was a better way to live.

The lad made another discovery. There was a way back from where he was. The story reads: "When [the boy] had spent all, a mighty famine arose in the land and he began to be in want and no man gave to him." Alone and deserted with nothing left but shame, the boy must have felt hopeless. As he thought about it, however, it became apparent that he didn't have to stay in the fields with the pigs. "I will arise," he said, "and return to my father."

We are often told that there are "points of no return" built into life. There are opportunities that cannot be recalled when they are passed. But there are other opportunities. Hopelessness need never be a human predicament unless we want it to be. There are always open doors if we look for them.

The Apostle Paul was an early advocate of Christianity. He traveled the ancient world talking with people everywhere. One day Paul ran into conflict with some folk who thought him a threat to their power. They put him in jail. Paul thought his work finished. But Paul had a talk with himself and found a new way to tell his story. He wrote letters from his prison cell, and those letters have become some of the most important documents ever written. They now constitute a major part of the New Testament.

Mary Pickford once said: "Today is a new day . . . If you have made mistakes, even serious mistakes, there is always another chance for you." That's a thought worth remembering. Too many people imagine all is lost. Such a notion needs to be challenged. There are always open doors if we seek them. The boy in our story didn't have to stay with the swine. He had a talk with himself and concluded that he could go home again.

The young man in our story made a third discovery. He found that his old home was better than he thought.

Remember his words: "How many servants in my father's house have bread and to spare." Living on his father's farm was tough. The discipline was rigorous and the work was hard. But the boy found himself taking a new look at things. At least there was food to eat, and that was far better than living with the pigs.

Sometimes it takes the absence of a thing to make us appreciate it. Our freedom is a priceless possession, but we don't always recognize that until we are deprived of it. We take our health for granted, but when it is gone, we quickly conclude that nothing quite compares with a strong mind and sturdy body. Work can seem like drudgery until we can't work. We then observe that the one thing worse than having too much to do is having nothing to do. Our families seem to require endless time and effort. But life without loved ones can be immensely lonely. The boy in that ancient story is an eternal reminder that some of the things we treat so carelessly are in fact our most priceless treasures.

Talking to yourself! Perhaps such verbal conversations are abnormal, but the process of introspection is not. Every now and then it

169

helps to sit down and do a bit of soul-searching. Life could be better than it is for most of us if we could learn to accept what must be, take the doors that are open and, most of all, try to appreciate the good things of life as we come to them.

The Quest for a Creed
Seeking Life's Purpose

About 30 years ago, a French artist exhibited a series of paintings depicting the mental and spiritual anguish tormenting the 20th century. On one of the canvases, there was the portrait of a man searching for a missing paper in a room filled with disarranged filing cabinets. Drawers were pulled open and papers were scattered over the floor. Behind the man there was a satanic imp holding the missing document over the frantic searcher's head. On the lost paper one could see the faint image of a lighted candle. Underneath the painting there was a caption: "The Search for Truth."

In many ways this artist described a universal quest. The human mind is always in search of truth. One area where this search is most intense is the effort to understand the meaning and purpose of life. Most of us at times ask the question, "Why are we here, and what is the reason for our lives?" The possible answers are many. They range all the way from the conviction that life makes sense and that we count for something to the belief that human existence is meaningless and life is a "blind leap in the dark." Between these options, our quest for answers goes on. Like the man in the painting, we seek the lighted candle. Three things need to be said about that search.

First, life requires the acceptance of a creed. No generation has possessed a greater accumulation of facts than ours. In 1768 when the *Encyclopaedia Britannica* was first published, there were three volumes. Today, there are more than 20 volumes, with new ones being added each year. This explosion of information is so massive that we can no longer rely on the printed page. We have complicated electronic storage systems that work with lightning rapidity, but the mere accumulation of knowledge provides us with little satisfaction. Facts must be interpreted. It's not enough to know *how* we were made. We want to know *why* we were made.

Those of us who work behind the counselor's desk confront that question daily. It is not uncommon to find highly trained people who believe their lives are meaningless. Life for these people is a daily grind of endless monotony. They yearn for a sense of purpose. They want to know if their struggles have a reason. These people frame the question in many ways, but we who listen have learned that their search is for something to believe about life. They are looking for a creed.

There is a second thought. The creed we accept is an act of faith. A few years ago, someone did a study of the great movements that direct our culture. The study revealed an interesting phenomenon. Almost without exception, great movements have small beginnings. Someone gets an idea and stays with it until it gains momentum. Others join the movement and it grows. Sometimes the originator of the idea gets lost in the growing tide. But the evidence of that study is clear. One person can count for something.

You and I must make up our minds about the conclusion of that study. The choices are simple. We can believe that we are worthless and whatever gifts and talents we possess have no value; or we can believe that regardless of our limitations, we can make some difference. It's a matter of faith—what we believe about ourselves.

It needs to be said here that our faith in ourselves must not hinge on our possessing extraordinary abilities. Most often it's the ordinary people who have made a difference. Edison once declared that genius was a 1 percent inspiration, and 99 percent perspiration. Our forefathers had a quaint but true expression, "God never made a person he couldn't use." This was their way of saying that it matters who we are, our contribution is important to the world.

A third consideration: Our creed regulates our lives. Henry David Thoreau once suggested that the differences among us may well be that we march to a different set of drums. Thoreau was saying that at the center of every life, there is a rhythm that determines its pace. Change that rhythm and the pace will change. Establish what a person believes and you can predict that person's behavior.

About 150 years ago, a slave was sold from a ship anchored on the Mississippi River. The man showed no fright, but carried himself with confidence and dignity. The auctioneer told the prospective buyers that the man was the son of an African king. "It will be hard," he said, "to make him a slave."

That auctioneer stated a basic truth. We live by what we believe ourselves to be. Either we are the victims of blind fate and we can change nothing, or we are the unique creations of God, who can use what we have to make a difference in our world. Each person needs to make a decision about this matter. Too many of us muddle along with our energies unfocused. If we can learn to believe in ourselves—to believe that what we have is important and needed—life will be an exciting adventure.

It's How You Call It
Taking the Longer View

Russell Conwell, in his famous address, "Acres of Diamonds," told about a South African farmer who grew tired of working the rocky soil of his old homestead. One day he sold his farm and set out to find his fortune. He traveled the world with no success. Finally, his resources exhausted, he decided to return home. When he arrived, he discovered that on the farm he had sold someone had discovered one of the richest diamond mines on earth.

Conwell told that story thousands of times across America. His purpose was to remind his listeners that opportunities can be found everywhere, no matter where we live or who we are. That thought has been reflected on countless times by those who examine the way life works. The truth contained in this thought is of such great significance that it must not be ignored by those who would live successfully. Three things should be said.

First, the importance of any want is not determined by the want itself. Years ago in Decatur, Illinois, there was a story told about a boy who ordered a book on photography. The publisher made a mistake and sent instead a manual on mind reading, magic and ventriloquism. The little boy was troubled about this mistake, but he read the book anyway. We are glad he did. Edgar Bergen got a wooden dummy, named it Charlie McCarthy and charmed millions with his talents.

That incident suggests an age-old truth. It's not the want itself, but the use of the want that determines its importance. Recently, a widely known political leader in this country declared, "In every victory, there are seeds of defeat; in every defeat, there are the seeds of victory." This was his way of saying that the winners and losers in any game are not always determined by the final score. That observation is profoundly true. Every circumstance provides its opportunities, and every difficulty can be a steppingstone. The old proverb, "An ill winde that bloweth no man to good," isn't quite right. The more correct statement would be "An ill wind always blows good—if we look for it."

A second thought: You can't determine the significance of a want when you examine it at any given time.

About 130 years ago, there were two articles in a London paper. One was on the front page. It was about a tiny showman who gave a performance before England's Royal Court. Tom Thumb's tour of Britain made the headlines of the world's papers, especially his appearance at the palace. In the same London paper that reported Tom Thumb's travels, there was a short article on a back page. The article was about the work of a little-known naturalist named Charles Darwin, who had written a

173

book entitled the *Origin of Species*. Both stories made the news that day in London, but the wrong story was on the front page. The world has almost forgotten Tom Thumb. It will be a long time forgetting the work of Charles Darwin.

So much of life is illustrated by those news stories. We don't really know when we have a good day. Sometimes the best days turn out less than good, and the worst of days prove to be our finest hours. Too often we judge too much of life from too short a vantage point. It's a wise person who takes the longer view. Time renders its own verdict on the significance of the wants of life. It's a mistake to become discouraged about any circumstance. People who find life exciting are those who wait for the ill wind to blow its good.

A third thought: More often than we imagine, we decide the significance of the wants of life.

There is an old story about a major league baseball umpire named Bill Klem. Klem was always in charge when he called a ball game. One day a batter hit a ball into left field. The third-base runner dashed for home plate. In doing so, he collided with the catcher. The players in one dugout shouted, "He's safe," while the other side shouted, "He's out." Klem was standing at the plate when the dust cleared. His fist was raised as he shouted so all could hear, "He ain't nothing until I've called it."

There is a profound lesson in that story. The wants of life become significant largely as we decide them. A circumstance can knock us down and keep us down, or we can use that want as a ladder to victory. It depends on how we "call it."

A long time ago, there was a kind and gentle teacher, who for strange and unjust reasons was brought to trial for his life. When execution seemed inevitable, the man waged no counterattack. He went to his death on a Roman cross with courage and dignity. Time has exonerated this man of all guilt. Today, despite these efforts to silence him, the voice of that carpenter from Nazareth is heard to the ends of this earth. This man stands as an eternal reminder that no want of life need destory us. Every circumstance is filled with opportunities if we have the will and the courage to call them that way.

Rewriting 'The Serenity Prayer'
Using the Inevitable for Good

There is an old prayer that often appears in offices and homes across our land. The origin of the prayer is unknown, but there is evidence that it was written in the Middle Ages by an unknown author, who was greatly troubled about life. You have seen that prayer many times: "God grant me the courage to change the things I can change, the serenity to accept the things I cannot change, and the wisdom to know the difference."

Most of us have read this sentence and accept it because it seems to make sense. If there are things in our lives that are wrong, then we are under obligation to change them. If, however, there are things that we can't change, it is a waste of time and energy to wrestle with the impossible. The problem arises in the difficulty of distinguishing between the two. How does one know what can be changed and what must be left alone? A lot of people struggle with that problem, trying to sort out the changeable from the unchangeable. Many of those folk are not comfortable with their decisions. Perhaps the entire prayer needs to be reexamined in the light of a single question, "Is there anything in the whole world we can't do something about?" Consider these thoughts:

First, there are some things in our lives that can and need to be changed.

In one of the oldest books in the world, there is a story of the creation of humankind. When the Creator finished his work, he said to the man and woman he made, "Fill the earth and subdue it, and have dominion over everything in it." If the point of this ancient story is right, then it is apparent that we are intended to help in making our world.

Once in a while, someone seeking to comfort us about that problem will advise us to take things as they come. In some ways that is the most dangerous advice we can receive. Suppose Abraham Lincoln had taken things as they were. Suppose no doctor ever challenged disease. Suppose the teacher had accepted as changeless the ignorant mind. What a terrible world it would be if someone had not said, "Give me the courage to change the things I can change."

There is a widely known minister who talks a lot about what he calls "possibility thinking." His point is that in every circumstance, there are opportunities. No situation is hopeless. If we look long enough and carefully enough, we can find an open door. The problem is that we give up too soon. It is a good prayer always, "God give me the courage and the determination to change the things I can change."

175

Here is a second thought: *Some things do appear to be inevitable in our world.*

There is an account in the Bible about some men who were trying to decide how to stop the Great Teacher from his work among the hungry and sick people of his day. One man stood and addressed his comrades: "Let this teacher alone. If his work is wrong, he will not succeed. If he is right, then we can't stop him."

That's sound advice. There are some things that the Creator intended to prevail in our world. Take the law of gravity, for instance. That's a principle not open to vote. No legislature can repeal the law of gravity. If everyone in the world were against that law, it would still hold. The same is true of the law of cause and effect. If we sow bad seed, we will get a bad harvest. If we sow good seed, we can expect a good harvest. This principle prevails and we can only accept it.

There is some sense to that timeless proverb, "Never cry over spilled milk." We can't undo the past. What's done is done. We need the serenity to accept that.

What, then, is the problem with the ancient prayer?

Centuries ago, St. Paul wrote an interesting sentence, "I can do all things through divine strength." Paul didn't mean that he could change the law of gravity or repeal the principle of cause and effect. Paul had something far more important in mind. A few years ago someone writing on this sentence penned Paul's thought another way, "I can *handle* all things." If you read the life of Paul, you will discover that's exactly what he did.

In that long-ago day, Paul stood against the cruel power of the civil authorities. Because of his defiance, he was threatened with arrest. "Do what you will," he said to his persecutors. "If you put me in jail, I'll find a way to work from there. If you put me out of the city, I'll go to another one. If you execute me, I'll die in such a way that the world will always remember. Whatever happens to me, I'll find a way to 'use it.' "

The example of this ancient man is worth remembering. Nothing in this world can finally defeat us unless we let it. Some things in life are inevitable, but even these things can be used for good. "The Serenity Prayer" needs to be rewritten: "God give me the courage to change the things I can change, the strength to wrestle with the things that can't be changed, and above all the wisdom to use everything that happens for something good."

Running for a Reason
Avoiding a Tragic Waste of Life

There was an editorial in a newspaper recently about a steamship line operating out of a southern port city. Among the voyages listed was one tour that was extremely interesting. It seems that the company had a steamer that left port and sailed in the direction of the Bahamas. Sometime after leaving port, the ship changed directions. It wandered around aimlessly for awhile and then returned home. The purpose of the voyage, it seems, was to appeal to people with limited funds. Apparently there are some folk who want to write home and tell their friends they are on a cruise. The title of the editorial was intriguing—"A Journey to Nowhere."

Back in one of the oldest books in the world, there is a similar story. A king's son had been killed in battle, and someone was needed to take the sad news to the king. Two runners were available. One was extremely fast, but incapable of telling a coherent story. The other was slower, but far more accurate in his reporting. The slower man was dispatched. The other runner was disappointed and insisted that he be sent. The general of the army asked the disgruntled runner a significant question, "Why will you run when you have no news to take?"

There is a serious thought in that ancient story. Life can be a journey to nowhere. We can leave port, sail around for awhile and then turn homeward empty-handed. The question thoughtful people raise is this: "How do we avoid this tragic waste of life?" Three things need to be remembered.

First, we are all runners on the stage of life. This imagery often appears in literature. The Bible compares life to a race, a voyage or a journey. Poets often speak of the stream of time or the flight of time. Of course, no one needs to tell us about this. We sense movement in living each time we think about it. We are running. We may not know where we are going or why, but as the old song puts it, we are "moving on."

It is so easy to forget this mobile dimension to life. We sometimes live as if we were here to stay. Every now and then, however, we are jolted back to reality. Birthdays seem to come with increasing rapidity. Our children grow up and, before we know it, have children of their own. Retirement, which once seemed ages away, suddenly looms on the horizon. We are all runners and, even more to the point, we are running fast.

This is why that ancient general's question is so important. Why are we running? Is life a journey to nowhere? Are we running for a reason?

177

Such a question faces a second consideration. *Intelligent running demands serious planning.*

There is a story about a famous wit of the 19th century who made a thoughtful comment when someone told him that a new invention called the telephone would enable people in Maine to talk to the people in Texas. "Suppose they don't have anything to say to each other?" asked the philosopher. There's the question again, "Why are we running?"

A college dean said recently that a surprising number of young people are finishing college without the slightest notion of what they want to do. They have not faced the question, "Education for what?" But college students are not alone in this. A lot of us are slaving life away in our offices, in factories and in our homes. We are running without a reason—with little concern over delivering the goods on arrival, if we even know where we expect to arrive.

A prominent psychologist once asked a client, "If this were your last day, what would you do, say or think?" That question has a way of putting important things into focus. Limited time demands a consideration of priorities. Thoughtful people are always thoughtful planners. That ancient general was on target when he told the foolish runner, "You need to have some news if you are going to run."

A third thought: *Every life needs a worthy goal.*

Recently, a striking sentence appeared in a popular magazine: "If you get what you want, will you want what you have." One of the hard facts of life is that some of the things we seek prove disappointing even though they seem attractive from a distance. Wealth quickly loses its glitter, great power can become a stifling burden and the thundering applause of the moment dies quickly into silence. Remember the pathetic lines of the poet, "I have spent a lifetime seeking things I have spurned when I have found them." No wonder so many runners go to pieces at the end. They have been running without a reason.

Cardinal John Henry Newman once closed a prayer with these words, "Then in thy mercy, grant us a safe lodging and a holy rest and peace at the last." Peace at the last! That is the prize worthy of pursuit by anyone, but it never comes by accident. It comes by premeditated intent. And those who find it suggest it cannot be bought. Neither does it come by the selfish pursuit of fame or power. It comes by an entirely different road.

Two thousand years ago, a man came into our world. By the measurements we use in determining success, he was a failure. He never led an army or commanded a kingdom. He owned little, if anything. He died at 33, as a criminal by execution. Yet he stood before his accusers, on his last day, untroubled and with perfect peace. This was his secret: He invested his life in the lives of others and gave himself to causes he believed to be just and right. We have learned through centuries of experience that those who live by this man's plan find their hearts growing quiet and steady in an unshakable peace.

178

Running with the Horses
Preparing for Stressful Times

Several years ago there was a television program about three men on a hunting expedition. During the hunt one of the men was killed. News coming back from the scene failed to identify the victim. The three families were jolted from the pleasant routine of their daily lives as they awaited final word as to which man had lost his life. The question raised by the drama was this: Can one prepare for the greater moments of stress in life?

Most people are far too busy to spend much time contemplating the possibility of catastrophic events. Now and then, however, all of us wonder how we would react should we have a rendezvous with unexpected fate. Long ago there was a man named Jeremiah who had fallen on troubled times. Reflecting on his problems, he was seeking encouragement. Instead of encouragement, this thought came to him: "If you have run with the footmen and been weary, what will you do when you race with the horses?" There are implications in this thought that are important for all of us. Consider these things.

First, there is the hint that life tends to move from simplicity toward complexity. Jeremiah had run into conflict with the power structure of his little hometown. The political leaders there had threatened him. He was chafing under these threats when he remembered that the day would come when not only the local authorities but the whole nation would be angry. Indeed, he had been running an easy race facing only local opposition. Soon he would be running with horses.

Jeremiah's experience parallels that of most people. The running gets harder farther on. A schoolchild begins with simple arithmetic; before long there are the complicated equations of algebra and calculus. The intensity increases with every grade. Graduation does not ease the pace. The pressures of business and professional life, the responsibilities of parenthood and the necessary choices of every added year contrive to make life more complex. Even retirement only shifts the nature of the race. Stop anywhere and look back. The problems of yesterday seem like child's play when compared to those we face today.

Second, life requires prior conditioning. Jeremiah's thought suggests this, too. Handling the increasing pressures of life demands the building of a line of defense. How we meet the big things in life is determined by the way in which we stand up to the little things. We must learn to run with the footmen if we expect to race with the horses.

Psychology defines habit as the fixed tendency to perform certain acts in a certain way. The repetition of a certain act not only makes it easier to perform, but habit also makes possible the performance of more complex actions. Handling a complicated mathematical calculation begins with the simplest rules governing addition and subtraction.

The habits of the spirit follow the same rules. Facing the difficult situations of today with courage enables us to handle ever-increasing degrees of shock. We build confidence by living through hard circumstances. Inner strength comes to those who have been tested in the fires of tough times.

Someone tells of a group of people caught in a hotel fire. It was not certain that any would escape. According to the reporter, in those solemn moments of uncertainty every person revealed his true colors. Even their faces reflected their inner strength. That's not surprising. When we are forced to run with the horses, we can always tell those who are accustomed to running. They have endurance, if nothing else.

All of this leads to a third consideration. *The ultimate strength of our lives is designed by our daily living.* Psychologists tell us that the memory stores every impression. Some impressions are imprinted in the conscious memory; others are filed below the surface in the vast unknown of the subconscious. The sum total of these impressions determines the nature of the mind. It is becoming increasingly clear that our lives are controlled by the things we think about. If we fill our minds with the trivial, there is little wonder that in the moment of crisis we go down.

Somewhere in his writings, Henry Grady, the famed Atlanta newspaperman, refers to the profound impression which his mother's religious faith made on his life. One morning as he was leaving home for the city, his mother followed him to the gate and said to him "Son, always remember who you are." "What my mother didn't know," said Grady, "was that she had taught me her faith so firmly that nothing could destroy it. The faith she kept has been the faith that has kept me."

There comes a time in every life when what we do depends on what we firmly believe. Such a faith is not the fruit of sudden emergency. It is the process of long accumulation. It comes from courage gleaned in day-to-day combat with little things. It is born of regular decisions made by the highest and best we know. The verdict of human experience is clear. If we have learned to run with the footmen, we have a real chance of making it when we must run with the horses.

180

The Blessing of Being Tense
Experiencing the Richness of Life

In countless bookstores across our country there are shelves of books dedicated to helping Americans deal with stress. Such books are desperately needed in these "pressure cooker" days. Physicians tell us that the tensions in contemporary life can be deadly. These tensions lead to sleeplessness, depression, health disorders and even death. It is not surprising, therefore, that people skilled in the art of living are trying to help us. Their books on stress management are invaluable.

It needs to be said, however, that all tension is not bad. There are times when stress is not only necessary but also essential for healthy living. Contrary to the thoughts of many people, tension is not always a curse; it may be a special gift of the Creator to us. Years ago someone suggested a few thoughts on this matter that merit consideration. These thoughts may be of real value to those who are struggling to handle the frustrations of daily living.

First, there are tensions we cannot avoid. In one of the oldest books in the world there is a story of creation. The ancient writer describes in rich symbolism the creation of the world and the beginnings of humankind. In the closing sentences of his story, the author imagines the Creator giving his creations a divine mandate. Here is the sense of that mandate: "And God said to man, 'Fill the earth and subdue it.'" The word "subdue" is not a passive or inactive word. This long-ago writer wanted us to know that from the beginning people have been situated in the circumstances of tension.

The reason, of course, is that only out of tension does growth occur. The struggle to acquire a trained mind results from the frustrations of being ignorant. The human body grows healthy through proper exercise, and exercise always involves stress. In many ways tension is the normal predicament of human existence.

Years ago a famous boxer said of an opponent who declared he would outrun the champion in the ring, "He can run, but he cannot hide." That is a fair description of life. Try as we may, we cannot always avoid the pressure cooker. If you are going anywhere at all in life, if you are trying to accomplish anything worthwhile, you must become accustomed to living under stress.

Second, there are tensions we can avoid. A lot of stress we create for ourselves unnecessarily. We come at life the wrong way. For instance, we seek success at any price, and pack too much activity into too short a time. We take shortcuts that lead nowhere except to trouble.

181

A while back, one of America's better-known counselors was writing on this theme. She left a bit of advice worth pondering: "Sometimes when you are debating a course of action, it helps to ask if you could sleep on a stormy night." That counselor's point is valid. We can be relieved of a lot of tension if we live our lives so that when we are alone we are not ashamed of what we see. It is a bad thing to spend our days always looking back to see if someone is gaining on us. The people who have untroubled minds are usually those who play by the rules.

Third, there are tensions we should not avoid. One of the great images in American history is that of Abraham Lincoln standing amid the smoking ruins of war trying to build a nation where all people could be free. He knew that our land could not survive half-bound and half-free. Someone had to come to grips with that problem and Lincoln took upon himself the task of dealing with it. As a result he led a tormented life, but the world is better because he did. Could it be that life would be better if, instead of trying to rid ourselves of tension, we sought to bear some of the loads of our world?

I once saw a football player sidelined by a minor injury. His team was losing and the boy kept pleading with the coach to let him back into the game. Reason would suggest his request to be foolish. It was safe on the bench. It was rough and dangerous on the field. But every football player understands the lad's request. Peace of mind comes from getting into the game and doing what you can.

There is a kind of tension that lightens your own load. People who do what they ought to do tend to sleep better on stormy nights. And those who give a bit of themselves to help others find their own tensions easier to handle. It is a serious mistake to avoid stress at any cost. Sometimes through stress and tension, life takes on its richest meaning.

It's All Right to Worry
A Place for Constructive Anxiety

Several years ago one of America's greatest humorists wrote a book in which she made an interesting confession. "I am an orthodox worrier. There are days when everything seems to go right. Such days nearly drive me nuts." Not many people are candid enough to make such a confession. Although not listed among the cardinal evils, worry is not considered healthy for a well-adjusted life.

There is, of course, good reason for this. Many, if not most, of our worries are mentally and emotionally destructive. Someone tells of a sign on a barbershop door in a sleepy little town: "Closed on account of improved financial condition. May open next week, but a lot depends on financial conditions then." To some degree, that is a great way to live—doing only what you have to do and never being apprehensive over what is coming next.

Any virtue pressed too far can become an evil. If anything is worse than taking life too seriously, it is taking life too lightly. There is a place for constructive worry and anxiety. Even the Great Teacher was aware of this. On one occasion he said to his followers, "Now is my soul troubled." Here is the clear admission that even in the best of lives there is a place for positive concern. A bit of thought will suggest two or three such places.

Consider, for instance, concern about the world as it is, as opposed to what it should be.

A few years ago at the funeral of a widely known American, the speaker made this observation: "There are those who see the world as it is and ask 'Why?' There are others who see the world as it should be and ask, 'Why not?'" The latter part of that statement describes the mind set of those who make our world livable. These are the people who have pulled us up the long hill toward a civilized society.

George Washington will be remembered for many things, but the finest portrait we have of him comes from that terrible winter at Valley Forge. We are told that he walked among his cold and hungry soldiers worrying about their welfare. Out of this sort of struggle our nation was born—a nation committed to the noblest and highest aspirations of humankind. We owe an unpayable debt to people who have worried when things were wrong and were dedicated enough to try to right them. Worrying for the proper reason is the way life needs to be lived.

Worry is constructive when the focus is on what can be done about a bad situation. It is wasted energy to spend time lamenting what has already happened. "Crying over spilled milk" leads to emotional and

183

mental disorder; but facing the circumstances and asking what can be done about them not only changes the world but it also builds mental and spiritual muscle. It is all right to worry if we worry in the right way and about the right things.

There is a place, too, for concern about the difference between the achieved self and the potential self. Have you ever heard someone say, "I have arrived." That observation is appropriate only as an epitaph. We should never feel we have arrived as long as we have life. There is always a difference between what we are and what we can become.

Recently, in a television interview, a highly respected American statesman was reflecting upon the people who had influenced his life most. He singled out an elementary schoolteacher whose name was unknown to his listeners. "She was kind but firm," he said. "Time after time she would hand back our homework with one sentence written across the top: 'You can do better than this!'" People who "trouble our souls" when we are less than we can be are not our enemies; they are our friends.

Wise is the person who wrestles for self-understanding. Life can be wasted in anxiety over the lack of certain abilities or talents. The "wishing well syndrome" is futile and destructive to our well-being. An intelligent analysis of self, however, and the determination to be the best we can be make for exciting and healthy living. There are really no inferior people. We all have our strengths and weaknesses. When we utilize our strengths, our weaknesses are minimized.

In one of his finest essays, Emerson made a thoughtful observation: "There is a time in everyone's education when one arrives at the conviction that envy is folly and imitation is suicide . . . My life is for itself and not for a spectacle. What I must do is all that concerns me, not what other people think."

We are all unique. No two of us are alike. To surrender our individuality is to destroy a special part of creation. The happy people are those who do not waste time worrying over what they are. Happy people dream about what they can become and keep worrying with that dream until they find a way to make it come true. It is all right to worry when you worry that way.

Magnificent Friends
Giving Credit for Your Success

Several years ago a widely known American retired from a long career in business and public life. At a dinner held in his honor, the man made a brief address in which he reflected on the events of his life. The striking thing about his address was his claim that he could take little credit for his success. "I am indebted to some magnificent friends," the man declared. "These friends fall into three categories. There are friends I see regularly, there are those I will see no more and there are friends I have never seen." This observation offers food for thought for all of us. Most of us share this man's experience. Much of what we accomplish in life we owe to our friends.

Think, for instance, about the friends we see regularly.

There is an old saying that contains solid wisdom. "The best way to deal with any problem is to talk it over with three people: God, yourself and a friend." Not many of us give enough attention to the latter part of this proverb. Fortunate indeed is the person who has someone with whom the difficulties of life can be shared.

Psychologists have long been aware of this. One of the techniques they use in helping people is creative listening. They simply encourage their patients to talk about their problems. Often no other therapy is needed. Many times bottled frustration can be relieved if the matter is brought into the open.

Back in days of the Roman Empire, the legions of the emperor conquered the known world. These soldiers moved from nation to nation bringing into subjugation people from the coasts of Spain to the borders of India. There was, however, one band of people the Romans never conquered. These people were the followers of the Great Teacher from Bethlehem. Historians have long since discovered that one of the reasons for the sturdiness of this folk was their habit of meeting together weekly. They shared their difficulties and stood side by side. In doing so they found the courage to defy the Roman armies. In the end Rome did not conquer these people. These people conquered Rome.

We could well profit from this example. Wise is the person who cultivates personal friendships. Loners seldom manage life successfully. They are usually miserable and tormented. People who lead happy and exciting lives are those who work at making friends. Hard times are easier to handle if you do not have to handle them alone.

Think, too, about the friends we will see no more.

In the Old Testament there is a story about a king named Saul. Saul was facing a critical hour in his reign and needed assistance. He remembered an old friend whose name was Samuel. Samuel had helped him in former years, but Saul had treated the friendship lightly. One of the tragic scenes of history is that of Saul standing one dark night in Samuel's hometown, muttering to his servants, "Bring me back Samuel." But Samuel was dead, and Saul had lost a trusted friend.

We should never treat lightly people whose absence would impoverish our lives. All of us are indebted to folk who have inspired us and guided us on our way. It may have been a parent, a teacher, a business associate or a neighbor. These people came into our lives at critical moments and made the difference between success and failure. Time has taken these people from us but their influence lingers. Often we do not recognize how important these friends are to us until they are gone. But to these people we are debtors. We owe a lot to friends we will never see again.

Finally, there are friends we have never seen.

On the banks of the Potomac there is a lovely cemetery—the resting place of some of the great leaders of our land. Here are the graves of such people as Robert E. Peary, Richard E. Byrd, John J. Pershing, George C. Marshall and many others; but the best-known memorial there is the Tomb of the Unknown Soldier. On the monument that marks that grave is this inscription: "Here rests in honored glory an American soldier known only to God." They keep a continuous honor guard there, and rightly so. We need to be reminded of our debt to the Unknown Ones—the people we never see.

The simple fact of life is that no one is independent. We stand on the shoulders of countless people who have gone before us. Every time we eat a meal we gain from the labors of another. Each visit to our doctor utilizes the sacrifices of people who have struggled with the complicated secrets of illness and disease. Every trip in our automobiles or in an airplane makes us debtors to courageous explorers and the pioneers of science. It is a mistake to believe that we have earned our way. We are the recipients of countless gifts from the past.

The word from that retirement dinner is profoundly true. Most of what we are and have we owe to magnificent friends. Some of these people we see every day, some we will not see again and some we will never see. Thoughtful people remember these friends and with gratitude try to pass on to others something of what they have received.

How to Keep Your Cool
Maintaining an Even Perspective

The other evening a national news commentator reviewed the events of the preceding week. He mentioned the hijacking of an airliner in the Middle East, the bombing of a car in Lebanon, the starving millions in Central Africa, and the discovery of mass murders on the West Coast. He concluded his report with the terse comment, "That's the news, such as it is!"

It required little imagination to observe that the news reporter was discouraged. On any given day in our world there is good reason to be pessimistic. There are other days, however, when the news is not nearly so bad. There are stories of plane loads of food going to hungry people, cease-fires that have been signed and word that arms talks are making progress. We live in a world where the news alternates between extremes. One day there is concern as to whether we will make it into the next century. The next day there seems to be hope.

As the mood of the times oscillates between extremes so do our individual attitudes. In the folk music of our land there is an old spiritual which begins, "I'm sometimes up and sometimes down." That is the way life goes for most of us. We have good and bad days. The trouble is that when we have a good day, we are apt to overlook the grim realities that we will face on other days. Somehow we cannot seem to keep ourselves balanced between the extremes. We cannot remember the good times well enough to keep our wits during the bad times. Nor can we remember the bad times well enough to be responsible during good times.

The youth of an earlier generation had an instruction we need to follow. They said to us, "Keep your cool." What they meant was that we should maintain an evenness of temperament. The problem is, how do we do it?

It helps to remember that the "sands of time" have always shifted between good and bad directions. In this respect life has changed little. Centuries ago there was a king who was reflecting on the events of his life. He wrote, "Oh, that I had the wings of a dove that I might fly away and be at rest." On another day, this same king wrote some songs filled with such joy that they were written on the pages of the Bible. Life was so good at one point in this country that we refer to those years as the Gay Nineties. Hard on the heels of those years came economic depression and the outlook was correspondingly bleak.

In the news a few years back there was a story of a restaurant owner who was usually calm, serene and happy. One night he went into a rage because one of his employees drank coffee from a saucer. The rage was so intense that the man had a heart attack and died. The world has been going up and down like a yo-yo since the beginning. We are not the first people to find life oscillating between the good and the bad.

In one of the world's oldest books there is a story about a man who had been jailed by his enemies on a "trumped-up" charge. The cell was dark and damp—nothing more than a limestone cave with an iron door. The furniture was a chair, a table and a bed. The only light was a smoking candle. Miles away he had some friends who tried to help him. They sent him some gifts to enable him to endure. The man wrote a letter to these friends—a copy of it we still have. In that letter he thanked his friends and then added this line: "I'm grateful, but I want you to know that I have learned in whatever state I'm in, to be content." You have to know about this man whose name was Paul to understand his secret.

One of the things Paul had learned was that he did not know how to determine when he had had a good day. He had been a highly ambitious man, holding a political position of great power. He had lost that position and thought he would no longer have any influence in the world. But Paul was wrong. Shortly after he lost his position, he took up writing. His writing brought him immortal fame. We still read his works on the pages of the New Testament.

Paul reminds us of one unalterable fact. It is humanly impossible to assess the importance of any event. John Bunyan's loss of freedom inspired his writing of *Pilgrim's Progress*. John Milton's blindness resulted in an immortal contribution to literature. Dante, in the anguish of exile from his beloved Florence, wrote his *Divine Comedy*, usually recognized among the classics in any language.

Triumphs are not always lasting and defeats are not always permanent. Remember the lines:

> *Speak, history! Who are life's victors?*
> *Unroll thy long annals and say,*
> *Are they those whom the world called victors,*
> *Who won the success of the day?*
> *The martyrs, or Nero?*
> *The Spartans who fell at Thermopylae's tryst?*
> *Or the Persians and Xerxes?*
> *His judges or Socrates?*
> *Pilate or Christ?*

History is clear about this. Everyone has been sometimes up and sometimes down, but few people have known which was which at the time. Those young people were right when they admonished us to "keep our cool." There is a hand in this world constantly working to bring the good out of the bad. Every day may not be a good day but if you hang on, things have a way of changing. Somehow right things float to the surface. It helps to remember that when the news coming in is all bad.

Living with the Past
Determining the Opportunity

There was a story in the news recently about a man standing on the edge of the roof of a 40-story building in New York City. He was poised ready to jump. The man was in his middle 40s and had behind him a successful career in business. A few months earlier, his business had fallen on troubled times. A part of the problem was the man's embezzlement of funds that had been entrusted to his care.

A passing priest was called to the scene. The priest managed to crawl to within a few feet of the desperate man but was unable to reach him. The only alternative left to the priest was to try to persuade the man to surrender. The newsman reporting the story asked an interesting question: "What do you say to a person who has decided that the past makes the future impossible and believes that suicide is the only way out?"

Few of us will ever confront the circumstances faced by that priest; but all of us, at times, talk with people who live on the edge of desperation. Sometimes we feel that way about our own lives. The events of the past are such that we believe there is no hope for tomorrow. How do we deal with such feelings? How do we live with a past that seems impossible? There are at least three things we could well remember.

First, the past for all of us is a mixture of good and bad. About 20 centuries ago there lived a man we have come to call a saint. Paul's name is synonymous with everything good and decent. The impact he had on the world is for the lasting benefit of humankind. We forget that the early life of St. Paul was far from that of a saint. He participated in at least one murder and likely was involved in the execution of other innocent people. The life of St. Paul is a constant reminder that few if any of us have a perfect past. All of us leave behind a trail mixed with good and bad.

Any student of biography is aware of this. More often than not the greatest of our heroes have dark and shady splotches on their records. St. Augustine's early years were so wild that his mother feared for his life. One of America's greatest generals had long bouts with alcoholism during which his behavior was anything but exemplary. If a questionable past could shut out the future, then history would have lost some of its greatest leaders. It's a rare person indeed who can look back and be proud of everything.

Second, preoccupation with the past is useless except as it is used to guide us in the present and the future. George Santayana is credited

189

with saying that those who cannot remember the past are doomed to repeat it. There is nothing unhealthy about looking back as long as our purpose is to learn from it. But living with the past can destroy us if we spend our time simply lamenting our mistakes and dwelling on our failures.

The reason is obvious. The past is unalterable. The past reminds us that the "Moving Finger" writes and moves on and neither worry nor tears can erase its lines. The record stands as it is written. Squandering time lamenting mistakes is a foolish way to live. It robs life of its potential and wastes precious opportunities.

The real question is not how can we change the past, but rather how can we profit from it. We learn not only from the good but also from the bad. The brutal experimentation during the early years of modern medicine was terrible but out of these horrible days many lifesaving techniques were discovered. The way to handle the past is to learn from it and then ask what can be done under the circumstances as they now exist.

Third, it is possible to redeem the past by living responsibly in the present. There is a timeless proverb that everyone should remember. "God never allows one door to close on us without opening another." The point of that proverb is that life is so arranged that no circumstance is completely impossible, and we are never boxed into a totally closed room. There is an open door somewhere, and we can find it if we have the will to look for it.

Alcoholics Anonymous has worked for years on the principle that there are no hopeless people. To prove their point they have pulled people out of every kind of circumstance and helped them to find new life. What AA has demonstrated in the field of drug and alcohol addiction is true in every other area of life. St. Paul and St. Augustine outlived their pasts. That American general now occupies an envied place in our history. There are always open doors if we have the will to look for them.

The next time you find someone living in desperation over a troubled past, or if you feel that way yourself, try recalling these things: Not one of us can look at the yesterdays of life completely unashamed; but what is done is done and nothing can change that. Above everything, however, is this clear fact of history. Life is so arranged that the most hopeless problem has its opportunity. We can find it if we take our minds off what might have been and think about what can be.

Escaping the Treadmill
Finding a Useful Purpose

Sometime when you are in a busy city, take a moment and observe the people who pass by. Some of the folk appear to be happy and excited. They smile when they meet others and often stop to chat even with strangers. There are other people who shuffle along at a dull and lifeless pace. Every step seems an effort. They stare into space with eyes clouded in futility. Think for a while about the differences between these two kinds of people. Has one group discovered a secret the others have not found?

A long time ago an ancient writer described his people in this fashion. "In the morning they wish it were evening. In the evening they wish it were morning." Such people are still around. Life for them is a treadmill. They have plenty to do but their work has no meaning. They arise in the morning so they can go to work to come home in the evening so they can rest for work in the morning. Existence for these people is a monotonous circle. They wonder if it is possible to break out of their endless prison.

In one of the oldest books in the world there is an interesting passage. "Why spend your money for less than bread and your labor for that which does not satisfy? Eat that which is good and feed on that which will sustain you." Two or three things are evident in this thought. Among them is the inference that people are hungry creatures. We are hungry physically, mentally, spiritually and emotionally. It is the search for the satisfaction of these hungers that governs our behavior.

A recent study by a management consulting firm supports this. In a questionnaire asking why people work, the consultants discovered that earning money was only one of the reasons people seek employment. Some folk were interested in status, some were seeking release from boredom, others said they were looking for their "place in the sun." In every case the people questioned indicated they were trying to satisfy some deep-seated hunger. Apparently we are all alike in this regard. We are hungry people in search of food.

It is possible, however, that some of the foods we seek never really satisfy. A plane went down in the Pacific a few years ago. The survivors drifted for days before they were rescued. "The maddening thing about it all," said one of the survivors, "was the presence of water everywhere and none to drink." Every sailor knows of the dangers in drinking salt water. One of them is that salt water does not ultimately quench thirst. It only intensifies it.

Many of our young people are concerned about some of the phony values of our time. Their concern is not without cause. They have seen their elders spend their health to gain their wealth and then spend their wealth to regain their health. They have observed, too, that the passion to possess can rob us of being able to enjoy what we already have. We can be so busy maintaining status that we are miserable with it. A wise man was once asked, "How much money does it take to make a person happy?" The reply was interesting: "Just a little more."

One of Tolstoy's best-known stories is about a man who was promised all the land he could walk around in a single day. At the first blush of dawn he started out, leisurely at first, but with every moment his pace quickened. As the rich, black soil seemed to draw him on, the word "more" began to throb in the man's heart and brain. At the last rays of sunset he flung forward, his hands reaching onward. But his pace had been too taxing. The man died as he fell. That long-ago author was right. Life can be spent in pursuits that never satisfy.

There are ways to satisfy our hunger with foods that strengthen life and give meaning to it. Centuries ago there lived a young man in a far corner of the world. He was wealthy and influential but he was also tired and bored. He was known for his wild, undisciplined living. One night his friends held a party for him and crowned him King of the Revels. A few days later riding along a narrow path he met a leper. Revolted at the sight he turned aside. Later, filled with shame, he rode back to help the man. For the first time the young man felt meaning and direction to his life. He joined a colony of lepers to help them. When his father threatened to disown him, the boy took his clothes and piled them at his father's feet. He dedicated his life to helping others. We now remember St. Francis of Assisi as the Troubadour of Joy.

There is a lesson to be learned from St. Francis. Nothing gives greater meaning to life than finding a useful purpose. If life seems less exciting than it should be, the reason may be that we have no compelling purpose. A good way to change that would be to find something to do every day that will make the load lighter for someone and the world a better place. People who live this way discover that life is no longer a treadmill, but a thrilling journey.

Changing What We Are
Can We Shape Our Destiny?

About 300 years ago, a German physician named F.G. Gall became interested in the behavior of the criminally insane. Among his many ideas was the theory that human mentality has to do with the shape of the skull. His findings received tremendous publicity, and for many years he was regarded as the authority in the field. He insisted that intelligence is related to the size of one's forehead. It was from this physician that we picked up the word "highbrow." The higher the hairline, the greater the brainpower.

Gall's "highbrow" theory has long since been discredited, but a few of his notions are still around. There are some behavioral scientists who insist that what we are is determined by environmental and hereditary forces that are beyond our control. This theory followed to its ultimate extreme suggests that we are totally at the mercy of cosmic powers. Our destiny is already shaped and there is nothing we can do about it.

Despite the arguments of these scientists, not many of us subscribe to the theory of absolute determinism. We believe that we do bear some responsibility in what happens to us. Because of this belief we struggle with vocations, practice safety and health precautions, and go to school to train our minds and improve our thought processes. Outside forces may have considerable influence upon us, but these forces do not have the final word. Most of us believe that to some degree we can change what we are into what we want to become. The fact is, whether we realize it or not, we are constantly changing what we are. This is true for at least two important reasons.

First, what we do consistently determines in large measure what we become. There is an old fairy tale about an unscrupulous villain who fell in love with a lovely maiden. The maid refused to marry the man, declaring that he did not have a kind face. The man sought out a mask maker who made a special mask and fitted it to the man's face. This time the man wooed the girl and won her. One day, years later, an old enemy sought out the man and, in the presence of the man's wife, tore off the mask. But when the mask was removed a kind face was revealed. The man had become what he had practiced day by day.

C.S. Lewis once said, "Every time we make a choice we are turning the central part of ourselves into something different." This is but a reminder that a conscious choice made often enough becomes an unconscious habit. We must, therefore, exercise care lest our choices make us into something we do not want to be. To become the person we would like to be requires selective action, and the change comes about gradually. We do not learn to appreciate great art at one sitting. We must cultivate a taste for it over years of conscious choices. Eventually the choices become habitual. Wise is the person who gives serious thought to what he or she would like to become and then makes deliberate choices in that direction. We are becoming something different every day whether we want to or not. The pressing question of life is to choose the kind of person we would like to be.

Second, the set of our minds determines to a great degree our lives. An office manager was having great trouble keeping the thermostat suitably adjusted for all his people. Everyone kept tinkering with the controls. One night he brought in an engineer who installed a new thermostat out of sight where no one could find it. He left the old control on the wall but disconnected it. When a complaint came in about the temperature, the manager directed the person to the old thermostat. The person would fiddle around with it for awhile and go away completely satisfied.

James Allen wrote a classic little book entitled *As a Man Thinketh.* That title was gleaned from the Bible. The verse in the Book of Proverbs reads: "As a man thinketh in his heart so is he." The point of that verse, Allen contended, is that the mind is like a garden which may be intelligently cultivated or allowed to run wild. If we put good seeds into this garden we determine our lives. This is true because our deeds, and our character, spring from the thoughts of the mind.

How completely Allen's thesis could be defended by the discoveries of modern psychology is open to debate. It is true, however, that the way we decide to look at things determines in large measure their meaning for us. If we look for the good and the beautiful in the events of life, then life tends to take on a joyous and happy glow. If we choose to see only the evil and the bad, our minds become sad and troubled. Someone has rightly said, "What gets our attention finally gets us."

So important is this principle that hundreds of books have been written on it. The books may vary in content but their premise is always the same. Life is determined by the direction we choose to look. Every event in our lives poses both problems and possibilities. We decide which we will see. By that choice, more than we imagine, we are determining what our lives will be.

Telling Your Own Fortune

A few years ago a Texas author named Charles Welborn related an incident from his childhood. One night, after his mother had put him in bed, Welborn said he began reading an adventure story about a young man named Don Sturdy. Sturdy and his friends were on an ocean trip searching for a deep-sea monster. Inadvertently, Sturdy had fallen overboard and was locked in the viselike grip of an octopus. Just as the story reached its critical moment, Welborn's mother came in, pulled the covers about the lad and turned out the light. "That's enough reading for tonight," she said. Welborn lay in the darkness worrying about his hero, Don Sturdy. Unable to stand it any longer, he climbed out of bed, took the book into a closet and flicked on the light. He did not turn to the page he had been reading. Instead, he went to the last page of the book and read hurriedly. Welborn said he closed the book with a sigh of relief. His hero was all right. He was back at home planning his next adventure.

All of us at times share the predicament confronted by Charles Welborn. We face a critical moment in life and find ourselves wondering about the outcome. We wish for some magical way to look into the future. Unfortunately, much of the future is hidden from us. It is a rare person indeed who dares claim the gift of predicting what tomorrow will bring.

There is a sense, however, in which the future is not as obscure as we imagine. To a degree, it is possible for all of us to take a reliable look at tomorrow and determine how things will turn out. To achieve this insight into the future we need to remember two or three things.

First, we must remember that we live in a cause-and-effect world.

On January 11, 1958, space scientists thrust into the sky a pencil-like cylinder that orbited the earth every 115.8 minutes. It was not an easy task. For years scientists had been searching for the conditions necessary to put a satellite into orbit. People such as Sir Isaac Newton, Albert Einstein, Albert Michelson and Ernst Mach had been probing the universe searching for the natural laws governing space travel. One by one these laws were discovered. The space engineers obeyed these laws, and today we make regular and predictable excursions into the "great beyond."

We have learned that we live in a dependable universe. Certain conditions produce certain results. Doctors understand this. If they want to treat a particular disease, they seek to understand the conditions under which healing from this disease takes place. The gardener works by this same principle. He knows that the seed he sows will determine the harvest he gathers.

The principle of cause and effect prevails throughout our world. An ancient writer once declared, "Be not deceived. What you sow, that you will reap. Sow the wrong seeds and you will reap the wrong harvest. Sow the right seeds and you can expect the right harvest." A second thought: The chief business of life is to choose the right goals and then meet the conditions necessary to achieve those goals.

A few years ago one of America's most widely known ministers said when he was a boy he went to a high-school Halloween carnival. One of the games at the carnival was called "Fishing." You paid a quarter and selected a string from a bundle hanging on a screen. You pulled the string and received the prize tied to the other end. Said this minister, "Be careful about the strings you pull in life. You always get what is on the other end."

The warning of that minister sounds ominous, but it should not be. The fact that we get what is tied to the strings we pull is really a marvelous promise. It is this principle that makes it possible for us to establish goals and achieve them. If we desire a reputation for honesty and dependability, we must handle our personal and business affairs with that goal in mind. If we want a successful, long-term business, we will seek to give good service and honest value. If we want a close-knit family, we should set aside time and build family ties. If we want friends we will cultivate friendships.

There is very little magic involved in building a life. A good student learns that the price of scholarship is study, and an accomplished musician finds no substitute for practice. Building a life is like building a house: put the proper materials into the effort and we get the expected results. We get the kind of house we build. Life, then, is a matter of choosing a direction and working toward it. If we meet the conditions, we can predict the outcome.

Finally, we must learn to wait.

Abraham Lincoln was often asked how he managed to endure the constant criticisms of his foes. But, as he once put it, "If I am right, then nothing my enemies can do will defeat me. If I am wrong, then all the angels swearing I am right will not help me." Lincoln had discovered the most precious secret of life. If we meet the right conditions and learn to wait, we finally come out at the right place.

Sometimes it takes years for the seed to come to harvest. Lincoln did not live long enough to see his cause vindicated. He died while still a target for the unjust charges of his detractors, but Lincoln knew that someday, somewhere, he would prevail. He was right. Today no American holds a more hallowed place in our history.

All of us would do well to remember this lesson. Those who meet the right conditions finally come out at the right place, but it takes time. Plants seldom produce their fruit overnight. There is always a time lag between seedtime and harvest. People who live with serenity and peace understand this. They establish their goals and work toward them. They know that as long as we live in a cause-and-effect world, someday they will arrive at the right place. Like the boy who read the last page in the book, they know where they are coming out.

Standing at the Crossroads
No Decision Need Be Fatal

He was 22 years old and just out of college. Confronting him was a vocational decision that would have long-range effects on his life. In one direction was a fabulous salary, but there would be constant travel, often to the far corners of the earth. The young man had just married his college sweetheart. He wondered how the extensive travel schedule would affect his marriage. In the other direction there was a far more modest salary and the opportunities for advancement were limited, but it was a good job and he could depend on being at home. "What shall I do?" pleaded the young man as he chatted with his minister. "How can I be sure I am making the right decision?"

Most of us can identify with this predicament. Life is filled with decisions. Time after time we stand at the crossroads debating directions. The question we ask is, "How do we make the right choice?"

Much could be written on this question, but there are a few simple things all of us should remember. One is that making decisions and life go hand in hand. Someone has said that human beings are free but they are not autonomous. This is one way of saying that while we are free to say "yes" or "no," we are not free to evade saying one or the other. Indecision is not possible in our kind of world. We either decide or our failure to decide becomes a decision.

The reason, of course, is that life is an ever-moving stream. We are as tiny vessels traveling on a river that never stops. Along the way we pass many tributaries where new courses are possible and other streams can be taken. Each time we pass one of these tributaries a decision must be made. If we refuse to decide, the stream moves on and makes our decision for us.

James Russell Lowell, in his famed poem, "The Present Crisis," declared, "Once to every man and nation comes a moment to decide . . . And the choice goes by forever. . . ." Life is hardly that rigid, but Lowell was right when he suggested that we never confront the same choice twice. Every moment brings a slightly different set of alternatives. We only pass this way once. The stream of life always moves one way. We must decide or time will make the decision for us.

Another thing we need to remember is that once a choice is made it is foolish to look back. There is a somber verse that many of us recall: " For of all sad words of tongue or pen, the saddest are these: 'It might have been!' " Perhaps it is natural to wonder how life would have been different had we made a different decision. Suppose we had chosen another profession or married a different person? Suppose we had moved to another place or gone to a different school or college? We can waste precious time reflecting on what might have been, but such thoughts seldom help. There is really no way of knowing how our world might have been different.

The most important thing to remember, however, is that while our choices are final, they need not destroy us. One of the most popular records of recent years had the unlikely title, "The Ten Worst Songs Ever Recorded." An enterprising salesman dug down into a stack of records and found some tunes no one would buy. He put them together on a single record and made a fortune. The adage, "Where there is life, there is hope!" is profoundly true. We may not be able to take the same road again but we can always find another one.

It is said that Henry David Thoreau once wrote a book no one would publish. He decided to have it published at his own expense. That was a mistake. He sold only 214 copies; the remaining 700 were delivered to his doorstep. But the "Unconquerable Resident of Walden Pond" recovered quickly. "I have," he said, "a library of 900 books, 700 of them I wrote myself." Those 700 books are now almost priceless. Life can work that way. Even "bloopers" can be made to turn a profit.

Long ago a writer penned a sentence the world still remembers: "All things work together for good for those who love God." This ancient author had discovered one of life's most precious secrets. No decision need be totally destructive if we live in faith and trust. Even bad things can work for good purposes. Life demands that we make decisions and once a decision is made, in some ways, that choice is forever. The river of life, however, has many tributaries and one is always on the horizon if we look for it. The key to successful living is to make decisions when they need to be made. But do not spend your time looking back. If the decision proves to be wrong, start looking for a way to make it right. You will find it if you are willing to look long enough.

Choosing the Right Window
Discovering the Secret to Abundant Living

Someone tells about a house in New England to which the owner attached a unique tower. In each of the four walls of the tower there was a window fitted with a different color of glass. The owner would often take his visitors to the tower and ask them to look at the world through one of the windows. In one direction the glass was red, suggesting the fiery heat of summer. In another direction, the glass was blue and through that window the landscape took on the cold, icy tint of winter. One glass was brown, suggesting the color of autumn. The fourth window was green, hinting at the beauty of spring. What the visitor saw in the world about the tower depended on the window through which the world was viewed.

What was true in that tower is also true in life. The world is greatly colored by the window through which we view it. In some measure this factor determines how we live and the attitude we have toward life. Consider this premise in three areas.

First, the window we choose makes a difference in the way we see other people.

Will Rogers often said he never met a person he did not like. Another well-known American declared that "a sucker is born every minute." Both men saw the same people. One viewed the people around him with warmth and friendliness; the other man looked at others through the eyes of a cynic. The men saw the same people but they saw them through different windows.

There is an old idea in psychology known as "imputation." The suggestion is that people tend to conform to what is expected of them. Child psychologists often point to this. Treat a child with trust and respect and the child tends to become trustworthy. View the child with distrust and doubt, and the child will likely move in those directions.

A wider application of this principle can have a bearing on the way all people respond to us. Leaders are those who sense the possibilities in their associates and then inspire these associates to achieve the possibilities. It is a wise person who searches for the best in other people. People who do this form lasting friendships and discover friends who are dependable. They also achieve positions of leadership more readily than other folk. Always look for the best, not the worst; concentrate on the positives, not the negatives; and look for the victories, not the defeats, in the people around you. It makes a difference when you look at others through the right window.

Second, the window we choose makes a difference in the way we read the events of life.

Centuries ago an ancient writer penned a letter to some friends in a far-away corner of the world. In that letter he made this declaration: "All things work together for the good of those who love God." The author of those words had little evidence to support this claim. For most of his life he had been a hunted criminal, and many of his days were spent in jail. But this man knew that the laws that made him a criminal were unjust. "Our cause is right," he said to his friends. "And because it is right it is backed by the powers of the universe. Some day we will prevail if we do our best." Time has proved this man to be right. His cause did prevail. Today this man's writings are a part of the world's most important book—the New Testament. Those who know this ancient author's biography know that even his obstacles became his stepping stones.

They usually do! The old adage, "When life hands you a lemon, make lemonade," remains with us because it suggests a profound truth. Every circumstance, no matter how bleak, has its opportunities, but we cannot discover these opportunities by looking through the windows of despair. Life must be seen through the windows of hope and expectation.

Finally, the windows we choose make a difference in the way we see ourselves.

There is an old Roman fable about a day when the gods grew tired of people complaining about their troubles. They established a time when every citizen would go to the pool in the center of the city and throw his troubles into the pool. Each person would then be given an opportunity to select from the pool the troubles that best suited him. The people gathered on the appointed day, threw their troubles in and began to select new ones. When the scramble was over, each person had selected the very troubles he brought.

There is a lesson here with many applications. We spend far too much time measuring our lot in life against the circumstances of others. We lament our lack of talents when measured against the talents of others. We do not spend enough time concentrating on our strengths. It is through this window that life is found to be exciting. The happy people are those who remember that no one has everything but everyone has something. The secret to abundant living is to discover yourself and then develop your strengths to their highest potential.

Finding the Way to the River
Learning the Importance of Brooks

In the 1960s a Canadian author wrote a book entitled *Twenty-four Hours to Live*. One of the chapters in that book was entitled, "Following the Brook." According to the author, the title for that chapter came from James Howell Street's book, *The Gauntlet*. In Street's book there was an account of a young, bewildered minister seeking what he called "the river of truth." About this search Street remarked, "In seeking a great river, the young man hadn't learned the importance of brooks."

That sentence is worthy of reflection. Sometimes the most important destinations are reached along simple roads. Most great achievements come about a step at a time. Back in the 1920s one of America's first radio stations went on the air in Pittsburgh. Countless people began building crystal radio sets, tinkering with what was called the "cat's whisker." The vacuum tube soon replaced the crystal detector, and the transistor replaced the vacuum tube. We now talk about minicircuits and microcircuits. We followed one steppingstone after another. We reached the river by following the brook. Most of life's important achievements come that way.

Consider the business world. In the biography of one of America's best-known business leaders, the author reports on a young man's beginnings in the automobile industry. The fellow's career did not begin in the president's office. His first assignment was at the furnaces where the steel was made. He began as a number-three helper. He worked his way through manufacturing, sales and so forth, until he knew the industry from the lowest rung of the ladder. Not many people begin at the top and remain there successfully, not even the boss' relatives. Most people get to the river by following the brook.

Is not the same thing true in the physical and intellectual world? Strong bodies are built through endless hours of exercise, proper diet and sufficient rest. A boxer spends weeks in training for a fight. An Olympic winner often begins work in early childhood.

A trained mind is the product of following the steppingstones. Reading begins with simple words. The complexity of words increases until the most complicated documents can be read and understood. The mathematician begins by working with the easiest problems of addition and subtraction. Only after these lessons are learned does the math student move to the more difficult fields of trigonometry and calculus.

Most great literature begins by the brook. A British author who had become widely known for his writings was asked by a reporter how it felt to awake and find himself an overnight success. "Madam," replied the author, "I was not an overnight success. Before I was a success I spent 15 years as a drudge." Most important achievements come about a step at a time. You get to the river by following the brook.

Remembering this is especially important in developing stamina for life's tough places. Robert Goodrich wrote a book once with an intriguing chapter he entitled, "The Night Shift." "All of us now and then," he declared, "go on the night shift." Goodrich was not referring to working after dark. He was talking about those times when life seems to make no sense. Those moments come to all of us—a time of severe illness, the loss of a loved one or some other inexplicable tragedy. How do you stand up to dark days?

The building of spiritual stamina is not an overnight achievement. You build for the dark days while living in the sunshine. You decide on the answers to such questions as the meaning of life or whether human existence is confined to the limits of this one world. You decide whether there is help beyond human hands. It takes time to work through such questions. It requires reading, meditation and reflection. Little by little, answers get fixed in your mind. As they do, you develop anchors you can hang onto when you go on the night shift. You discover strength you did not know you possessed. But that strength does not come instantly; it comes gradually. The Canadian author and Street were right. You reach the great rivers by following the brooks.

Handling the Giants
Winning Despite the Odds

In the year 1779, a refugee British naval captain named John Paul Jones sailed his tiny ship, the *Bonhomme Richard*, into the North Sea. For months the Revolutionary War had been raging. Jones and his men were fighting on the side of the American colonies. On the afternoon of September 23, the captain and his crew ran into a British convoy led by a British battleship. The battleship commander fired a shot across the bow of the *Bonhomme Richard* and demanded that it halt. Jones, fearful that his small vessel would be sunk, pulled alongside the rail of the battleship and tied on. The captain of the battleship saw the *Bonhomme Richard* tied to his rail. Thinking Jones had capitulated, he asked, "Do you surrender?" That afternoon, John Paul Jones wrote his name into the history books of the world with his now-famous reply: "Surrender? I have not yet begun to fight." Three hours later the commander of the battleship turned over his weapons to the captain of the *Bonhomme Richard*.

History is alive with events such as this—little people taking on giants and doing the giants in. In one of the oldest books in the world there is a story about some nomadic people who were looking for a homeland. One day the leaders of these people sent a dozen scouts to survey the nearby territory. Upon their return ten of the scouts reported, "There are giants in that land. Compared to them we are as grasshoppers." Two of the scouts, however, gave a different report. "Those people are not giants. They are as we are. Let's go up and take the land." The ancient story raises an interesting question. Why do some people look at the world and see giants while others looking at the same world see none? Why do some of us feel overwhelmed by life while others feel adequate and secure? What makes a giant?

One thing seems clear. The answer is not because we live in different worlds. Life is not usually easy for any of us. Of course, some people have better opportunities, live in better situations and have more ability, but the winners are not always those with such advantages. The records are filled with victories won by unlikely people—people who win despite the odds.

In many, many ways we confront the same problems. No one is immune from illness or free from the chance of accidents. The most skillful business leaders can suffer reverses through no fault of their own. Death knows no strangers. It is a tough, dangerous world for everyone. Some people see this world and are overcome by it. Others stand up to these realities and refuse to surrender to them. What, then, makes a giant?

If we can believe the record, giants are made by the people who see them. By the same token, what appear to be giants can be reduced to normal size by people who refuse to surrender to them. The Most Valuable Player in the 1986 Super Bowl was not a first-draft choice of the pros. He was well beyond the 200th player picked when college players were chosen. When asked how he managed to be the MVP of the Super Bowl, this player declared, "You have to have a dream and believe in yourself."

This is not to suggest that we can do anything we choose to do. Sometimes there are giants and they are too big to climb over. The only alternative is to go around them. There are handicaps we cannot ignore and circumstances with which we must live. But one thing is certain: we never confront any situation that we cannot do something about—not even death.

A long time ago a man stood before a Roman court. Convicted of a crime he did not commit, he was sentenced to die. The method of execution was to be a cross. He was only 33 years of age. There were so many things he might have done if only he could live, but the verdict had been rendered and the man had no choice but to die. That man determined to die in such a way the world would always remember his name and his cause. He succeeded. Today this man's cross has become his eternal throne. His life is the dividing line of history. From his birth we date our calendars. This man stands as a constant reminder that nothing can finally conquer us unless we surrender. There is always a way to handle the giants if we look for it.

Who Is Winning the War?
Building Well Ensures Genuine Success

During the Second World War, a soldier fighting in the South Pacific wrote a letter home to his father. In his letter, he described the unbelievable horror going on about him. He named his comrades who had fallen in battle and talked about the danger he faced daily. He closed his letter with this question: "Dad, please write and tell me, who is winning the war?"

It is not difficult to understand the reason for that question. When you have been working away at your part of the battle, it is easy to become preoccupied and miss the larger picture. This happens not only on the battlefield; it also happens in life. Young people who work diligently to prepare themselves for a vocation wonder if there will be a world around in which to work. Parents struggling to rear a family wonder if their children will be caught up in global war. Older people who have struggled to build a better world often wonder if their efforts have been in vain. Who is winning this war is a question all of us ask at times. We want to know how the total conflict is going.

The answer to such a question is important. The way we handle any battle depends on what we believe about the ultimate outcome. There is an old story about a man named Elijah who found himself protesting the inhuman policies of a wicked queen. The queen threatened Elijah's life. Deciding his cause was lost, Elijah fled. Somewhere out in a remote hiding place the man contemplated suicide. But a message came to Elijah. He was told, "You are not alone in your struggle. There are others fighting on your side." The record reports that the man took new courage; he returned to his homeland and worked at his cause until he prevailed.

There is always a connection between despair and surrender. The will to struggle is directly related to the possibility of victory. A few years ago, a man in New England received a letter from his son who was away in college. The son asked, "Why should we do our best when the world is going to hell?" In other words, "If you know you cannot win, why keep on trying?" The answer to that question is important, whether we are talking about an international battle or a personal skirmish. Wise leaders understand this. There must be some hope of victory or all effort ceases. This principle is true in business; it is true in political and civic matters. It is true in all areas of life.

There are only two ways to make a judgment on who is winning the war. The first is to decide on the basis of single events. In that old story, Elijah discovered this. He thought he was all alone. He did not know that countless others were working on his side.

We can stand so close to our little battles that we lose sight of the total picture. Many of us do this. We judge the total direction of the world by the headlines of one paper. We are rendered hopeless by one setback in our personal affairs. It is a mistake to judge the whole world by one event. Not all young people are bad because a few step out of line. All is not lost because one promotion fails to go through. Your children are not doomed forever because of one bad report card. Misfortunes come to everyone after a while; but so does good fortune.

The second possibility is to judge the outcome against the longer view. Elijah should have done that before he left home. If he had, he might not have fled. In any event, when Elijah returned to his homeland, he discovered he was not alone in his battle with the queen. The record states that 7,000 people were working on his side.

Many of our dilemmas result from our failure to read the events of the moment against the wider picture. As a consequence, we make serious mistakes. We take shortcuts trying to find success. We forget that genuine success comes only to those who build carefully and with proven procedures. In the end, these are the people who win the war. They may lose a battle now and then, but the final outcome finds them at the right place.

The Great Teacher told about a couple of men who set about building their homes. One builder was in a hurry. He did not take time to lay a good foundation. The other builder was wise. He worked long and hard to set his house on solid footing. Finally, when both builders were finished, a storm struck the two homes. The foolish builder found his house falling into the sand.

There are lessons to be learned from these two builders. If you want something solid and dependable, you do your building that way. Far more often than not, the people who are successful in their vocations prepare carefully for them. Parents who try diligently to rear their children usually discover that after a while their efforts prevail. People who struggle to build a better world will finally make a difference. The reason is this: The world is so made that seeds reproduce their own kind.

We should never forget this when we are struggling with our battles. Those who build well eventually win. Maybe not today, perhaps not tomorrow, but after a while they are the winners.

Pulling the Right Strings
Life Demands Choices

One of America's greatest journalists, Horace Greeley, was a specialist in the use of language and word meanings. He often engaged in debates with his reporters about their grammar. One day he became involved in a discussion of the word *news*. Greeley insisted the word was plural; the reporter said it was singular. Finally, Greeley sent the reporter a message, "Are there any news?" The reporter fired back, "No, not a single *new!*"

Greeley lost his argument, but his pursuit was important. If we are to have proper communication, we must have precise definitions and usage of words. There is a phrase we often misuse, Greeley said. That phrase is *human freedom*. We frequently take this to mean one thing when it really means another. Human freedom, many of us assume, is the complete absence of restriction or restraint. If that is the proper definition of *freedom*, then humankind is never free. There is no life completely unencumbered. Wendell Jones was correct when he said, "We may have freedom of choice, but not freedom from choice." That is a thought worthy of reflection.

Consider the fact that we are never free from the necessity of choice. It was Thomas Kelly who said that most of the muddle of contemporary life results from our attempts to pursue goals that are incompatible with each other. Someone tells about a sign in Europe posted on high-tension electrical pylons. It read: "Danger! High Voltage! Anyone touching these pylons will be instantly killed!" Underneath that sign was this notice: "Violators of the above notice will be prosecuted." These two signs suggest a conflict that demands attention. Our goals cannot be contradictory. We must have directions that are compatible.

There are countless examples of this. Physical fitness requires discipline, an education demands study and friendships require cultivation. There is no long-term business success without integrity and dedication. Years ago, someone asked a successful English writer how it felt to awake one morning and discover himself an overnight success. The writer replied, "I was not an overnight success. Before I was a success, I spent 15 years as a drudge." That British author was right. Some things go together. Life demands a choice.

Remember, too, that while we may be free to choose, we are not free to choose the results of our choice.

There is an old idea in theology called predestination. In its strictest meaning, predestination suggests that every event in our lives has already been determined. We are simply robots following through on a drama written for us from the beginning. Expressions of this idea are heard every day: "You won't die until your time comes"; "What is to be will be"; or "Fate is against me." While we often repeat these phrases, we do not really believe them. We wear seat belts to protect us even if our time has come, and we work hard to change "what is to be" into what we think it should be. Pure predestination is untenable. It suggests that we have absolutely no control over our lives, making all effort completely useless.

There is a sense, however, in which our lives are predetermined for us. Certain choices make certain circumstances inevitable. As children attending high-school carnivals, we often played a game called "Fishing." Prizes were tied to strings and then hidden from sight. We paid our money, chose our string and pulled. We always got what was on the other end. Life is like that. We choose our strings and pull. Life has a way of bringing to us what is tied to our strings. A student chooses to become a musician. Practice becomes the inevitable result. There is a price to be paid for every choice. That is a law of life, and it is written into the scheme of things.

These thoughts lead us to a final conclusion: Only as we are bound do we become free.

In one of the oldest books in the world there is a powerful sentence: "Keep these commandments that it may go well with you." Here is one of life's most profound paradoxes. Only in discipline is there freedom.

When an artist first begins painting, every movement of the brush is painfully made, often erased and corrected. But as practice continues, the hand begins to move more accurately and with better or no conscious effort. A doctor engages in grueling study; but in time he or she does in minutes and almost instinctively what once took hours. Life works this way. Keep pulling your string and eventually you get what is on the other end. Only in discipline is there freedom.

One of America's best-known authors in one of his books describes "The Land of Look Behind." It is a mythical land where criminals go to escape punishment. Yet, he said, these people are never free. They live in constant fear that the past will someday overtake them. Most of us live some part of our lives in that kind of land. Consequently, we are often filled with anxiety and apprehension. To the degree, however, that we have disciplined ourselves to seek the finest and best things in life, we are free. We have the assurance that pulling the right strings finally gets us the right things.

Is It Wrong to Love Yourself?
Self-Pride Can Be Virtuous

When Theodore Roosevelt was president of the United States, one of his critics complained that the president suffered from severe egomania. He said Roosevelt once declared that when he got to heaven, he planned to organize a choir. In that choir, Roosevelt reported, he wanted 10,000 altos and 10,000 tenors. When asked who would sing bass, Roosevelt boasted, "I will."

Whether Roosevelt ever made such a statement is questionable. It is true, however, that he was a man of great confidence and self-assurance. Such qualities of personality are essential for successful living. A long-ago teacher once said to his followers, "You shall love your neighbor as yourself." We usually imagine that the instruction here is to be concerned about others and to forget ourselves. Indeed, we are often told that concern with self is a character flaw. This, of course, is not completely true. Pride in oneself is not a fault but a virtue, provided that it is a proper pride. That is a thought that needs consideration. We need to understand what constitutes proper self-pride.

First, proper pride does not mean self-idolization. It is said that Dorothy Parker once attended a social gathering. In the group was a celebrity who was vain and proud. During the conversation the celebrity declared condescendingly, "I always try to be gracious to my inferiors." "How wonderful," purred the disarming Parker. "But tell me. Wherever do you find them?"

Nothing is quite so destructive in human relationships as an unrealistic estimate of ourselves. It builds barriers that separate us from others. The result is loneliness, apprehension and fear. People tend to avoid those who are concerned only with themselves, leaving them isolated and friendless. The failure to have friends may not be the fault of others; it may be in ourselves. The old proverb, "He who loves only himself will have no rivals," is true. People who idolize themselves lead lonely lives.

Second, to be proud of oneself does not mean self-satisfaction. An artist was once commissioned to paint Oliver Cromwell. The artist made an attempt to minimize the blemishes in Cromwell's face. Cromwell was enraged. "I want to be painted warts and all!" he declared. Cromwell's individuality is to be admired, but not necessarily his approach to life. To be satisfied with unnecessary blemishes of body, mind or spirit is to settle for less than the Creator intended.

A lot is being said these days about the importance of accepting oneself. Properly understood, self-acceptance is a splendid attribute.

If, however, we mean that we are to be content as ignorant, childish, angry, irresponsible people, then self-acceptance is both wrong and destructive. Life is exciting only for those who are unwilling to accept themselves as they are. Rather, they strive to be what they can become. Self-acceptance is not equivalent to self-satisfaction.

Proper self-pride means simply the appreciation of our significance and uniqueness as individuals. Emerson once said that there must be a point in everyone's life when one discovers that imitation is suicide. A well-known movie producer stated that his biggest problem was keeping young actors from trying to mimic the academy stars. Our highest obligation is to appreciate our own talents and opportunities and develop them to the fullest. The miserable people are those who repudiate themselves by trying to be someone else. To live by imitation is to be counterfeit.

It is a serious mistake to spend life hating oneself. If for no other reason, such an attitude is always reflected in our outward behavior. If we are insecure inside, we will be undependable outside. If we do not trust ourselves, we have no capacity for trusting others. When we are afraid within, we are usually uncertain without. People who hate themselves usually hate others.

But how do we come to appreciate ourselves? Years ago, Rabbi Joshua Liebman left for us a clue to the kind of thinking which should help us with this: "Not one of us escapes limitations. Some people are gifted with their hands; some people are gifted in the realm of art or music; some people are gifted in the realm of abstract ideas. Almost no one is gifted in all these realms. But we need to recognize that we can do what others cannot do, that we can contribute what others cannot contribute. Let us then learn how to accept ourselves, accept the truth that we are capable in some directions and limited in others, that genius is rare, that mediocrity is a portion of almost all of us, but all of us can contribute—to the storehouse . . . of our common life."

Liebman was on target. Not one of us is so limited that we cannot count for something. The people who find life exciting and worthwhile are those who refuse to measure their gifts and talents by the gifts and talents of others. Instead they spend their lives examining who they are and what gifts and talents they possess. They then live out their days attempting to develop who they are and what they have to the fullest.

Working on Our Mental Houses
The Need to Feed the Mind Properly

A few years ago, an American psychologist gave an address in a southern city. Among other things, this psychologist declared that the human mind is a vast repository of impressions. "The mind is so intricately designed," he said, "that it never loses anything." The accuracy of that observation may be open to debate. It is clear, however, that the mind records its impressions and stores them more or less permanently.

Modern psychiatry has demonstrated this. One of the assumptions of the psychiatrist is that when an impression is registered in the central nervous system, it always leaves behind a trace or a group of traces. Often, when there is a need, the physician can probe the mind and by a very special set of skills uncover events and experiences that happened to us long ago. Some of these experiences have dropped below the level of consciousness; but despite the fact that these impressions are beyond present recall, they still affect our lives. How this happens no one fully understands, but it does happen; because it happens there are some things we need to remember.

About 2,000 years ago, a man wrote a letter to some friends in an ancient city. In that letter, the man admonished his readers, "Whatever things are true, whatever things are just, pure and winsome, think on these things." What prompted this ancient writer so to advise his friends is not wholly clear, but surely one of the things this author had in mind was that the health of the mind is dependent upon its food.

All of us understand that what we eat affects the health of the body. A group of dentists recently did a study of some people who live in a remote jungle area. They observed that the teeth of these people were terribly discolored and decayed. The reason, they discovered, was that these people lived in the land of sugar cane and from early childhood had nibbled on the sweet stalks. The regular exposure to sugar had produced its effects. The health of the body is conditioned by its food.

Much is being said these days about the potentially harmful chemicals that filter into our food supplies. The indiscriminate use of pesticides and the careless disposition of waste materials pose a serious threat not only to us but also to generations to come. There is an increasing emphasis, too, on the importance of a balanced diet if we are to maintain good health. "We are what we eat." This may not be the complete truth, but it is close enough to be a working rule.

The human mind is not greatly different from the body in this respect. If the mind is a storehouse where impressions are filed with more or less lasting effect, then its health is in some degree dependent on its diet. What we fix our minds upon does affect our lives.

This is why we are so careful to guard the mental sustenance of our children. We want to fix their minds on things that will help them establish proper values. We try to impress upon them the significance of simple but important virtues such as honesty, trustworthiness and respect for others. These early years, we believe, are crucial. If we can feed a young mind the proper diet, the health of that youthful mind will be affected for good.

We must remember that proper food is not only important for the youthful mind; it is also important for minds of any age. What gets our attention finally gets us. If we concentrate on the trivial, the negative and the unlovely, our lives tend to turn in that direction. We become trivial, negative and unlovely. On the other hand, if we give attention to the important, to the positive and to noble ideals, our lives tend to assume a corresponding nature. This is why the books we read, the television programs we watch, the amusements we pursue and the people we associate with are of crucial importance.

In light of this, we need to remember that what we put into our minds today produces its harvests tomorrow. This principle can be of strategic importance in helping us weather the hard times which finally come to all of us. President Abraham Lincoln declared that in the dark hours he faced during the conduct of the Civil War, he was sustained by the faith his mother taught him. It works that way. We live through the hard times of today on the stamina built in other days.

One of the oldest stories in the world is about two carpenters who set out to build their homes. One built in a hurry, not establishing proper foundations. The other set his house firmly on the rock. When the houses were complete, a storm came through the area. The foolish carpenter lost his house, while the other enjoyed the comforts of a well-built home. The lessons of that story are clear. We are all builders working on our mental houses, and we must live, finally, in the structures we build. The pressing business of life is to focus on those things that make for a sturdy house. What gets our attention finally gets us.

The Salt Is Missing

There is an old story that makes the rounds among educators about a paper received by a third-grade teacher. A list of words had been given to the teacher's students and the children were asked to supply definitions. One of the words given the students was "salt." One youngster came up with this interesting thought: "Salt is what you don't notice until someone forgets to put it in."

Whether or not this definition originated with that youngster is of no consequence. His answer, however, does suggest something that has profound implications for life. We take a lot of things for granted unless, for some reason, they are absent. There is an ancient parable about a military guard who was given a prisoner to keep. Apparently the prisoner was important, because the guard was told that if the prisoner escaped the guard would forfeit his own life. We don't know what happened, but the record states that when the guard was finally called to accounts the prisoner had fled. The soldier gave this excuse: "As I was busy here and there, the prisoner was gone." That's a pathetic confession. It is also a frequent occurrence. Consider these things.

First, there are some things vital to us that we never miss until they are gone. There was an ad in an American newspaper recently: "Dear Jane, I love you more than duck hunting!" It was signed "Bill." No one knows why the ad appeared in the paper, but one wonders if it was not the result of a domestic quarrel. Bill must have been spending too much time hunting. Jane had issued an ultimatum. In anger Bill left home. When emotions cooled, Bill discovered he had lost more than he had dreamed.

That's a perfectly human discovery. Someone has said that if the stars could be seen only one night each year, everyone would see them. As it is, many people never look up to see them. This principle also applies in other areas. Few people really appreciate clean air and pure water until the air and water have become polluted by careless wastefulness. Few of us really appreciate our families as we should until we are deprived of them by death or extended separation. The real value of a friend is seldom recognized until that friend is gone. This is also true of health, meaningful work and a host of other important things.

There's a second thought worth remembering. *Sometimes we become preoccupied with lesser things and lose sight of the more important things.* Christopher Morley wrote a poem entitled "End of August." When you read it, you get the picture of a person who takes time for granted: he has many things to do but none of them seem pressing. Hear the final lines of the poem:

Chattering voltage like a broken wire
The wild cicada cried, Six weeks to frost!

Those lines give cause for sober reflection. Life has a way of slipping by much more rapidly than we dream. That's why the admonition of a few years back—"Don't sweat the small stuff!"—is so important to us. Don't waste life on small things—things that in the long run do not matter. Never postpone happiness or waste the present trying to live in the past.

A final thought: *Remember the importance of the "now."* In 1913, Sir William Osler gave an address at Yale University. This was his theme: "Live neither in the past nor in the future, but let each day's work absorb all your interests, energy and enthusiasm. The best preparation for tomorrow is to do today's work superbly well."

Arnold Bennett wrote a book which became a classic in its time. He called it *How to Live on Twenty-four Hours a Day*. One idea from that book still makes the rounds: "You wake up in the morning and lo, your purse is magically filled with twenty-four hours. It is yours. It is the most precious of possessions. Its most effective use is the matter of highest urgency." That's the point of those lines from the poet:

Tomorrow's fate, though thou be wise
Thou canst not tell nor yet surmise;
Pass, therefore, not today in vain
For it will never come again.

Life needs to be lived in the "now." It takes only a moment to feel the freshness of a crisp morning or to glance at a tree laden with new snow. An evening by the fireside with family and friends, who so often want only a little attention, can be an unforgettable experience. It isn't how much time we take to "smell the roses"; it's how we use the time we have. The uncertainties of life press the question upon us. The time to start living is *now*. It may be the only living we will have time to do.

Who Needs a Witch?

On the eastern edge of the Mediterranean Sea there is a vast and fertile valley known to history as the Plain of Esdraelon. Located at the crossroads of the ancient world, this plain has often been called the Battleground of the Ages. The chariots of Egypt rolled across this valley on their way to meet the empires of the north. Armies from Nineveh, Babylon and Damascus have camped in its fields.

One night about 3,000 years ago, the valley was the scene of preparation for one of its many conflicts. An army under the leadership of a king named Saul set up camp to await battle. That evening by the fireside Saul found himself on the verge of panic. What would tomorrow bring? His thoughts turned back to other days. He was searching for something that would bring him a bit of hope. Suddenly he remembered a wise and trusted counselor who in earlier years had offered him wisdom and friendship. But somewhere along the way Saul had pushed this friend aside and forgotten him. Now the old friend was dead. That night as Saul faced the most crucial hour of his life he yearned for an opportunity to talk to this friend once more. Not far away in a little village called Endor lived an old witch who claimed the power to communicate with the dead. Slipping away in the darkness, Saul made his way to the cave where the old woman lived. "Bring me back Samuel," Saul whispered to the witch. "Let me talk to my friend once again."

The story of King Saul standing before the cave of Endor is one of the unforgettable dramas of history. Perhaps the reason is that this story reflects a circumstance common in human experience. Many times we find ourselves confronting uncertain and troubled times. We wonder if there is any way we can hear a word about the future.

Foretelling the future is an inexact science. It is possible, however, to arrange our lives so that we can get at least some insights into what tomorrow will bring. We are, you see, creatures of choice, and our choices always bring consequences. Thoughtful persons, therefore, will give serious attention to the consequences their choices bring.

There are choices, for instance, that restrict and diminish life. Kierkegaard had a story about a wild duck flying south with other ducks. Suddenly the duck noticed, in a barnyard below him, some corn that a farmer had scattered for his tame ducks. The duck fluttered down and joined the tame ducks in the barnyard. He ate the corn and decided to stay a few days, since the corn was free. He remained day after day. Spring came, and it was time for the wild ducks to fly north. The duck heard his mates calling as they went overhead. He tried to join them, but he could not fly. He had stayed too long on the ground and had lost his strength.

An athlete who refuses to practice little by little limits his opportunities. An artist who will not rehearse soon has nothing to rehearse for. A businessperson who is interested only in today's business will not be doing business tomorrow. A person who places no value on integrity and trust will be trusted with less and less. People who use their friends have no friends to use after a while. There are choices that diminish life. You don't need a conversation with a witch to discover this. You need only observe the way life works.

There is another side to this that should be remembered. There are choices that enhance life and widen its possibilities. There was a story in one of our southern papers about a man who had been released from prison several years earlier. He had been a high-school dropout and had no training for any job requiring any skills. The man was determined to start over. He got a job as a laborer and went to school at night. He took college entrance exams and enrolled in a community college. He stayed with it, and now he heads his own business. "I am amazed," he said, "at how many people will help you if they know you are trying. Doors have opened that I never dreamed were there."

It's a wise person who tests every decision with this question: Will this direction enhance my life and widen my opportunities? A positive answer to that kind of question is within the reach of everyone. Now and then someone will imagine a circumstance to be hopeless. It never is. No matter how hemmed in life may appear to be, there is always at least one step that can be taken in the right direction. It may be a small step, but the world is so arranged that if that step is taken another will become evident. Soon many other doors will appear. You don't need a witch to know about the future. The best way to know tomorrow is to make the right choices today.

At Wits' End

The other day a counselor in a large industrial firm was making his rounds through the offices of the corporate headquarters. He passed the desk of an employee who was usually cheerful and bright. That day, however, this employee sat with her face to the wall. She toyed absent-mindedly with papers and pencil. Suspecting something wrong, the counselor paused for a moment and asked, "Are you all right?" "I shouldn't be here today," was the response. "I'm at wits' end with nowhere to turn."

Said this counselor, "In a large company such as ours you encounter people like this every day—people who are living on the edge of desperation. Through the years I have tried to come up with something to say to them. I remember something I found in a book years ago: 'Some things that are wrong, if left alone, will right themselves; some things, no matter what we do, cannot be righted; and some things, if we try, can be made right.' That counselor's words are worthy of thought. All of us at times live at wits' end. How to handle the events of such days is important.

First, some things, if left alone, will right themselves. Among the oldest living things on this planet are the giant sequoia trees found on the Pacific coast. The secret of their longevity is the ability of this tree when damaged to repair itself. Foresters have discovered evidence that lightning struck many of these trees hundreds or thousands of years ago. But as soon as the lightning strike is over, the tree begins the process of repair.

Given time, a lot of things correct themselves. When Jesus of Nazareth died, he was labeled a criminal. He is not considered a criminal now. A short time before Lincoln was shot, a newspaperman called him the "original gorilla." Our estimate of Lincoln is far different now. Time has a way of correcting injustices. Right is self-authenticating.

Sometimes in the dark moments of life it helps to remember that, given time, right prevails and wrong defeats itself. Adolf Hitler promised his people an empire that would last a thousand years. He missed by 988 years. The system of slavery failed despite every effort to preserve it. On occasion all of us have been wronged. The temptation is to seek revenge. That never works. We simply inflict further injury on ourselves. The people who make it through bad times are those who know how to wait. Patience is not so much a virtue as an essential to successful living. In the long run integrity, honesty and justice prevail. There is validity in the maxim: "Truth crushed to earth will rise again."

Second, some things, no matter what we do, will not be righted. There is an old prayer that contains the line: "Give me the grace to accept

218

the things I cannot change." That's a worthy thought. It is useless to waste precious energy on things that will remain the same no matter what we do. Take the past, for instance. The poet was right when he said,

> The Moving Finger writes; and, having writ,
> Moves on: nor all your Piety nor Wit
> Shall lure it back to cancel half a Line,
> Nor all your Tears wash out a Word of it.

We may make the present or the future different, but the past stands as written. Wise is the person who accepts that and moves on.

There are also things such as handicaps that don't go away. We can work with them and compensate for them, but the handicaps stay. In one of the world's oldest books there is an account of a man who had what he called "a thorn in the flesh." "I tried in every way," he said, "to rid myself of that handicap but it remains." All of us have some physical limitation which is more or less permanent. The secret of successful living is learning to live with that limitation. That's what psychologists have in mind when they admonish us to accept ourselves. It doesn't do much good to keep measuring our gifts against those of others and envying the talents they possess. The key to life is to discover who we are, the assets we possess and how we can use these assets to compensate for our limitations. Wise indeed is the person who knows what can't be changed and moves on to other things.

Finally, there are some things that, if we try, can be made right. To these things, and to these things only, the truly wise give their energies. This, too, is in the same old prayer: "Give me the courage to change the things that I can change." There are a lot of things like that in our world. Consider our lives, for instance. Heredity may determine to an extent the broad outlines of our abilities, but within those outlines we have fabulous opportunities to develop our skills and talents. The "hand of fate" may sometimes decide where we must live, but what we do while we are there is largely up to us. Circumstances may be pressed upon us, but how we react to those circumstances is largely up to us.

A while back a line worth remembering appeared in a widely read book: "Happiness is not something you carry in your hand; it is something you carry in your heart." The point of that is clear. Tangible possessions do not guarantee happiness. Great multitudes of affluent people in our world are miserable. Happiness is an aspect of the spirit. It is a determination *we* make. It is one of those things we can have if we choose.

Living at wits' end—life doesn't have to be that way. Our lives can take on new meaning if we will learn that some things, if wrong, right themselves; that other things, no matter what we do, can't be changed; that still other things can be changed, if we try. We must give our energies, therefore, to those things that we can do something about.

The Quest for Inner Peace

About 25 years ago a widely known author published a book that contained some interesting statistics. In the last 5,600 years there have been only 292 years of general peace in the world. Since 3600 BC, 14,513 wars of major or minor importance have been fought. During these wars, slightly more than 1.2 billion people have died. In the past 3,200 years, 4,700 treaties have been made. Of these, 4,687 have been broken. The accuracy of these figures may be open to debate. If, however, they are reasonably correct, one thing is clear: our search for world peace has not been an outstanding success. The fact is, we have known astonishingly little of it.

It may be that in our time the folly of war is becoming evident. It is just possible that we will find other ways to settle our differences. But even if we achieve that goal, another problem will remain. Not only do we seek a world free of outer conflict, we also look for peace within. It may be that this latter search is of greater intensity. Pascal once said, "Man wants inner peace and only peace. He cannot wish otherwise." Pascal is saying that this quest is the motivation for all our behavior. It drives us to drink or away from it. It pushes us to seek success or to spurn it. We all look for inner peace in one way or another. The question is: *Can* we find it?

One thing must be remembered: the possibility of inner peace depends on how we define it. There are three things inner peace does not mean. *The first is escape.* A recent news story concerned a man who got fed up with people, the rat race and related problems. He bought a boat and set out across the Pacific alone. He was picked up a few weeks later. He was disillusioned and glad to see people again. "Loneliness," he said, "has its own set of problems." This man discovered a basic fact of life. When you run from one problem you always run into another. You can't run away *to* inner peace.

Second, inner peace does not mean contentment. A lot is being said these days about self-acceptance. We need to be careful about how we define that. If we are trying to say that peace within results from accepting things as they are, then that is the most dangerous kind of escapism. Historically, those persons who have found genuine inner peace have been those most dissatisfied with themselves and their world.

A long time ago a man was wrongfully imprisoned in a Roman jail. From his cell he wrote a letter to some friends. "I have learned," he said, "that whatever state I'm in, I'm to be content." But contentment to him did not mean accepting things as they were. This man used even his jail cell to help him carry on his work. When he said he was content, he meant that he would accept everything that happened to him and use it for something good. This man's resolve should be an example for everyone.

Third, inner peace does not mean outer tranquillity. Centuries ago there was a king who was haunted by difficulties. One night he wandered out to the roof of his palace to listen to the street battles being waged below. As he reflected upon all that confronted him, he uttered a sentence that is still preserved for us: "Oh, that I had the wings of a dove, that I might fly away and be at rest." That wish is a tempting one for us, too. The trouble is that it is impossible. There is no such thing as outer tranquillity. The search of all history has been for the tranquil world. We have sailed the oceans and crossed the continents. But every place has its set of problems. If inner peace is dependent upon finding outer serenity in a world free of conflict, then the peace within will always elude us.

How then do we find peace? In one of the world's oldest texts there is a curious phrase: "Peace is a gift." Reflection upon that phrase suggests that peace is not something we can seek directly. It is the byproduct of another kind of search. A student, for instance, is troubled about a final examination. The anxiety is not relieved by ignoring the examination, but by careful preparation. The more prepared the student, the more likely it is that he or she will find peace within. Peace comes that way. It is the fruit of another pursuit.

On the front of a farm calendar published years ago there was this sentence: "When you do what you are supposed to do, life becomes what it's supposed to be." There is wisdom in those words. When we give ourselves to our duty, when we live with integrity and honor, when we work at causes that are right, then our troubled and anxious spirits come to rest. Peace is not an impossible dream. It's a present reality for those who try to live life as it needs to be lived.

221

Life-Changing Words

Not long ago, a funeral was held in a large southern city. In attendance were hundreds of people, many of whom had come great distances. The funeral was for a man who had chosen to be a teacher rather than to pursue the more lucrative career for which he had been trained. Few people, however, had touched more lives than this man. He was among the most widely respected community leaders in America.

One of the persons speaking at the funeral commented on the way in which this teacher had influenced people. "He was always interested in others. It might be a phone call or a note, but on regular occasions you could depend on hearing from him. His interest in me changed my life."

About 20 years ago, a Scottish writer, Dr. William Barclay, wrote an essay entitled "Life-Changing Words." He based the essay on a quotation from the Old Testament: "I have been given a tongue that I may know how to sustain with a word him that is weary." Said Barclay, "People are seldom changed by force or power. They can be changed by words of encouragement." That is a thought worthy of reflection.

Never underestimate the power of the spoken word. Adolf Hitler's oratory almost brought the world to its knees. He might have succeeded had not Winston Churchill's equally inspired voice lifted the world to its feet. Words make a difference. They can inspire as well as defeat and destroy. Consider the words of *congratulation.*

In an article on one of America's leading chief executive officers, a news reporter made an interesting comment: "This man always gives credit to those who deserve it. He will take time even from the busiest day to recognize an associate's achievement." One can understand the secret of that CEO's success. Few things encourage a person more than for someone to call, write or visit and say, "You have done a good job." That's especially true if the road has been difficult and the journey long. It's a wise person who takes time to congratulate another for special achievement. It affects the lives of all concerned.

A few years ago, the students in a college psychology class decided to greet their professor with concerned expressions for his health. Whenever they saw him they would say, "You are not looking well," or "You look tired." At first the professor countered these comments by asserting that he felt fine. But gradually his replies became less positive. Finally he actually became ill. What we say affects the lives of others. We can make people ill. We can also strengthen and encourage them. Consider the words of *appreciation.*

The president of an international civic club told of leaving his office after a long, hard day. It was raining. Out in the rain he found a small boy who was crying. He asked the boy about his problem. The boy said his father had sent him to the store but he had lost the money. "I am afraid to go home," said the boy. The man pulled some money from his pocket and gave it to the boy. The lad ran hurriedly down the street. At the corner he stopped and came back. He paused only long enough to whisper, "Gee, Mister, I wish you were my dad." The man said he was so overwhelmed by the boy's gratitude that he walked a mile in the rain that night to look for other boys who might need help. How important words of appreciation are. They give new vitality to life.

Finally, there are words of *sympathy*. No one makes it through this world without walking through dark valleys. Life puts on all of us its sorrows as well as its joys. There is a sense in which each person bears his or her burden alone. Franz Schubert once said that no one really understands the grief of another. The old spiritual had it right: "You gotta walk that lonesome valley by yourself."

It does, however, bring courage and strength to know that others are thinking of you. In my work I often hear people say, "I never knew how important my friends are." Or, "I couldn't have made it without my friends." These are testimonies to the importance of extending a caring word to someone else. Such words need not be eloquent or studied. All that is needed is the simple phrase, "I care."

Life-changing words! They are immensely important. Countless people are struggling with life. Many have worked diligently to obtain only a small victory. Others are depressed and discouraged by fate or misfortune. A helpful word either from or to another could alter their lives. Never be hesitant to share a word of congratulation, gratitude or sympathy with another. The people who express these concerns make an interesting discovery: Like the harvest of planted seeds, such thoughtfulness is always returned.

Shortcuts to Paradise

There is an old book tucked away in the great literature of the world that contains the wisdom of a people who lived thousands of years ago. The book, known as the Book of Proverbs, is a valuable resource for those who would learn from the experiences of the past. It covers a variety of subjects ranging from the problems of being a parent to the ingredients necessary for achieving a successful life. Not all of the messages in this book have meanings that are readily evident. Some of them require a lot of thought. One of the most provocative messages reads in this fashion: "There is a way that seemeth right to a man, but the end thereof is death."

The author of this sentence may well be suggesting that some approaches to life seem to have great promise, but in the end they destroy us. He admonishes us to look carefully at the roads we take. It's mighty easy to be deceived.

For one thing, we often succumb to the attraction of the effortless. Several years ago an American author wrote a book containing an essay entitled, "Shortcuts to Paradise." The essay dealt with humanity's persistent attempt to find utopia by easy roads. Evidence of this tendency is everywhere. The standard advice given is "Hang loose," "Play it cool," "Don't sweat it," "Take the shortcut." We buy computers to help us think. We use power equipment to do our work. We pay public officials to perform our civic duties and hire actors and athletes to entertain us.

This, of course, is not all bad. It is this yearning for the easy way that brought us modern medicine, the Industrial Revolution and the electronic age. Someone has said that the machine age is the result of our inherent tendency to be lazy.

It must be said, however, that most of our finest destinations can't be reached via the shortcut. A strong body and a trained mind are always the result of toil and struggle. Remember the old Spanish blessing, "May God deny you peace and give you glory." Complacency seldom produces anything worthwhile. Great living comes to those who are willing to pay the price. History's heroes were always tormented people: Lincoln, Gandhi, Moses, Jesus, and the list goes on. We gain the high ground by struggle, not by the easy road.

We can also be deceived by symptoms. This, too, is a perfectly human reaction—the attempt to ease the pain without getting at the cause. Many years ago someone asked a tired, bored Englishman why he spent so much time at the pub. "It's the quickest way out of London!" came the caustic reply. A lot of us travel such roads. We imagine we cure our ills by suppressing the pain. This is why Jesus was crucified and Socrates poisoned. If we dislike the news, we want to kill the messenger.

A driver's license examiner was giving a test to new motorists. Among the questions was this one: "What is the most dangerous part of a car?" One youngster wrote, "The driver." That's a good insight. Problems are resolved when you deal with causes. That's true whether it is a personal problem, a business problem or a family difficulty.

A *third reason for being deceived is our tendency to be preoccupied with the present.* It is an old and well-known parable, that story of a wealthy builder who one day called in his assistant. "Jim, I'm leaving on an extensive trip. I want you to build a house. Here are the blueprints, and here is a check to cover the costs. Spare no expense. Make it the best we've ever built." When his employer was gone the assistant thought he saw a way to gain a fortune. Wherever they could not be seen, he put in cheap and inferior materials and put the money he saved in his pocket. One day the employer returned and went to see the house. "How do you like it, Jim?" the employer asked. "It's magnificent, sir," came the reply. "I'm glad you like it, Jim," said the employer. "It belongs to you. I wanted to express my gratitude for all you have done for me."

A long time ago the Great Teacher told a story about two carpenters. One was wise; he took a long time to anchor his house on a good foundation. The other carpenter was foolish; he was a man in a hurry. "Foundations are not important," he thought, "except in a storm, and a storm may never come." So he built his house on an insecure footing. But the storm did come and his house went down.

Building a life is much like building a house. We have to live in what we build. We can shave the corners and take the shortcuts, but that road always ends badly. Wise is the person who takes his or her own right road, no matter how steep and hard it may seem. Paradise is only available to those who dare to climb the heights and scale the high mountains. It's a good prayer, that Spanish blessing: Grant us not peace, but glory.

What Keeps Us Going?

Two days before Christmas 1986, Dick Rutan and Jeana Yeager landed a small, fragile airplane in the Mojave Desert in California. They had just completed a nonstop flight around the world. While this was not the first such flight, it was the first global atmospheric trip to be made without refueling.

Upon the completion of their voyage the two aviators were interviewed by newspeople from around the earth. When asked how they were able to endure more than nine days in a cockpit the size of a phone booth, one of the team declared: "At times we almost gave up. But we kept going because of the people who had helped us and the unconquerable faith that we could complete the journey."

The question posed by those newspeople is age-old. How does one keep going in a world where the roads are long and hard? That is a question all of us ask at times.

In one of the world's oldest books there is a story about a man named Nehemiah. Nehemiah had been taken from his homeland by a conquering army. He was kept in exile for years until one day a benevolent ruler released him. Immediately, Nehemiah returned to his native land. There he found his hometown a shambles. Nehemiah set out to rebuild the city. There were people in that land who for various reasons did not want Nehemiah to succeed. They came by at regular intervals to stop the project. "Come down, come down," they demanded. The world still remembers Nehemiah's answer to their taunts: "I am doing a great work and I cannot come down." From this ancient story come some insights for those who find it difficult to keep going.

For one thing, this story reminds us that to keep going we must believe in ourselves. In the 1950s there was published a provocative little book entitled *Through the Valley of Shadows*. The book was written by a priest who had been a leader in the Nazi resistance movement. Said the author, "You could tell the difference between those who had deep convictions about themselves and those who did not. People who had deep-seated beliefs about the meaning of life, who knew who they were, were simply not afraid anymore."

Countless people who have learned how to keep going report that at least one of the ingredients for endurance is an understanding of oneself and the meaning of one's life. They believe that every life has a purpose. They know that not one of us can do everything but that all of us can do something.

Another thing we must have to keep going is hope. In that story about Nehemiah several things are worth noting. One of them is that Nehemiah's dream of rebuilding may not have been possible, but

226

Nehemiah believed it could be done. It was this hope that kept him going even though he worked alone. One of America's most distinguished psychologists wrote recently, "Destroy hope and civilization will perish. Keep it alive and humanity will survive." That's profoundly true.

This is a thought that needs to be remembered by all of us. If we would have people succeed, then we must help them believe that they can be successful. This is true in our families, our businesses, wherever people look to us for guidance. We must never lose hope ourselves, and we must not let those about us do so.

A third thing that helps us keep going is a compelling sense of purpose. One of the runners in the last Olympic Games was heard to say, "There is more fun in running the race than in winning it." This may not be entirely true, but one thing is clear: those who can see the goalpost are more likely to have endurance. There is nothing like a sense of purpose to give us a second wind. Nehemiah knew what he was about. Despite his critics he would not turn back.

Sometimes it helps to break long journeys into measurable steps. Wise is the parent who helps offspring establish concrete, possible objectives. Wise is the business leader or manager who helps employees understand the whole picture and how they themselves fit into the larger effort. People do not fare well when they don't know what they are about.

It's been a long time since the days of Nehemiah, but his story still speaks to us. It may be tough at times to keep going, but it's a lot easier if you believe in yourself and if you can find a compelling purpose. Only then can you run any race in life with patience and hope.

Fire Makes the Steel

Several years ago there was a story in one of America's papers about a man who accidentally touched off an explosion and blew himself to pieces. When he awoke in the hereafter he looked around and said, "I am going to like it here. I can rest all the time. I'm glad the accident happened." As he sat enjoying himself an attendant came up and asked, "Is there anything I can do for you?" The man replied, "No, I have everything I could wish for!" About a thousand years later, the man was becoming restless—he had so little activity—when he spotted the attendant again. He said, "I believe I would like to play golf." "Sorry," said the attendant, "we don't have a golf course here." "Well," responded the man, "let me go over there and work in the garden." "I'm sorry," said the attendant. "Our guests are not permitted to work in the garden." "All right," said the man, "I'll just go gather some apples." "You can't do that either," declared the attendant. The man was furious. "See here, I don't understand. No golf, no gardening and I'm not to gather fruit. If I'm not allowed to do anything, what's a heaven for?" "Mister," said the attendant, "you are not in heaven!"

It's easy to see the point of that parable. Someone has said that the only thing worse than having too much to do is having nothing to do. Sometimes we imagine work to be a curse. That thought, however, usually comes to us when we are harassed by crowded schedules and too many demanding responsibilities. In our better and more sober moments we recognize that our work affords us rewards far beyond the dollars we receive as compensation.

Reflect for a moment on two things:

First, it is work that gives meaning to our lives. Long ago a poet wrote:

When the twilight has fallen on gray
And all of life is complete
They know who work
If rest is sweet.

Those lines suggest that there are byproducts resulting from our labors. It should be added that sweet rest is not the only one.

Many years ago there was a story about a group of natives who wanted to honor their doctor. The doctor had given his life to serving people in primitive lands. The people were asked to bring gifts. One man traveled for miles to the celebration. When he arrived he presented the doctor with a small wooden bowl his family had carved. The other people who lived nearby had given the doctor far more expensive gifts. But the man was not embarrassed. As he presented the bowl to the doctor, he said with great satisfaction: "Long walk is part of the gift." The man was right. His life, if not invested in the gift, was invested in the walk. And in that he found a sense of well-being. That's often one of the results of one's labors.

Some of us may have work that is so routine that it seems meaningless. If that should be true, then the business of life is to find ways to give our work meaning. Sometimes this can be accomplished by discovering how our work can fit into the total scheme of things. Back in the New Testament there is a story about a man named Barnabas. Barnabas was an associate of one of the giants of human history, the Apostle Paul. Barnabas traveled with Paul, but Paul was so talented that Barnabas had little to do. I am sure he wondered if his life counted for anything. One day, however, Barnabas found in their traveling party a young man named Mark. Mark was erratic and undependable. But Barnabas worked with Mark, and as a result Mark eventually became one of the really indispensable citizens of the ancient world.

It has been rightly said that if your life is worthwhile, it is not because you found it that way, it is because you made it that way. Not many of us find jobs that shape history. All of us *can* find vocations that we can make count for something if we work at them. There are always opportunities to make contributions and thus find satisfaction. The real question of life is not how to find a job that counts, but rather how to make the job you have count.

A second thought: It is out of the struggle of work that we find our best selves. There are many things to be gained from work, and they are more valuable than monetary compensation. There are a lot of people in the marketplace these days—and not because of salary needs. Indeed, research suggests that for most people money is not the primary consideration. Their rewards have to do with such things as the satisfaction derived from working and the need to count for something. The struggle involved in honest toil leaves a good mark on human character.

Several years ago a New York minister surveyed his congregation, asking what experiences had been the most meaningful to them. The results were not unexpected. The people usually listed the hard roads they had traveled. It is through struggle that sturdy character is achieved.

Robert Browning wrote these words:

> *I walked a mile with pleasure.*
> *She chatted all the way,*
> *But left me none the wiser*
> *For all she had to say.*

> *I walked a mile with sorrow,*
> *And ne'er a word said she;*
> *But, oh, the things I learned from her*
> *When sorrow walked with me!*

The poet had in mind the lessons that come through hardship, but the messages apply in other places. Honest labor can be used to pay a dividend.

In a southwestern city there is a man who once had a terrible speech defect. The only job he could find was as the stock clerk in a large chain store. But he learned the merchandise and practiced meeting customers. He has become one of the company's highest executives. On his desk he keeps this sign: "Where there is no pain, there is no gain." That statement may not be either terribly original or completely true, but the point is worth a little thought. As steel is tempered by the fire, so are we tempered by our toil.

Things That Are Certain

The speaker had their attention and achieving that wasn't easy. College graduation exercises always seem to have speeches, but not many people are interested in what is being said. Most graduation addresses are devoted to challenging the new graduates to take the problems of the world and solve them. This speaker, however, had chosen a different theme. He titled his address, "Things I Know for Certain." The students tuned in immediately. In a world where moorings are constantly shifting, these students wanted to know if there was anything dependable. The graduation speaker that day identified three things.

First, said the speaker, life is short.

Today in America, the average person can expect to live in excess of 70 years. This is a longer average lifetime than any people in history have had. But this extended number of years doesn't take from us the feeling that life is short. Even those who live the longest discover in retrospect that the days have slipped by at an incredible pace. Indeed, the longer we live the more compressed time seems to be. It is not uncommon to hear an older person say, "What has happened to the years? They have gone by at a terrific speed."

It is because our years seem so limited that we make every effort to preserve our youth. We want to slow the race, but it seems to get faster as we near the finish line. We search for ways to push back the boundaries and extend our days. We try all sorts of health programs designed to prolong our stay here. We even look with interest at gadgets that promise to add to our years. A Swedish chemist, a few years ago, came up with a special metal bracelet designed to make people live longer. The bracelet sold well until the chemist died at 48. Life *is* short. It's short even to those who live the longest.

Second, said the speaker, the most important moment in life is now.

Long ago the Great Teacher said to his people, "I must work while it is yet day. The night comes and no one can work." That's but another way of saying that since life is short, if there is something that should be done, we need to do it now. This is the reason the graduation speaker reminded his young friends of the importance of the *now*. When you are young, life seems without limits. But very quickly we reach the point at which the days and weeks run together. We have such a short time to get what life has to offer. If we miss a day, it's gone forever.

On the front page of a western newspaper there was this sentence: "If you are not happy now, you never will be." That's a point worthy of reflection. Too many people live their lives in the future tense. We imagine we will be happy when we get our next promotion, when the children are grown, when we retire or when we reach some other goal. But people who are waiting for tomorrow to be happy always discover that tomorrow never comes. We are happy now or we never will be. Life must be lived in the now.

Finally, we make our own decisions or time will make them for us.

There is a story about Lou Gehrig, who one day let the umpire call the third strike on him. It was the last inning of a crucial game. As Gehrig threw down his bat, he seemed to be muttering to the umpire. This was totally out of character for Gehrig. A reporter asked him what he was complaining about to the umpire. Gehrig replied, "I was not complaining to the umpire. I simply said to him that I'd give a thousand dollars for a chance at that last ball again."

There is food for thought here. Wait too long in making a decision and time will make it for you. John Oxenham once wrote some thoughtful lines:

> *But once I pass this way and then no more.*
> *But once, and then the silent door*
> *Swings on its hinges, opens, closes*
> *And no more I pass this way.*

Life is like a river with streams branching off along the way. Our lives are as tiny rafts with no power except to steer. We are constantly passing opportunities to take a different channel. If we fail to make a choice, time and the river make it for us.

The key to successful living is to make our own choices rather than allow our direction to be decided by default. It's a serious mistake to allow chance to determine what our lives are to be. Life is too precious to be used that way. If a business decision should be made, make it now. If there is a personal crisis to confront, face it today. If there are friendships that need to be strengthened, or a mistake that needs to be corrected, there is no better time for action than now. Maybe we just need to take some time to smell the flowers. Today is the best day we will ever have to do what needs to be done. Life is much too short to be wasted in inaction. We need to get on with what should be done, for the "night does come."

Hearing the Small Voices

Many years ago there was a young man who enrolled at a famous German university. The boy had an inquiring mind and a compelling curiosity. He toyed with ideas that are considered unacceptable by the responsible people of his day. One day in a class session the lad began exploring some of his radical thoughts. The professor became so impatient with the young man that he sent him from the room. The boy never quite recovered from the professor's harsh treatment. Out of his hurt he began to formulate some strange theories. His writings may have had long-range effects on history. There are those who believe that Adolf Hitler was profoundly influenced by the thoughts of Friedrich Nietzsche, the young man who was expelled from class by an impatient college professor.

Someday a qualified historian needs to take a long look at the past and uncover the origins of the great movements that have altered history. In almost every case the historian will find that such movements began with small events that are almost lost from the record. Many years ago a French physician was watching some children at play. One of the children began to tap on a board with a small stone. At the other end of his plank another child listened. The doctor continued to mull over what he had seen. Out of that reflection came the invention of the stethoscope, one of the primary tools of modern medicine.

For a long time tires were made of solid rubber without inner cushions of air. While such tires were much more comfortable than metal or wood, the ride was still unbearably rough. One day a man was watching his son ride his bicycle over cobblestone streets. Seeking some way to make the tires absorb more shock, the man came up with the idea of an inner lining made of canvas. In that inner lining he pumped a quantity of air. John Dunlop didn't know that day that his invention would have a lasting effect on history. Today the world rides on compressed air encased in rubber tires.

If the records of the past suggest anything, they shoud remind us of the importance of little things. Most of the time our lives are not changed by gigantic events but by happenings so small that we almost miss them. Centuries ago there was a minor official in a small Roman province in Asia Minor. One day the local courts sent a case to him for review. A carpenter from a nearby village had been charged with civil disobedience. The lower court found the carpenter guilty. The Roman official was supposed to review the case, but he felt that it was of such little consequence that he didn't need to be involved. He turned the matter back to the lower court for disposition. Pilate, that Roman governor, did not know that day that his decision would affect history forever. The carpenter from Nazareth would become the

233

most powerful person of all time. We date our calendars from the year of his birth.

Recently a widely known business consultant led a seminar for middle-management people. In one of his lectures he made this observation: "Most managers want to handle major decisions and leave the details to others. We need to remember that most major decisions are finally made by those who have handled the details." That observation may not be completely accurate. Every human endeavor needs someone to set overall directions. But it is true that more often than not the people who set such directions have earned that right by handling smaller things. People who are careful about little things can be trusted to handle larger things.

We need to remember also that unless the smaller things are cared for there may be no larger decisions to be made. Success hinges on giving attention to little things. Businesses survive on such tiny matters as satisfied customers—customers who are carefully treated with courtesy and respect. Factories stay in business by paying attention to small parts made and fitted with precision. Sloppy workmanship will eventually destroy the largest company. Homes are knitted together by small deeds of kindness. Friendships are sustained by those who work at meriting trust and confidence. In life it is the little things that count.

There is a story about a little boy who, one night at dinner, suddenly picked up his plate and smashed it on the floor. His mother sent him upstairs to his room. The next evening at dinner the father said to the family: "I want you to hear something. Last night I discovered I had left my dictating machine on during dinner. By chance I recorded our conversation just before Johnny threw his plate on the floor. Listen to what went on." The father turned on the recorder. There were the sounds of laughter and small talk. Then, in the background, could be heard a tiny voice, "Pass the butter!" No one seemed to hear the small voice so it came again, "Please, pass the butter!" Still the laughter and talk continued. Again came the wee voice, not much louder, *"Please pass the butter!"* Nothing happened. Finally there was the sound of the crashing plate.

Life is filled with tiny voices often lost beneath the noise and clatter of a busy world. The people who manage life successfully are those who listen carefully for the wee voices and who are alert for the small things. Never overlook the details. Someday, when you least expect it, one of the tiny things could change your life.

Friendly Persuasion

Several years ago a national consulting firm asked some of America's leading corporations what quality they sought most as they selected managerial people. Contrary to what many expected, the quality sought most was not skill in business, sales or technical know-how. The first quality wanted in managers was the ability to work with people. All other skills, said the respondents, are of secondary importance when compared with the skills involved in working well with others.

It is often said that the major hindrance to success in business is the "people problem." The persons who function best at the management level are those persons who are able to bring out the best in other people. Consequently, most corporations plan management training for their employees. This training includes specialized courses in the motivation and handling of people. Such skills are of crucial importance to those who aspire to leadership positions. Most often these courses require knowledge of intricate and complicated theories. There are, however, a few simple principles which all of us can use to great advantage if we want to improve our interpersonal relationships.

The first principle is "imputation."

Webster defines "imputation" as ascribing to others a fault or a virtue. A less formal definition is this: Imputation suggests that the behavior of people is determined in part by our expectations of them. This principle may not be exact in its application, but it is sufficiently precise to merit attention. People tend to conform to what is expected of them.

A long time ago the Great Teacher demonstrated the power of imputation. He gathered about him a dozen men who have brought about more changes than perhaps any other persons in history. The men he chose were not of exceptional talent or of high station. They were ordinary people. The secret to the success of these men was the trust the Great Teacher placed in them and the expectations he had of them.

One of America's finest parliamentarians was once asked what he considered the most important principle in *Robert's Rules of Order.* He declared, "The most important rule is not necessarily in the book. It is this: People are more important than rules. When people believe they count for something and their ideas are important they usually rise to their best." Good managers are always those who place the highest value on their associates. They look for the strengths and abilities of those who work with them and then expect of them their finest. More often than not these associates come through.

Imputation is important for those who want to be leaders. Management by threat and intimidation seldom produces lasting results. Managers who trust people to do their best and expect it of them are seldom disappointed.

The second principle involved in working with people can be labeled "exemplification."

There is an interesting scene in a popular book on American folklore. A grandfather is sharing some of his wisdom with his grandson. "Never be lazy in front of people," he declares. "It pure riles hardworking folks to see a fellow having fun at anything. This is why fishing was invented. A fellow who is fishing can be lazy without anyone knowing it." There is truth in this homespun wisdom. Managers generally get from us no more than they ask of themselves.

It is said that when Napoleon was trying to conquer Europe, he appointed Marshal Ney to hold a certain line while he gave attention to other fronts. The marshal tried, but he couldn't hold back the enemy attacks. All his soldiers were killed or captured, and the marshal barely escaped with his life. Napoleon demanded an explanation. Unlike others who were called on the carpet by Napoleon, the marshal seemed calm and serene. "I've done my best," he said to the emperor. "How do I know you have done your best?" inquired Napoleon. Ney responded with complete confidence, "Sir, I would ask of you no more than I have done!" It is easy to understand why Ney was a leader of excellence. He always asked as much of himself as he did of others.

It has been said that the successful manager says, "Let's do it together." The manager who fails says, "You do it." Success says "we"; failure says "I." Success gives credit to others; failure takes personal credit for achievements. Success takes the blame for errors and mistakes; failure places the blame on others. Success leads by precept and example; failure manages by threat and intimidation.

In one of the world's oldest books there is an instruction worthy of thought. "Why do you behold the splinter in your brother's eye and ignore the plank in your own?" Or, put another way, "Beware of finding fault with another until you have taken a look at yourself."

There *may* have been a time when people could be treated as animals and motivated by fear or force. Our world, however, is different. Today people respond best when we trust them and set before them the right example. The best managers are those who know how to use the tools of friendly persuasion.

236

The Way the Cookie Crumbles

Near the southern tip of the Sinai peninsula there is a small chain of mountains known in ancient times as Mount Horeb. It is rough and desolate country with arid valleys and rocky mountainsides. One day long ago a man came to those mountains. He was nervous, despondent, afraid. He had been running for days, hiding out in the caves of that deserted country. A few weeks before, he had been involved in a disagreement with a powerful queen. The queen threatened his life. Believing himself completely without friends or defenders, the man fled for his life. For more than a hundred miles he roamed those hills.

Finally, completely exhausted, he sat down to rest. That day something happened to this man. We do not know exactly what. He may have had a dream or a supernatural vision. In any event, he heard a voice asking, "Why are you so despondent?" The man replied, "My life has been threatened. I have no one on my side." The voice spoke to him again: "Get up and return to your home. There are many things you can do. There are 7,000 people in your hometown who will be on your side." There are lessons in this story worth remembering.

One of these lessons is this: *It is possible in the face of hardship to surrender a cause too easily.* This ancient man thought there was nothing more he could do, so he gave up. That is a common circumstance among us. It happens every day to hosts of people. They surrender at the slightest resistance. If these folk would only remember that nothing worthwhile is accomplished without the risk of hardship. Remember the Beat Generation? Someone has suggested that the current crop is the Beaten Generation. That's likely an exaggeration, but it is not far-fetched. There are many people who want success but do not want to pay the price for it. Figuratively speaking, a lot of us wander in the desert, driven there because life in the real world seems too hard.

There is a second idea in our story: *No circumstance is hopeless.* There is always a handle we can work with if we look for it. We are not bound in hopeless determinism. There is a way out of every situation if we look for the door.

Sometimes our problems are so great that a solution seems impossible. One of America's best-known ministers made an observation recently. He said that gray is not a basic color. Gray comes from mixing white and black. If, in other words, we take gray paint and look at it under magnification, we would see particles of black and white. The point this minister was making is this: We can break our larger problems into smaller ones and find handles that will allow us to do something about the total circumstance.

237

There is a timeless proverb that suggests an interesting thought: "Things turn out for the best for those who make the best of the way things turn out." No problem is so large we can't do *something* about it. Sometimes we need to break our larger problem into its smaller components. When we do, handles begin to appear. The interesting thing is that as we work with one handle, other handles become visible.

There are no hopeless people and no hopeless circumstances. People who manage life successfully do so not because they live in an ideal world. Rather, they take a less-than-ideal world and transform it into what it can become. No one need spend a lifetime on Mount Horeb.

There is one more thing in the story of the ancient man. *As we work at our problems, other hands work with us.*

Anyone who has worked with carpentry tools knows that it is far more difficult to drive a nail in a ceiling than in a floor. The reason is simple. When we drive a nail overhead the forces of gravity are against us. If we drive a nail into the floor, then these gravitational forces work with us. All of life is like this. There are forces in the world that support us if we give these forces an opportunity. Honesty, truthfulness and integrity finally prevail. Dishonesty, selfishness and wrong eventually defeat themselves. If we take the right road and stay with it long enough, we eventually come out at the right place.

The lessons in this ancient story are worth remembering. As we struggle with our problems, we need to be reminded not to surrender too soon. Every worthwhile achievement has a price that must be paid. We need to remember, too, that there is always at least one handle with which we may grasp our problem if we look for it.

Finally, if we seek worthy goals, there are forces in the universe that work with us. No one needs to live on Mount Horeb in despair. There is hope for every person in every circumstance.

A New Look at Home

There was a movie on national television recently about a husband and wife who were having marital difficulties. One day while his wife was away with the children, the husband removed all their possessions from their home and claimed them for his own. He declared he would give no support to his wife and children until forced to do so by the courts. The legal battle went on for months. The man's family became desperate. They searched trash heaps and rummage sales to find cast-off furniture for their modest apartment. Finally the divorce was granted. Because of a quirk in the law, the man was allowed to keep most of what the couple had owned.

One day after the divorce the father came by to visit his children. He told the kids he was now ready for them to come live with him. Bundling them into his luxurious auto, he took them off to see his new penthouse. "This," he said, "is the home I've been preparing for us." The children wandered about for a while. They remembered the hard times they had had trying to get by without their father's help. "Please, may we leave?" they asked. "We want to go home." In the final scene of the movie the father was standing alone in his elegant apartment. In gaining the things that mattered least he had lost the things that mattered most.

You may remember the dramatic story of a boy who one day got tired of the discipline of home. Taking his share of his father's estate, he went down to a bustling city to live in the fast lane. After a time of extravagant living his money ran out. The only job he could find was as the caretaker of a swine farm. His new job was not a happy one. He began to reflect on what he had left behind. When seen from the pigpen, the home he thought so terrible was not so bad after all. This story is nearly 2,000 years old, but the lesson is timeless.

There is here the vivid reminder that perspective establishes the relative importance of things. Several years ago one of America's finest religious leaders, Bishop Herbert Welch, died at the age of 105. In one of his last interviews, Welch said, "In the waning light of day you see more clearly the things that are important." That's profoundly true. The things that seem important in the sunny morning of life have a way of fading when you get a better look at them from a little farther down the road.

Caring for a family can be a dreadful drag when you are trying to get ahead in business or manage a successful social calendar. Children must be looked after. Someone has to drive them to scouts, music lessons or school functions. You are always under pressure to attend PTA or church activities. On occasion you must neglect business opportunties to attend Little League or dance recitals. The temptation is to go single or stay that way. But in later years no one is quite so lonely as the person who has never had time for anyone but himself. Bishop Welch was right. At waning time you see what is important.

The importance of family and friends, however, is not just reserved for the evening of life. Sometimes the storms of life can put things in perspective. Think about that runaway boy. Things were great for a while, but one day a depression hit. The boy tramped the streets all day long looking for work. Everywhere he went the vacancies had just been filled. At night there were no friends or family to offer consolation. He huddled in a farmer's barn trying to keep warm. Morning came, bleak and cold. The boy muttered to himself: "What a fool I've been. Life was tough at my father's house, but at least there are people there who care."

Life gets complicated for everyone now and then. Out there in the storm we can get battered and beaten. We live in that kind of world. The desperate need in such times is for a shelter and a retreat. Our families and friends can be that for us if we have worked at these relationships thoughtfully and carefully. Home and friends offer acceptance. Here are the people who care for us, not for the victories we've won, the successes we've attained or the honors we've received. Fortunate is the person who has such a hiding place in the time of a storm.

Handling Murphy's Law

No one knows exactly where it originated. We call it Murphy's Law of Perversity, and it reads as follows:

> *Nothing is as easy as it looks.*
> *Everything takes longer than you expect.*
> *If there is a possibility of several things going wrong, the one that goes wrong first will be the one that will do the most damage.*
> *Left to themselves, all things go from bad to worse.*
> *If you work on a thing long enough to improve it, it will break.*
> *If you think everything will be okay, you have surely overlooked something.*
> *Mother Nature always sides with the hidden flaw.*

Most of us at times believe we are the victims of Murphy's Law. Sometimes we even imagine that these perverse principles prevail universally. But despite Murphy's Law there are people who manage to live happily even in adversity. How do these folk achieve this? That's a question worth exploring, especially if at times you feel depressed and discouraged. There are three things you need to remember.

First, *happiness is an attitude of the heart and not a function of circumstance.*

A thoughtful poet once wrote: "Two men looked out from prison bars. One saw mud, the other saw stars." The truth of that observation is evident to any student of life. Happy people are found in every conceivable circumstance and at all economic and social levels.

Recently a news reporter in a southern city wrote a series of articles on the street people in his city. In order to research his story he decided to live as they lived for a two-week period. He adopted their mode of dress, let his beard grow, and left all his money and credit cards at home. He made some interesting discoveries. Among them was the fact that many of the people seemed to be happy despite their circumstances. "I found," he said, "that there were about as many happy people living in the streets as there are in affluent suburbia, where I live." It is difficult to imagine how people who have nothing and who live daily at the mercy of the elements can be happy. Perhaps the poet was right. Perhaps there are people who always see the stars, even from behind prison bars.

This isn't to suggest that we should be content with our circumstances no matter how difficult they are. We should strive constantly to improve our lot. Indeed, the great discoveries—the wheel, electricity, the internal combustion engine, radio, television, etc.—have resulted from the work of someone who was discontented with the way things were. We do need to remember, however, that we can be happy in any circumstance. Happiness is not a function of circumstance. It is an attitude of the heart.

Second, *the ability to cope with life depends upon the philosophy we have about it.*

One of America's largest corporations conducted some experiments with assembly-line workers. Two groups were chosen at random and given identical tasks. One group was told that they were a part of a planned study. The other group was told nothing. Both groups were then subjected to stringent working conditions such as poor heat, improper light and long hours. The informed group showed little change in production, while the other group slipped far behind. Those conducting the study concluded that informed people soon develop a sense of purpose that rapidly shows in their work.

Karl Menninger tells in one of his books about a group of doctors who survived a Nazi slave labor camp while their fellow prisoners, living in identical circumstances, died by the thousands. The doctors organized themselves into a medical society. They met regularly, gave papers and swapped medical information to be used in their practices when the war was over. During night hours they treated as best they could their fellow prisoners who were ill. Said Dr. Menninger, "Those doctors were kept alive by hope and purpose." Dean Samuel Miller of Harvard was right when he wrote: "Life without a philosophy of life is a wheel without a hub. What we believe gives our lives perspective, motivation and direction."

Finally, *happiness comes to those who learn to work and wait.*

There is an old proverb that says, "If you take the right road and hold it, after a while you come out at the right place." Ours is a cause-and-effect world, despite the claims of Murphy's Law. If you push the right buttons you can get predictable results.

William Cowper, who lived a sad and finally tragic life, often suffered from "seasons of madness." He never understood why this was his lot. He was sustained, however, by an unfaltering trust. This is what he wrote:

God moves in a mysterious way
His wonders to perform.
He plants his footsteps in the sea,
And rides upon the storm.
Ye fearful saints, fresh courage take;
The clouds ye so much dread
Are big with mercy, and shall break
In blessings on your head.

Sometimes the events of life are bewildering. It isn't always easy to know the direction or determine the significance of what's happening to us. We walk a lot of dark roads and wonder why so many painful and difficult things seem to push us down. The greatest resource we can have is the deep and certain faith that if we have taken the right road, we will come out at the right place. There is, as Benjamin Franklin put it, a "hand that governs in human affairs." Murphy's Law is not universal. If we give life our best, somewhere, sometime, the seeds we sow will bring the right harvest. We can stake our lives on that.

Things Worth Keeping

One of America's best-known columnists wrote an article on the ordeal of moving from one home to another. He said one evening some friends came by to help them with their packing. Sometime during the evening, one of the family lost something no one seemed to find. After a long search, the man's wife declared, "I believe I threw that away. I didn't think we would ever need it again."

Anyone who has ever moved understands that predicament. When you are packing for a new home, you realize that everything cannot be taken. Some decisions are fairly easy; the choice is between something of value and something that is worthless. But how do you choose between two things when each has value? That's a dilemma confronted not only in moving; it is also a dilemma of life. How do you make such decisions in life? Three things need to be said.

Wise living depends upon finding a standard against which values may be measured. There is an old and silly story about a fellow who was riding his motorcycle on a cold day. The zipper on his jacket was broken, so the rider stopped and put the jacket on backward to shield him from the wind. A bit later, the rider had an accident and was knocked unconscious. He stayed in the hospital for weeks. The doctors said the boy wasn't hurt much in the wreck, but he was severely injured when the policeman tried to turn his head around to match his jacket.

Standards are essential as reference points. A man's coat is supposed to zip up the front and the policeman made his judgment against that custom. If the standard is wrong, then the resulting decision will be wrong.

We never escape the need for reference points. A great teacher declared that we cannot serve two masters. A divided allegiance always creates tension. We never find peace until life is brought together under a single flag. Most of the stress and anxiety of our age results from our failure to choose one flag.

A second thought: *All of us face the constant necessity to choose values.* Minton Johnson tells about a young woman who told him she wanted to be a doctor but was troubled because she was spending her life at another job. Johnson said that after a conversation he discovered the girl's problem. She liked beautiful clothes, going out every evening and engaging in all the enjoyable activities that go with being young. These were all pleasant things, but she needed to forgo them for a medical education. In short, the young lady couldn't establish her values.

There is a phrase often used in business management seminars: "correlated objectives." The phrase implies that some goals and objectives are compatible. There may be nothing wrong with many of our goals when viewed separately. It's when we try to put such objectives together that they present us with trouble. An Old Testament writer declared, "There is a season for everything under the sun." This writer is right on course. There is a time for all things and we must choose those times. Sometimes we have to set aside one objective while we reach toward another.

Much of the tension in our lives is the result of our failure to choose correlated objectives. We rarely have to make a choice between the valuable and the worthless. Most often we must choose between two things of equal value. But choose we must, simply because some things don't go together.

The question is, how do we establish a reference point? Consider a third thought: *A good way to make decisions is to use the standard of the longest value and the greatest usefulness.* Wallace Hamilton had a little parable which speaks to this. "Suppose," he said, "you were moving to a far-off country where all standard currency was useless. The medium of exchange in the new country, let us say, is oranges. The very last thing you would do before leaving your old home would be to convert your present money into oranges so you might be able to make purchases in your new home." At the end of this parable, Hamilton commented, "Wise is the person who exchanges what cannot be kept for things that cannot be lost."

That's a thought worth pondering. There are some things that are fleeting. Success, power and fame slip away quickly. Wealth so often is "easy come, easy go." But there are some things that abide. The help we give to others, especially children, lasts beyond our lifetime. The love of family and friends stays with us long after fame and fortune are gone. A great teacher put it this way: "Whoever gives a cup of water to those who are thirsty, a crust of bread to the hungry, a visit to someone in trouble or a piece of clothing to those who are cold will have possessions that last forever."

245

Chasing a Dream

A few years ago, one of America's leading newspapers did a study on the perils of middle age. It was the story of two men struggling with the recognition that life was slipping by and they had not accomplished nearly all they had intended. The implication of the study was that the middle years of life are the most perilous. During these years many people develop serious psychological and physical problems.

It needs to be said, however, that middle age is not the only time of crisis. Every age has its special difficulties. Children wrestle with the problems of growing up. Older people face the complex matters related to retirement. In every stage of life we are beset with a unique set of problems.

The newspaper study suggested that at least part of the crisis of the middle years is the loss of one's dreams. In earlier years we have high and worthy ideals and ambitions, but as the years slip by we may well lose sight of them. According to some psychologists, such a phenomenon happens to everyone. As we grow older we lose our dreams.

There is a measure of truth in this contention. Many of us do lose our dreams with the passing years, but to say this process is inevitable requires more evidence than the circumstances present. It is possible to be a dreamer to the very end. Tucked away in an old book there is a commentary on a man named Abraham. About him the author said, "He died in the faith, not having realized his goals, but having seen them, pursued them even from afar." If you study the life of this man, you will discover he lived to be an old man, and he kept his dreams to the very end. There are lessons to be learned from him.

One of these lessons is that dreams are essential to meaningful life. There is an old legend about a soldier who was court-martialed before Alexander the Great. Dissatisfied with the verdict, the soldier asked for permission to appeal his case. Alexander quickly informed the soldier there was no higher court. The soldier replied, "Then I appeal my case from Alexander the *Small* to Alexander the *Great.*"

There is an important lesson here. All of us possess at least two selves. Both struggle for supremacy. There is the lower self—content to wander along on the "misty flats" without purpose or direction. This self is willing to settle for things as they are. No new brave resolves are made, and there is no deep soul-searching or struggle. Many people succumb to this lower self. They settle down in the stagnant waters of unrealized potential.

There is another self all of us possess unless it is stifled or suppressed. It is the voice that tells us no matter what heights we have scaled there are still more peaks to climb. The voice of that self will

246

never let us rest on achieved victories, no matter how great these victories may be. That voice tells us we were made for higher things.

It is the voice of this higher self we need to hear. There are people who would tell us that dreaming of impossible aspirations and goals could result in unhealthy frustrations. This doesn't need to happen. We may not achieve all our dreams, but even a partial victory can bring us some sense of well-being. Medicine, for example, has for its purpose the relief of all pain and release from all disease. No doctor will ever achieve such final goals, but every competent doctor will certainly try to move in those directions. The moment a doctor ceases to have these ultimate dreams, he or she will no longer be worthy of the profession.

It is the dreamer who brings about changes in our world and who finds the real satisfaction of living. Dreamers have explored the earth and have charted the heavens; they have been responsible for our great inventions. It is the dreamer who leaves the world a better place.

The middle years need not be the years of lost dreams. Indeed, these years can be the most productive of all. A study of the biographies of great people reveals that many of the people who have made the greatest contributions have made them not while they were young but when they were older. The verdict of human experience is clear; never stop dreaming. We may never achieve all of our dreams, but those who keep on establishing goals and working toward them are likely to achieve far more than those who have no dreams at all.

Why Me?

Those who sit behind the counselor's desk often hear a question for which there is no good answer. When someone is the victim of a serious calamity or misfortune, the question usually asked is *why me*? There is, of course, no real way to answer such an inquiry. Hard times often come to people without rhyme or reason. Not in the long records of human reflection have we ever been able to respond successfully to the question, *why me*?

It does seem interesting that we only ask for reasons when we are the victims of misfortune. Strange, isn't it, that we never ask *why me*? when we have a streak of good fortune. We often attempt to fix the blame for the bad things but fail to give proper credit for the good things. Most of us owe more than we imagine for treasures for which we can claim no credit.

Think for a moment about the good fortunes of creation. Charles Schulz, in his comic strip, had a marvelous line from Snoopy. Snoopy is watching Charlie Brown and Linus pass by. Snoopy murmurs to himself, "I wonder why some of us are born dogs while others are born people. Is it just chance, or what is it? Somehow the whole thing seems unfair." Then Snoopy adds this line: "Why should I have been the lucky one?"

Many of us could afford to ask Snoopy's question. Even with all our misfortunes we are still the lucky ones. No Berlin Wall runs along our borders. No secret police knock on our doors when we criticize our government. No garbage trucks are sent each day to pick up the bodies of our loved ones who died during the night. Few of us know what it means to be desperately hungry. The majority of our children do not die in the first year of their lives. What about the opportunities given to us by the accident of birth? Why are we the lucky ones?

We also owe a debt to a heritage that keeps us on course. There was a story recently in our papers about an eight-year-old boy addicted to heroin. It happened at the instigation or with the permission of his mother. How can an eight-year-old deserve that environment?

Hodding Carter once said, "Only two things can we give to our children: roots and wings." Fortunate indeed are those who have received such possessions. Our childhood home may be modest in size and our parents of very average means, but if they have given us anchors for our lives, we are indeed fortunate people. We certainly did nothing to deserve being born into such a home any more than others deserve to be born into an opposite environment. Why are we the lucky ones?

We owe something also to the things that did not happen to us. In the Old Testament there is a story of a man who had enormous wealth. About him the author declared, "He was the greatest of all the people of the East." One day the man lost everything—his wealth, his health, even his family. In the story of this man's life there is the recurring theme, why has this misfortune come to me? Not once in his story does the man ask why he received his good fortune.

A hundred and fifty years ago we knew very little about alleviating pain. Countless people died from diseases which today would be considered minor health ailments. A lot of us owe great debts for the things that didn't happen to us. An ancient man once admonished his people not to think they did it all. We are debtors for things that didn't happen to us. Strange, isn't it, that we are the lucky ones?

Such good fortune imposes upon us obligations. In 1854 Ulysses S. Grant resigned from the army. Without funds and far from his Ohio home, he made his way to West Point and called on an old friend, Simon Bolivar Buckner. Buckner gave Grant some money. Eight years later, when Grant captured Fort Donelson, the surrendering general was Buckner. The other officers had fled. Later, Buckner said, "Grant never forgot an act of kindness. After my surrender, Grant followed me to my quarters, leaving behind his own officers celebrating the victory. There in the shadows, in that modest manner peculiar to Grant, he handed me his purse." A great teacher once said the lesson also revealed in that story of Grant: "Freely you have received; therefore, freely give." The next time something good happens to you, ask, *why me?* Then share your good fortune with someone else.

Half-Truths
Examining Promises from the Past

A few years ago in a southern magazine there was an article entitled "Traditions, Folklore and Hokum." The author pointed out that some things we believe to be true are not. The notion, for instance, that cherubs are pudgy little angels is not consistent with the way cherubs are described in the Bible. The biblical cherub is a fearful creature standing 15 feet tall with four faces, one of which is the face of an ox. And contrary to popular belief, the old saying *God helps those who help themselves* is not in the Bible. It was probably coined by a fifth-century playwright.

Quite often, the author continued, we take comfort in proverbs only to discover that we have not heard them right. There are times when we need to examine the truth of these sayings from the past.

Consider, for instance, *Everything happens for the best*. That axiom is often believed to be in the Bible. It is not. Most likely it is derived from the writings of St. Paul, who declared, "All things work together for good for those who love God." Often we read the first part of Paul's promise and not the condition stated in the latter part. But things do not always happen for the best. War, pestilence and disease are not good from most points of view. Things did not turn out for the best for Judas, the man whose betrayal of Jesus cost him his sanity and life. Only foolish people believe that everything turns out well no matter how they live.

The truth is that things only turn out for the best for those who work in harmony with the scheme of things. If we take the right direction—a direction that is honest and just—then the forces of creation work with us. Then, even bad things work for our good.

There is another proverb that many of us believe which isn't exactly true: *Time heals all wounds*. There is a folk song which runs, "Trouble in mind, I'm blue; but I won't be blue always. The sun's gonna shine in my back door some day." It does. Yet good times don't last forever either. After a while, the high roads lead back to the valleys.

Time doesn't necessarily heal. It would be more accurate to say, "Change is inevitable. Progress is not." Ignore maintenance of your house and time will destroy it. Neglect a garden and weeds will choke it. Time is neutral. It can heal or destroy. It can bring life. It also brings death.

Time is a friend only for those who work constructively. Lincoln died from an assassin's bullet, but he had worked at good and just causes. His causes are now prevailing. When we work at proper things, time is on our side.

One other example: how often have you heard the proverb *God will provide?* There is a little verse tucked away in the wise literature of the world:

It may not be in my time;
It may not be in your time;
But, in God's time, he will provide.

It is a mistake, however, to believe that the help of Providence is automatic, with no conditions attached. Providence does help those who help themselves. Here again we must work at honest and just things, and give these things our best.

All of this says to us that it is foolish to believe there is a cosmic magician at work in creation making everything right for us no matter what we do. We play an essential role in the events of life. Everything that happens can be used for good—if we are willing to work in faith and trust. Time heals all wounds—if we work at honorable and just purposes. Providence provides—if we have given our best in a good cause. The message of the age is this: If you take the right road, then somewhere, sometime, in this world or the next, you come out at the right place.

The Rules of Right and Wrong

There was a story in a southern newspaper recently about a guard posted outside a government building in London. So far as anyone could remember, he or his counterpart had been there for years—yet the positioning of the guard at that building made no sense. A student of British royal history did some research and came up with an interesting story: In the early 19th century, the Duke of Wellington would often ride his horse to the building, so a guard was posted there to hold the duke's horse. Somehow the order for the guard was never rescinded. For 125 years, one of the queen's finest was sent to that post, and no one ever asked why.

The story is not isolated. For example, it is said that the British civil service created a job in 1803 which called for a man to stand on the cliffs of Dover with a spyglass. He was to ring an alarm bell if he saw Napoleon coming. This position was not abolished until 1945.

So often traditions continue long after the reason for them has been lost. Now and then we wonder if this is not the circumstance in other areas. In this "enlightened age" we suspect that many of the old rules no longer hold true.

In recent years there has been a small revolution in the theories of physics. Einstein's theories have raised serious questions about some of Newton's laws. Quantum physics is also probing the validity of time-honored ideas.

A similar revolution has affected some of our ethical concepts. Ideals held by one generation may not be valid in another. Puritanism can be so negative and repressive that in our day it leads to emotional and mental disorders. Our forefathers in America may have been justified in clearing forests to make room for a growing population. But in our time other alternatives must be discovered. We now know that trees constitute one of our most important resources; to destroy them carelessly is criminal and wrong. The rightness of a given course may change with changing times. Does this mean there are no absolutes?

The best definition of morality can be said in five words: Morality is what creation intends. We do not establish right and wrong. The creator has done that. In the arrangement of the world some things diminish life; others enhance it. We don't establish these principles. They are written into the scheme of things. The fact that these principles are old does not change their validity.

If the foregoing is true—that in the process of creation the principles of right and wrong were established—then evasion of these principles is not accomplished without penalty. An ancient writer once said, "The way of the transgressor is hard." The writer was not just moralizing; he was reporting the results of human experience. There are unrelenting rules running through all creation. Living against these rules makes for a rough road to travel.

There are some principles, of course, that we *do* establish. Take fashions, for instance. Long hair, beards, casual dress and the like are not wrong; their suitability is arbitrated by public opinion. Such principles shift as attitudes change.

But some principles spring from a deeper level. This world is so made that some things work while others do not. The purpose of the Ten Commandments and the Beatitudes is to communicate these things. Here are listed the principles that work and are written into the scheme of things. They are not subject to public opinion. If everyone on earth voted against them, they would still be as binding as the law of gravity.

The secret to living, then, is to determine what was intended from creation and be obedient to that intent. Occasionally, someone suggests that only devoutly religious people need to be obedient to such rules. That suggestion is dead wrong. These rules, like the law of gravity, hold. They apply to everyone, thieves as well as saints. We either obey these rules or endure the consequences.

A few years ago one of America's most notorious criminals did an about-face. He completely changed his life. When asked why, he replied, "I have learned that certain rules prevail in this world no matter what custom and public opinion may suggest. The sooner we learn to cooperate with the inevitable, the sooner life becomes what it was intended to be." This man's conclusion is the collective verdict of the ages. Wise is the person who discovers it early in life and lives accordingly.

The Problem with 'Doing Your Own Thing'

Someone has estimated that of the 450,000 words in the English language today, only 200,000 would be recognized by William Shakespeare. Language is ever-growing; words move in and out of our vocabulary with changing times. Some remain for centuries, while others disappear almost overnight. A few years ago the "in" expressions included words like "hep," "go-go" and "teenybopper." Today these expressions are almost never used.

But there is an expression of recent vintage that has proven more durable. For some time now we have heard talk of people "doing their own thing." With this phrase we are trying to describe a kind of rugged individualism and self-determination. Such people live as they want to live and do what they want to do. The trend toward that kind of life-style is in some ways refreshing. Too often society tries to press us into a single mold, stifling our creativity. We live by standards set by others and become victims of conformity. It is delightful to find people with a strong sense of self, who are willing to live by their own values.

There is, however, a grave danger in all of this. Complete freedom in our world is as unreasonable as complete repression. We cannot throw off all restraints and live entirely as we choose. There are limits to doing our own thing.

About 3,500 years ago, there were some people who lived as slaves in Egypt. One day a man named Moses appeared before these people and declared that he would lead them to the Promised Land. Moses kept his promise, although he did not reach the new land himself and left the reins of leadership to Joshua. But when Joshua died, there was no one to succeed him. An ancient author wrote of these people: "Now in those days there was no king in the land, and each person did what was right in his own eyes." In other words, everyone did his own thing. History records the results of that long-ago experiment. Families fought with other families and among themselves. Personal, social and business affairs became chaotic and confused. Unlimited free expression resulted in terrible times.

Unlimited freedom is impossible for at least two reasons. First, there is the interdependence of people. No generation should be more aware of this than ours. The earth is a giant airship. What happens on any part of the ship has an effect on the rest. Stock markets are tied together. We buy goods from all over the earth. War in one quarter affects us all.

On a snow-covered highway recently, a driver traveling at a high speed lost control of his auto. The car careened like a gigantic cannonball into a bus loaded with children. That speeding driver was doing his thing. The result was a tragic reminder that whatever rights we have end where the rights of others begin.

But there is something even more basic than this. The reason unlimited human freedom is an impossible achievement is that our goals must be compatible with each other's. It is the failure to understand this that results in so much frustration in our times.

There is the story of a man who had a wonderful family he loved deeply. He also had an abnormal desire to win the approval of his peers. He wasted his money, throwing away great sums to impress his friends. About this man it was said, "He did not realize that in exercising his freedom irresponsibly, he was pursuing ultimately incompatible goals." In the end he lost both his family and his so-called friends.

Where in life does this principle not prevail? Can an athlete excel in a chosen sport while at the same time ignoring the discipline of practice? Can a marriage survive without some compromise of individual freedom? Can a business be respected while taking shortcuts to success at any price? It isn't that we are all repressed by custom or authority. This is simply the way creation is arranged. It's true, "You can't have your cake and eat it, too." Some goals simply don't go together.

Sooner or later all of us must recognize and deal with this reality. The best advice for us is not to do our own thing but to "get our act together." To do this we must understand the interdependence of people and the necessity of choosing compatible goals. We must ask ourselves what we want in life and what is necessary to achieve our dreams, but our choices must be such that in saving ourselves we do not destroy others. Those who make these decisions deliberately and intelligently are the only people who will find life exciting and worthwhile.

Present but Not Voting

There is a strange story about a wealthy man who died in London many years ago. According to the story, the man bequeathed a sizable gift to an English hospital. He stipulated that, as a condition of the gift, his remains be brought to the board room and placed at the head of the table. The record supposedly states that for more than 100 years the secretary of the board has added to the minutes this one line: "Jeremy Bentham, present but not voting."

There is something tragic about the situation this story describes. To be present and make no difference in what is happening is sad indeed. You wouldn't expect more from a dead man; but to be alive and still not count is a different matter.

Long ago one of the strangest trials in history took place. A man was charged with treason. Conviction meant death. He was innocent, but he needed at least one witness in his defense. The only possible witness was frightened and refused to say anything. Perhaps as the convicted man was being led away to his death, he begged for an answer from the potential witness: "Why didn't you say a word in my defense?" Before the witness could reply, the condemned man was taken away to a horrible death. The silent witness lived many years after that fateful night, and he never forgot it.

Years later, a biography of the witness bore this title: *Voting After the Polls Had Closed.* There are a few lessons here worth remembering.

It is possible to live all one's life and make little or no difference.

A fellow who was looking for a job stopped by a store to inquire about a friend named Henry. The store owner told him that Henry didn't work there anymore. The job seeker brightened. "Well," he said, "that means you have a vacancy." "Nope," said the businessman. "Henry didn't leave no vacancy."

Despite somewhat faulty grammar, the point of this story is clear. To live a lifetime and not leave a vacancy—to be present but not voting—is a distinct possibility. And it is indeed a dreadful epitaph.

It is often said that people fall into one of two categories: the "takers" or the "givers." Some people live their lives as parasites. They take for themselves and never give anything. There are others who try to make the world a better place.

They recognize that they are guests on this planet. They are constantly trying to put more into the world than they extract from it. These are the people who write their names into the history books, who are involved in civic and constructive activities, who see their efforts as a way of making a contribution to the world. These are the people who find life worthwhile.

Secondly, the past stands as it is written. Our days are like money—when spent, they don't come back. In the words of an old song:

Work, for the night is coming, under the sunset skies;
While their bright tints are glowing,
Work, while daylight flies.
Work till the last beam fadeth,
Fadeth to shine no more;
Work while the night is dark'ning, when man's work is o'er.

In a book entitled *A Night to Remember,* the author gave a minute-by-minute account of the sinking of the *Titanic* and told of the congressional investigation that followed the disaster. Legislation came out of the study that required a life jacket for every passenger on a ship. Congress so voted. For the people aboard the *Titanic,* however, the "vote came after the polls had closed." We cannot call back the past. The polls finally close and no one can vote.

It is possible, however, to reclaim the past. Consider the old English word, *redeem.* The root word in Latin means to buy back, or to give something in place of that which is lost. That is always a possibility. We cannot call back the past, but there is a way to make up for lost opportunities and to redeem a vote that is missed.

That man who refused to witness for his friend lived to see another day. The time came when he was able to speak and "vote" again. This witness helped to make the executed man's name live forever. We now remember that condemned man as the most influential man in history. We even refer to the birth of the Nazarene carpenter as the dividing line of history—between BC and AD.

It is never too late to start again. If we are haunted by the guilt of yesterday, we can begin afresh and discover that the load of countless blunders and mistakes is lifted. The polls are opened and we can vote again.

How's Your Hearing?
Listening to That Still, Small Voice

A tiny boy was seated at the dinner table in his highchair. Suddenly he threw his plate to the floor. His mother was furious. "Go to your room!" she ordered. "You will take your meals there until you learn to behave properly!" The little fellow tried to defend himself, but his mother silenced him. "You must learn to be courteous and polite," she declared.

That evening the father gathered the family in the living room. "I want you to listen to something," he said. "I had our new tape recorder on tonight during dinner, to see how it works. When I played the tape, I discovered something I think all of us should hear."

He started the recording, and the family heard themselves as they had sounded at dinner that evening. Everyone seemed to be talking at once. Amid the chatter, they heard a tiny voice say, "Please pass the butter." But no one seemed to hear. A bit later they heard the same voice, "Would someone please pass the butter?" After awhile, that little voice was heard again. "Please, please, pass the butter." Finally, they heard the crash of the plate as it hit the floor. There was that small voice again, but this time it was loud and clear, "Pass the butter!"

One of the problems of these turbulent times is the ever-increasing noise level around us. With the clatter and bang of today's technology—the wall-to-wall sound of contemporary music and the roar of trucks, trains and planes—many of the voices we need to hear are being lost in the general tumult. Physicians tell us that cases of deafness resulting from exposure to harmful levels of noise are increasing at an alarming rate. But physical deafness is not the only danger. As great a loss is that of the hearing of our minds and hearts.

Someone has rightly said that life's most important messages often come to us in whispers. Centuries ago there was a man who had been an adviser to kings and princes. As would be expected, the pace of his life was fast and furious. One day he realized that something was wrong deep inside his heart. An old record reports what happened to this man: he retreated to a remote corner of his world. There he began to listen again to what he called "the still, small voice" in his heart.

Deep in our spirit, all of us have a tiny voice that calls us to better things. It is this voice that sets before us the dream of what we can be, as opposed to what we are. It is also this voice that reminds us of the supreme importance of sturdy character and integrity. It is this voice that recalls for us the obligations of our blessings—the awareness that others have been less fortunate and thus have a claim on our compassion and concern. That still, quiet messenger suggests to us that friends and family are our most precious possessions. This is the voice that keeps us on course and prevents us from losing ourselves among trivial things. But this voice usually speaks to us in a whisper. Sometimes it is so gentle and quiet that we miss hearing it altogether.

A few years ago Mac Davis recorded what became a very popular song, "Stop and Smell the Roses." That song is a powerful reminder that we often get so caught up in the pressures of living that we miss life's most beautiful and valuable treasures. The lure of material success can be so strong that we hear nothing else but its tempting call. These sounds of fame and fortune get so loud that the "still, small voice" calling us to "smell the roses" gets lost in the roar.

There is a quaint story about a mountain man who lived in a remote and lovely valley. In the early morning he would sit on his porch and survey the breathtaking scenery about him. He would see the butterflies floating among the flowers in his yard. He would listen to the birds as they welcomed the new day. In the distance he could see deer grazing peacefully beside a tiny stream. It was a magnificent sight, and for the mountaineer it never lost its attraction. One day a traveler stopped at the man's house. The traveler was breathless and perspiring as he asked for directions to the next town. As soon as the mountaineer told him which road to take, the fellow was off at a dead run. The mountaineer called after him, "What's your hurry, Mister? You are going to run by more than you will ever catch."

There's great wisdom in those words. We can keep looking for the good life, listening to the roar and rumble of a world that is far too busy. We can drown out the tiny voice calling us to better and more important things. We hasten along looking for the good life, and yet all around us is beauty, love, friendship and the possibility of inner peace. These possessions can be ours if we will only take the trouble to hear the voices that call us to them.

Traveling by the Stars

One of the most interesting studies of history is the development of the science of navigation. In one form or another, this method of finding a way from one part of the earth to another dates back to the earliest days of civilization. The Chinese, it is said, invented a crude compass. With that compass they made charts and maps of the heavens. Using these maps, sailors made the stars their reference points.

Since these ancient times, navigation has evolved into a more exact science. Today we can pinpoint with fair accuracy any spot on the earth or in most of the known expanses of space. It is interesting to note, however, that despite our intricate direction finders and super computers, we must still check our equipment by the stars. We have not yet found a substitute for these cosmic reference points.

What is true in the realm of nature is also true in other areas. In life we often need reference points to help us chart our way through the bewildering confusion of a complex world. Sometimes life pushes us down and hems us in until we lose our bearings.

Several years ago, Dr. Donald Tippett wrote an essay entitled, "Stars Above the Freight Trains." The point of that essay was the contrast between the short and longer views of life. Tippett gleaned one sentence in the essay from an old prayer: "Help us lift our eyes beyond the shadows that we may see the light of eternity."

All of us at times get lost in the shadows. It can happen to us during serious illness or great sorrow. It can happen also in times of failure or stress. The question is how we can find our way through such difficult days.

Many people have discovered that certain thoughts can be helpful. One of these thoughts is found in an old folk song:

As I travel down life's highway,
Know not what the years may hold;
As I ponder, hopes grow fonder,
Precious memories flood my soul.

Every now and then, all of us need to reexamine our direction. One way we can accomplish this is by reflecting on the dreams and goals of earlier years. We need to reflect on the past and ask ourselves if we have made of life what we intended. Like the sailor who checks his direction with the stars, we need to measure our lives against those values we once deemed important. It is so easy to lose our bearings and to forget our finest hopes and aspirations. We need to see beyond the shadows of the present and take a long look into the past.

Think for a moment about the high resolves and dreams that once were a part of our lives. Remember graduation? What noble and worthy goals we set for ourselves. But somewhere along the way we lost sight of those dreams. Now, perhaps, we are floundering along the road without purpose or direction. Of course, the possibility of realizing some of these dreams is gone forever, because we have passed the doorway to these opportunities. But we must never forget that there are always other doors that are open for us.

Remembering the past, however, is not the only way we can find the stars. The future also has its promise. An old mountaineer was once asked to quote his favorite Bible verse. He replied, "It came to pass!" That exact verse, of course, is not in the Bible, but the mountaineer was suggesting a profound truth. No circumstance is here to stay. Something else comes to pass. Someone has rightly said, "Nothing is permanent but change." If that is true, then a circumstance that seems hopeless for the moment may change into a splendid opportunity. There are many doors in every room in life's house. There is no reason for despair as long as one of these doors is open.

So many of us are living in the shadows. We have surrendered too easily to the challenges and difficulties of life. Take a new look at the stars. Pick up the pieces of shattered dreams. Look beyond the gloom and shadows of the present to the almost limitless possibilities of the future.

There is a timeless proverb worth remembering: "If you take the right road and keep it, sometime, somewhere, you will come out at the right place." That's a star by which all of us can navigate. Don't give up just because you are going through the shadows. Hold to your course. After a while, you will come out where you are supposed to be. Honest toil will at last bring its reward. And that's one star you can depend upon.

The Laws of Growth
Good Seeds Yield a Good Harvest

Sometime near the middle of the last century a young man enrolled at the University of Berlin. He was a native of Treves, Germany, where his father worked as an attorney. Even in his early years the lad displayed a brilliant mind. At the university he took his studies seriously, but his professors noted that he had some unusual ideas.

One day during class, this student became involved in a heated argument with his teacher. Instead of taking time to understand him, the professor ordered him from the room. The young man never quite got over the harsh treatment of that professor. And his keen mind devised some theories that would one day have a tremendous impact on the world.

We will never know how history might have been different had that professor been more understanding of the young Karl Marx. In so many instances, the world has been changed by tiny events. Someone has said that the story of humankind is the story of small seeds growing to harvest. These harvests are brought about by certain laws that operate with unfailing dependability. Such laws are labeled by scientists *the laws of growth*, and are worth remembering.

One of these laws is that growth is *infinite*. The Great Teacher told about a man who planted some corn. The man cared for the seeds until they brought forth their harvest. "Some of the seed had a yield of a hundredfold," said the teacher. Any farmer would know that corn which produced a hundredfold would not be unusual. A bushel of seeds could easily produce a hundred bushels. The second year, if planted, the hundred bushels would produce 10,000 bushels, and by the third year, one million bushels.

Such figures illustrate the growing power of seeds when they are repeatedly planted. This principle operates not only in the garden but also in life. Seeds have a way of bringing forth a multiplied harvest. Our behavior today has its impact not only on tomorrow but also far into the years ahead. We keep gleaning the harvest from yesterday's thoughts, words and deeds. Good habits established in the present bring endless benefits in the future. Kindnesses extended today have a way of coming back to us, not just once but many times. The law of geometric progression is always at work in our world.

There is another law of growth that should be remembered: It is *gradual*. Among the oldest living things on this planet is a giant sequoia tree in the Sequoia National Park. Nearly 300 feet tall, the tree sprouted long before the birth of Jesus. Year after year the tree keeps growing, slowly adding to its size.

It is the gradualness of growth that often deceives us. We plant a seed today and expect a harvest tomorrow. Life seldom works that way. A reputation, for instance, is established one word or one deed at a time over a long period.

One of America's largest businesses was built on the slogan, "Satisfaction Guaranteed." That reputation did not happen overnight. It has resulted from the consistent application of fair play wherever that business has operated. The same gradual process works in other places. Physical stamina doesn't happen immediately. It comes about slowly as we practice proper health habits. A trained mind results from constant and disciplined study. There are no shortcuts to building a life.

Finally, growth is *neutral*. Centuries ago an itinerant tentmaker wrote a letter that is still being read today. In that letter, St. Paul wrote, "Whatever you sow, you will also reap." Sometimes that sentence is taken as a threat. It really isn't. Rather, it is a description of the way things work. There is a dependability in creation which requires a seed to reproduce its own kind.

There is nothing ominous about the neutrality of growth. Instead, it should be reassuring. It means that if we plant good seeds we can expect a like harvest. Young people should be especially encouraged by such a process. Good investments today can be expected to yield the right returns tomorrow. Good habits today bring the appropriate rewards in the future.

Charles Kettering once said, "You don't buy a fiddle today and play in Carnegie Hall tomorrow." That's true. But so is this: If you buy a fiddle today and practice faithfully, somewhere, sometime, such an investment will bring its harvest. Good seeds have a way of coming to a good harvest. The world is made that way.

The Law of the Shadow

Several miles south of Sanford, Florida, there stands what is believed to be one of the largest cypress trees in America. With an estimated age of more than 3,500 years, the tree stands 125 feet high, about 47 feet in circumference and 16 feet in diameter. The day Jesus was born in Bethlehem this tree was already a forest giant of 1,500 years.

For 35 centuries this colossus has weathered the storms that have roared across Florida. Here it has stood through the rise and fall of civilizations, giving shelter countless times to those who have gathered under its protective branches. It is an unforgettable experience to stand by this tree late in the day and watch this sentinel of the forest cast its shadow over the earth—its refreshing blanket of shade falling over the hot and humid countryside.

That a tree casts a shadow is a law of natural affairs. When any object of density towers in the sun, a darkened area in the shape of that object is an inevitable result. This shade makes a difference wherever it falls. Tender plant life, for instance, is protected from the hot and scorching sun. Shadows are important in the world of nature.

The law of the shadow, however, is not limited to the natural world. It is also a circumstance prevailing in human affairs. In one of the world's oldest books there is a story about a man who had achieved a reputation as a leader among his people. One day this man passed through the streets of an ancient city. Word of his presence spread like wildfire. An ancient reporter wrote this: "People were brought and laid in the streets that at least the great man's shadow might fall over them." Perhaps in an age of science such a practice might be considered superstition. There is, however, a thought here worthy of reflection.

Shadows can and do affect our lives. In 1859, the newspapers in England carried front-page pictures of a man named Charles S. Stratton, who, apparently normal at birth, had never grown to a normal height. P.T. Barnum discovered the little man and named him General Tom Thumb. Barnum took Tom Thumb all over the world, placing him on exhibition. On a certain day in 1859 the diminutive fellow appeared before the Queen of England.

As the years have passed, we now know the news of that day was not in the headlines but in the note on the back pages. In the same paper announcing Tom Thumb's appearance before the Queen there was a note about a book published by a man named Charles Darwin. For good or ill, Darwin's book, *Origin of Species*, has become one of the most important books in history. It triggered a whole new age of scientific exploration.

We have a way of only attending to the spectacular, easily becoming distracted by noise and speed. We headline the stories of those who lead armies and chart the course of nations. We so often miss the stories of those who quietly mold the future of humankind. Sometimes the real history of the world is to be found in obscure events that never appear in the headlines.

This sort of thing happens often in our personal lives. Someone has reported that five of this century's greatest physicists have come from a single school in Germany, all taught by the same teacher. Most of us can point to a teacher, a relative, a business mentor, a college professor or a counselor who came into our lives at a critical time and made a difference. These persons directed us in ways that have been lasting. Few if any of us achieve great heights on our own. There is always someone who spreads over us a shadow of protection, inspiration and direction.

Sometimes the persons who cast the shadows are unaware of what they have done. During a fierce Civil War battle, an army colonel had to lead his men in retreat. They fled over a burning bridge. The soldiers managed to escape, but the officer's orderly remembered that the officer's prize sword had been left behind and turned back to retrieve it. The orderly died that night in his attempt to recover his commander's sword. That army officer never forgot that young man. He vowed that from that time he would live two lives—one for himself and one for his orderly, Johnny Ring. For Johnny Ring, Russell Conwell wrote what became one of the most famous lectures ever given on this continent—"Acres of Diamonds." Conwell gave that address some 6,000 times, and from the proceeds helped to endow the famed Temple University.

There is a Johnny Ring in all our lives—someone who knowingly or unknowingly has touched our lives. It is also true that for someone we are, or can be, a Johnny Ring. Shadows are powerful. We need to be careful how we handle them.

It's All Right to Get Mad

They fired him on the spot, and it was a sad day for the man. He was as talented as any employee in the company. He was well trained and had all the skills anyone needed except one: He couldn't control his temper. Time after time he had been warned. Finally, one day in a fit of rage, he lashed out at his superior. There was really no other choice. The company had to let the man go. He was left with a family to support and no income.

Most of us know of similar incidents—people "flying off the handle" and creating havoc not only for themselves but also for the people around them. Sometimes the fits of rage last only minutes. At other times anger smolders for months, even years. But more often than not the results are devastating. Because of these destructive effects many of us believe anger to be evil. But such a conclusion is not completely warranted. Anger is not always bad. Three things about it should be remembered.

First, *all of us have impulses which are not necessarily evil; these impulses are divine gifts*. Think for a moment about the impulses we possess. We are capable of anger, fear, pride, ambition and the like. These impulses are as much a part of our lives as the instinctual response to hunger. This has always been true of people in every place and age.

There is a story in the Bible about the Great Teacher. One day he encountered some people who were selling merchandise in the temple. When he realized what was happening, the record says that he overturned the tables of these avaricious dealers and drove them away. Here you have it—a story of anger from the life of a man the world believes was perfect.

Most of us believe that anger is inherently evil. It isn't! Temper is an important asset in life. It makes the difference between iron and steel. A person without temper is too easily bent and often breaks. The Great Teacher was not acting out of character the day he drove away those profit-hungry merchants. Rather, he was exercising his innate impulses in a powerful way. We must not assume, however, that it is all right to get mad without restraint. There is a second consideration.

It is the way these impulses are used that determines whether they are good or evil. There is an old folk saying that goes, "The size of a person can be measured by the size of the things it takes to make him or her mad." Our problem is that often we get angry about the wrong things.

It was reported to Abraham Lincoln one day that one of his cabinet members had called him a fool. Lincoln only laughed and declared, "If Stanton said I was a fool then I must be one. For he is nearly always right." Here's an example of a person who refused to get mad over a trifle. But remember, Lincoln could be adamant when poor and helpless people were mistreated.

The causes of our anger determine our stature. We should get angry about injustices, betrayed trusts, sinister and evil forces that attack our families. We should get angry when people are mistreated. But, even then, our anger must not be an uncontrolled or irrational fury. There is a third consideration.

If anger is to be power, it must be controlled. When you read the complete story of the Great Teacher, this is evident. He never resorted to uncontrolled violence. When he got angry, he was angry with the evil, not the evildoer.

In the Book of Proverbs there is an interesting line: "He that ruleth his temper is mightier than he that taketh a city." The instruction in this sentence is not to destroy one's temper, but to control it. That is the lesson most of us need to learn.

Our problem is that we get mad about the wrong things: Someone cuts us off on the expressway, someone snubs us at a party, we get "dressed down" at work, the next-door neighbor edges over on our lawn, or the neighborhood dogs race across our yard. The list of these irritating trifles that come to all of us is endless.

Sometimes in a fit of temper over these trifles we do stupid and destructive things. Remember that we are "no bigger than the things that make us mad." When we begin to feel anger rising within, a good question to ask is, "Am I losing my temper over something that really counts?"

The Struggle for Good Purposes

In one of the world's oldest books there is a story of a tiny city held under siege by a great army. For days, all help from the outside had been cut off. The people inside the walls of the city were filled with despair. They had given up hope and were only waiting for starvation to take its course.

Near the edge of the city, just outside the walls, four men were huddled in serious conversation. Finally, one of the men addressed the others: "Why sit we here idle until we die? If we return to the city we will starve. If we remain here we will be caught in the crossfire. Let us cross over to the camp of the enemy and stage a small battle of our own." These four men made some discoveries that all of us would do well to remember.

First, *the men learned the value of helping themselves.* There were two sides to the city walls that night. On the inside the people had all but surrendered and were looking for a scapegoat. Some blamed their troubles on the government. Some felt that other people in the city had not fought hard enough. In any event, the people inside the walls had given up and were waiting for the end.

Outside the walls were four men who refused to accept defeat. "Why sit we here idle until we die? Let's be up and on the move. If we must die, let us die on our feet with our weapons in our hands."

There is a lesson here that many of us need to learn. The notion that the good life can be achieved without effort on our part is a myth. For the most part, life is what we make it. Someone has rightly observed that what happens to us is not nearly so important as what we make of what happens to us. A famed American basketball coach wrote in his autobiography that he always keeps a sign on his desk that reads, "Things turn out for the best for those who make the best of the way things turn out." Successful living is seldom a matter of luck. Those who find life exciting are those who work at it.

Second, *when the men helped themselves, the forces of creation began to work with them.* Remember that ageless proverb, "God helps those who help themselves"? On that long-ago day, the four men set out on their mission. Their nerves were taut and their hearts were pounding. They were not prepared for what they discovered. The enemy camp was deserted, apparently abandoned in great haste. The soldiers had departed in such a hurry that they had left all their provisions behind. The storyteller gives an explanation for the enemy's hurried retreat: In the night, the soldiers heard a great noise (perhaps a thunderstorm). Thinking they were about to be overrun, they had fled.

Something akin to this often happens in life. The forces of creation contrive to work with us when we give ourselves to worthy pursuits. When we take right positions, we can depend on the forces of right and justice working with us. Abraham Lincoln had this in mind when he said that if he were right, then his cause would prevail; but if he were wrong, then the angels swearing him to be right could not help him. We should never despair if our efforts are just and honorable. Sometime, somewhere, we will prevail. It pays to remember this if we are defending a lonely cause. Right has a way of coming to the surface.

Third, *when the men helped themselves, others worked with them.* When the four men entered the enemy's camp and discovered the abandoned supplies, the author of the story reported, they said, "This is a day of great rejoicing. Let us go into the city and get others to help us gather the food." When the besieged people in the city heard the report of the four men, they left the city to assist in taking over the enemy's camp.

There is a contagious quality to the courageous heart. While this principle may not work with mathematical precision, it is true that people are attracted to those who help themselves. Years ago in England there was a man who recognized the evils of slavery and set out to abolish the wretched system. At first his allies were few, but William Wilberforce continued to work for his cause. There came a day when countless people joined in his effort to see that slavery was destroyed.

Life tends to work this way. People are attracted to those who struggle for good purposes. A student who tries will tend to receive the aid of his teachers. An employee who works diligently at assigned responsibilities will win the support of her employers. It is difficult to resist helping someone who is honestly working to help himself. That "starvation committee" from long ago speaks to us. When you are working at something right and just, take heart. You will never work alone.